MARGARET ATWOOD'S VOICES AND REPRESENTATIONS

From Poetry to Tweets

Christine Evain

MARGARET ATWOOD'S VOICES AND REPRESENTATIONS

From Poetry to Tweets

Christine Evain

COMMON GROUND PUBLISHING 2015,

First published in 2015 in Champaign, Illinois, USA
by Common Ground Publishing LLC
as part of the New Directions in the Humanities book series

Copyright © Christine Evain 2015

All rights reserved. Apart from fair dealing for the purposes of study, research, criticism or review as permitted under the applicable copyright legislation, no part of this book may be reproduced by any process without written permission from the publisher.

Library of Congress Cataloging-in-Publication Data

Evain, Christine.
  Margaret Atwood's voices and representations : from poetry to tweets / Christine Evain.
    pages cm
  Includes bibliographical references and index.
  ISBN 978-1-61229-791-0 (pbk : alk. paper) -- ISBN 978-1-61229-792-7 (pdf)
  1. Atwood, Margaret, 1939---Criticism and interpretation. I. Title.

PR9199.3.A8Z64 2015
818'.5409--dc23

2015014383

Cover Photo Credit: "Margaret Atwood" by George Whiteside

Table of Contents

Acknowledgement	ix
Abbreviations and Publication Dates	x
Introduction	xii

Part I: Representations and Stagings of a "Voice" in Margaret Atwood's Poetry

Chapter 1
Introducing Margaret Atwood's Poetic Voice — 1

Chapter 2
The voice and the underworld — 15

Chapter 3
Representations of the Aging Voice-persona — 29

Chapter 4
Voices of the Powerful and the Powerless — 41

Part II: Identifying Margaret Atwood's Voice-print

Chapter 5
Atwood's Canadian Signature — 56

Chapter 6
Gaze and Voice — 60

Chapter 7
Trying to Capture the Atwoodian Voice-print — 64

Chapter 8
The Voices of a Two-headed Opus   90

Part III: The Poetic Voice and the Voices of the "Living Author" and of the Author's Public Persona

Chapter 9
The Need for Different Voices   105

Chapter 10
The Celebrity Culture, Atwood and Hyde   108

Chapter 11
The Atwood-Media Relationship Reflected in Fiction   118

Chapter 12
Atwood's Treatment of the "Iconized Voice"   125

Chapter 13
Atwood on the Internet: Epitextual Strategies and Categories of
Voices   136

Conclusion   163

Bibliography   171
Index   182

ACKNOWLEDGEMENT

I would like to thank Vanessa Guignery for her guidance and support. I would also like to thank Spencer Hawkridge for the careful proof-reading of my manuscript and for his constant encouragement throughout the project.

Abbreviations and Publication Dates

For all quotations from Atwood's work, the below abbreviations will be used:

Poetry (including prose poems)[1]

B	*Double Persephone*, 1961
CG	*The Circle Game*, 1966
AC	*The Animals in That Country*, 1968
JSM	*The Journals of Susanna Moodie*, 1970
PU	*Procedures for Underground*, 1970
PP	*Power Politics*, 1971
YAH	*You Are Happy*, 1974
THP	*Two-Headed Poems*, 1978
TS	*True Stories*, 1981
MID	*Murder in the Dark*, 1983
I	*Interlunar*, 1984
GB	*Good Bones*, 1992
MBH	*Morning in the Burned House*, 1995
EF	*Eating Fire, Selected Poetry*, 1995
Bo	*Bottle*, 2004
TT	*The Tent*, 2006
TD	*The Door*, 2007

Fiction

EW	*The Edible Woman*, 1969
S	*Surfacing*, 1972
LO	*Lady Oracle*, 1976
DG	*Dancing Girls*, 1977
LBM	*Life Before Man*, 1979
BH	*Bodily Harm*, 1981

---

[1] I will not refer to anthologies of Atwood's poetry except *Eating Fire* in which *The Journals of Susanna Moodie* is fully included.

BE   *Bluebeard's Egg*, 1983
WT   *Wilderness Tips*, 1991
HT   *The Handmaid's Tale*, 1985
CE   *Cat's Eye*, 1988
RB   *The Robber Bride*, 1993
LF   *Labrador Fiasco*, 1996
AG   *Alias Grace*, 1996
BA   *The Blind Assassin*, 2000
OC   *Oryx and Crake*, 2003
Pe   *The Penelopiad*, 2005
MD   *Moral Disorder*, 2006
YF   *The Year of the Flood*, 2009
Mad   *Maddaddam*, 2013

Main Critical Work

Surviv *Survival: A Thematic Guide to Canadian Literature*, 1972.
SW *Second Words: Selected Critical Prose*, 1982.
ST *Strange Things: The Malevolent North in Canadian Literature,* 1995
ND *Negotiating with the Dead*, 2002.
MT[2] *Moving Targets,* 2004
CP *Curious Pursuits*, 2005.
WI *Writing with Intent*, 2005.
Payback, 2008.
IOW *In Other Worlds: SF and the Human Imagination*, 2011.

---

[2] There are two other versions of the Canadian critical book *Moving Targets* : the English one, *Curious Pursuits: Occasional Writing 1970-2005* and the American one *Writing with Intent: Essays, Reviews, Personal Prose--1983-2005* published a year later, in 2005.

Introduction

"Where does it come from, this notion that the writing self – the self that comes to be thought of as 'the author' – is not the same as the one who does the living? Where do writers pick up the idea that they have an alien of some sort living in their brains?" (ND 38) The question of the double – "an alien" living in a writer's brain – resonates not just in *Negotiating with the Dead*, but throughout Margaret Atwood's work. From the images of a man who is "part of the grass", the sun shining "greenly on the blades of his hands" in "A Voice" (AC 58-59) to a voice staged in the form of a hothouse plant in her latest books of poetry (TT 21), Atwood is fascinated by representations of the poetic voice.

The term "voice" which Atwood uses both in her critical work and her poetry, not only feeds into themes of metapoetry but, at times, becomes a central concept. Indeed, as she moves beyond the metapoetical images of the romantic poets, which include puns associated with writing poetry[1], Atwood creates a complex network of images in which the concept of the "voice" holds center stage and becomes multi-facetted. Depending on the context, "voice" can be equated with a poet's specific writing or his/her gift or talent. A "voice" is either collective or individual. In Atwood's poetry, not only does it frequently shift forms (the collective and the individual become inter-related) but it is often staged as a persona. It is then defined by a number of things such as: who it belongs to, whom it collaborates with, whom it stands against, the way it speaks (in songs, or whispers, for example), where it is located, where it comes from, what its needs are, what its desires are, what it looks like (when physically incarnated and described), what it is called and whom it is calling. Not only is the voice a highly unstable concept, but it is also one that Atwood enjoys playing with. If one takes for example the three poems entitled "A Voice" (AC 58-59) or "Voice" (TT 20-23), published in different volumes, and another poem entitled

---

[1] Among the Romantic poets, we find puns on leaves, feet and so on. The leaves refer to the leaves of plants, and to the leaves or pages of a book of poetry. The feet refer to the body part, and to the metrical feet of a poem, etc. These metaphors can be connected with other images such as the foot sometimes associated with limping, chains, and binding.
Other types of metapoetry involve self-conscious commentary on the poem's own genre or on the process of creating the poem. For example, Billy Collins' "Sonnet":
"All we need is fourteen lines, well, thirteen now,
And after this next one just a dozen
To launch a little ship on love's storm-tossed seas,
Then only ten more left like rows of beans." (Collins, Sonnet 518)

"Shadow Voice" (AC 7), one can not help but notice the shifting position of the speaker from one poem to another: in "Shadow Voice" (AC 7), the speaker *is* the voice, in "Procedures for Underground" (PU 24-5) the speaker *hears* the poetic voice, in "Notes from Various Pasts" (AC 10-11) the speaker *catche*s words in her fishing net and the words are like fragments of the poetic voice. In another poem entitled "A Sibyl" (CG 48-50), the speaker *has* a voice (a sibyl in a jar).

But the distinctions do not end there. The poem "A Voice" (AC 58-59) offers a unique example of Atwood's playfulness with the concept. In this poem, the speaker comes to life or is spoken into being, by the voice: indeed, both the speaker of the poem and her companion are surprised at the voice's ability to "think us". In the same way the voice is surprised at his own ability to "think [them]" – in this case, the voice is referred to in the masculine (as "he"): "He sat/ He was curious/ about himself / He wondered / how it managed to think us" (AC 58-59). In other words, the speaker would not even exist if it were not for the voice – the "He" in the poem.

While the relationships between the speaker of the poem and the voice are varied – the voice being either in contrast to or similar to/ identifiable with or part of the speaker of the poem –, the concept of the voice as the speaker's double is perhaps the most frequently recurring concept which finds many variations when the speaker speaks in the first person singular and moves on to a plural ("my voice and I", "my sibyl and I"). The shadow voice (AC 7) however remains more distant, hinting at the ambivalence of the voice that is both foreign and familiar, much like Moodie's double voice in several poems in *The Journals of Susanna Moodie*.

This book will give us an opportunity to highlight occurrences of the voice, focusing first on mapping out the poetic images of the voice. When one holds up a mirror to the varied representations of the poetic voice, what does one see? A particularly striking image is that of the Sibyl crouched in an "ovaltine jar":

> wrinkled as a pickled
> baby, twoheaded prodigy
> at a freakfair
> hairless, her sightless
> eyes like eggwhites (CG 48)

But there are many other representations of the poetic voice. As the reader plunges into Atwood's fifteen books of poetry and discovers the Atwoodian voice in its various poetic guises, a number of questions arise revolving around issues such as: the differences between the "poetic voice", the "living author's" voice and the voice of the author's public persona; the relationship between distinctive voices and audiences; the characteristics of a "writer" as opposed to a tale-teller; the specific group(s) the poet belong to. These questions are not only related to Atwood's understanding of the poetic voice but also to her conception of language crafting and artistic creation.

The term "voice" needs to be explored, both in Atwood's use of the term and in the critic's understanding of the concept. While the idea of a voice as the reflection of a writer's personality has been rejected along with the rise of contemporary criticism (which takes its cue from Barthes who pronounced the author dead), the concept of "voice", in relation to the analysis of an author's work, is as relevant today as before Barthes's declaration. John Drury for example uses the term "voice-print" (343) to characterize an author's identifiable voice, that is the distinctive traits of his or her writing, the unique signature behind his or her work. For the purpose of exploring the concept of a voice, and before I return to Atwood's own use of the term, I will start with John Drury's definition of "voice": "The characteristic sound, style, manner, tone of a particular poet or poem. On the page, a poetic voice comprises diction (word choice), syntax (arrangement of words), attitudes, subject matter, rhythmic proclivities, line lengths, punctuation, the presence or absence of meter and rhyme, and especially the tone." (Drury 342-3). The subject matter, according to Michael Bugeja, is an important starting point in developing a voice: "When [well-known poets like Sylvia Path] matured as poets, they began to write about people and topics that thoroughly consumed them […] Once they had discovered their subject matter, voice followed." (Bugeja 140). In order to express his or her subject matter, the poet resorts to an imagery characterized by the world those images are taken from[2]; the originality of the images lies in their poetic construction as well as the aptness of the comparisons. The "tone" in Drury's definition suggests the very sound of the voice coming from the page, which is somewhat paradoxical since the page is silent[3].

---

[2] These images, in Atwood's case, include nature and technology as well as intertextual references and motifs which we will highlight in the present analysis.
[3] In her introduction to *Voices and Silence in the Contemporary Novel in English*, Vanessa Guignery quotes *A Midsummer Night's Dream* "I see a voice" (V, 1, 189), echoed in Jonathan Rée's *I See a Voice: A Philosophical History of Language, Deafness and the Senses*. Guignery comments: "This might very well reflect the experience of the reader who can see voices on the page but cannot hear them, since writing and reading are essentially silent activities." (Guignery 2009, 1)

How writers achieve tone brings into play other elements of voice like diction and syntax in relation to their subject matter. For example, Atwood's ironic tone is a result of a combination of a number of elements which include the subversion of popular images or expressions, puns and the ordering and laying out of the words on the page. Indeed, tone dictates what synonym to use for certain words; it will also affect the order of words (syntax). The order of words is dictated not only by rules of grammar, but also by the poet's desire to give weight to certain expressions (in order to highlight ideas, thoughts or comments) by displaying the words strategically on the page. The length of lines, the punctuation and rhythmic proclivities of the writing, the way these elements imply pauses, places to speed up or slow down or stop, give us a glimpse into how the author wants his/her poem to sound when read aloud. "The point to be made about the readerly experience [...] is that it incorporates both the visualist and the oral emphases [...]. This experience acknowledges two patterns, with a qualification that we can hear one and see the other" (Bradford 1993, 73). In other words, poetry must be seen as well as heard in order to reveal its full potency: "When we read, either silently or aloud but with a copy of the printed poem before our eyes, we experience both the progressive movement of language and its static visual configurations" (Bradford 1993, 73). The tension between the "movement of language" and "its static visual configurations" also constitutes an element which characterizes the voice.

The decisions a poet makes regarding subject matter, syntax, word choice and line arrangement work together to become the writer's "voice" – not to be equated with the voice of the writer as an individual, behind the words on the page. When analysing a poet's work, one gradually becomes aware of the poetic voice by learning to listen for it. It is surprising that so few critics have paid attention to the voice of Margaret Atwood's poetry in relation to that of her fiction. However, I was struck by Margaret Atwood's own reaction to her poetry at an event which included a reading of her work: it was clear that it had been years since she last re-read *The Journals of Susanna Moodie* and she seemed somewhat astonished as she thought back to the time in her life when she had written this book: "I wrote that? I was so young!" she exclaimed, clearly taken aback by the effect of the voice of the volume and hardly recognizing it as her own. Perhaps Atwood is so busy writing and then promoting her fictional work, that she hardly has the time to look back on her poetry. However, she does state that she considers poetry to be "the heart of language" (SW 346) and that, in her experience of writing, poetry infuses fiction writing.

The example of *The Journals of Susanna Moodie* (where Atwood stages a historical figure – Susanna Moodie – as the speaker of her inter-connected poems) provides me with an opportunity to introduce two other concepts I will be referring to in the present volume: the concepts of the "speaker" and of the "persona". Again, I will refer to a definition which includes both of these concepts and which John Drury provides:

> [The speaker is] the voice that is uttering, chanting, singing, or even thinking the words of a poem; the essential instrument through which a poem's words are channeled and delivered. It may be a careful way of describing the poet herself. It may be a narrator, as in a story.
>
> A poet can, of course, speak through the voice of a character [a persona], as Robert Browning impersonates a Renaissance painter in 'Andrea del Sarto.' Browning says of this practice, "I'll tell my state as though 'twere none of mine. (Drury 298-299)

In other words, the speaker can be seen as the figure that the reader imagines behind the voice. When the poet chooses to speak through the voice of one or several characters, the poet's own voice is comprised of these different voices, including the one of the speaker of the poem which rises above the voices of the other characters in the poem. The poet's unique and identifiable voice is then characterized by Drury's "voice-print" (343) which is as unique as a fingerprint.

Before I articulate the main points of this journey exploring Atwood's poetic voice-print, let me say a few words about Margaret Atwood herself, however unnecessary this may be. Biographical information concerning Margaret Atwood is available in biographical books, critical analyses, academic essays, journalistic articles, Internet pages, the Margaret Atwood Society, etc. Frank Davey's introduction to his book on Atwood's poetics is entitled "An Unneeded Biography", not because so much information on Margaret Atwood is readily available but because many writers claim (Atwood included) that biographical information on the writer is unnecessary[4]. I will therefore limit myself to a few words of presentation.

---

[4] In her introduction to *Novelists in the New Millennium, Conversations with Writers*, Vanessa Guignery quotes a number of writers on the subject: "Milan Kundera wished for the erasure of names: 'I dream of a world where writers will be required by law to keep their identities secret and to use pseudonyms. Three advantages: a drastic reduction of graphomania; decreased aggressiveness in literary life; the disappearance of biographical interpretation of works' (p. 148). In Postscript to *The Name of the Rose*, Umberto Eco proposed a more radical solution – 'The author should die once he has finished writing. So

Margaret Atwood, born on November 18, 1939, is a Canadian poet, novelist, literary critic, essayist and speaker who is an activist in various domains. She has been short-listed for the Nobel prize, is a winner of the Arthur C. Clarke Award and Prince of Asturias award for Literature, has been shortlisted for the Booker Prize five times, winning once, and has been a finalist for the Governor General's Award seven times, winning twice. In short, she is among the most-honored authors of fiction in recent history. With her partner Graeme Gibson, she is a co-founder of the "Writers' Trust of Canada", a non-profit literary organization that seeks to encourage Canada's writing community. While Margaret Atwood is best known for her work as a novelist, she is also a poet, having published more than a dozen books of poetry to date. Many of these volumes are hard to categorize because they can be considered either as long prose poems or short stories.

A countless number of critics have written about Atwood[5]. The early critics focused mainly on Atwood as a major figure in the Canadian nationalist landscape as well as in the feminist landscape. Some of these critics have revised their analysis of Atwood's work, such as Sandra Djwa indicating that Atwood changed from being "a Canadian poet" to an "international woman of letters" (Djwa in York 13-14). Indeed, critics may have started out labeling Atwood as a "Canadian" poet, but soon her work was understood to be relevant beyond the Canadian context. As her reputation as a novelist continues to grow, her poetry production is becoming less prolific, but her voice as a poet follows its journey, confirming the crucial place of poetry in Atwood's work. In her introduction to *Various Atwoods*, Lorraine York reflects on the diversity of Atwood, and her "multiplicity of approaches" previously underlined by Arnold and Cathy Davidson in their volume entitled *The Art of Margaret Atwood: Essays in Criticism* (1981). Fourteen years later, York says, the many facets of Atwood are "steadily increasing; just as Margaret Atwood's inventiveness continues to surprise and to impress her readers" (Djwa in York 1). When Reingard M. Nischik published *Margaret Atwood: Works and Impact* (2000), she turned to Atwood's critics and close collaborators such as agents and publishers, to portray the many facets of the author and her work. Contributors to Nischik's volume all point to Atwood's "quicksilver intelligence, her playfully wicked humour and sense of fun, her extreme perfectionism" (Seligman in Nischik 288), as well as

---

as not to trouble the path of the text' (p. 7) – which the narrator of Julian Barnes's *Flaubert's Parrot* comically echoes by exclaiming: 'the author to the guillotine!' (p. 88)" (Guignery 2013, 1-2).
[5] In their guide book entitled *Margaret Atwood: a Reference Guide, 1988-2005*, Shannon Hengen and Ashley Thomson list out nearly 3000 references of articles on Atwood written between 1988 and 2005 (press articles included).

her "insight into human behavior which goes laser-deep" (Talese in Nischik 289). All of these aspects of her personality and competence are illustrated both in her writing and in her reported professional interactions.

Now it is even more true that years after *Various Atwoods* and the above quoted volumes, Atwood's voice continues to venture out into many different fields, taking on many different forms. As I analyze the nature of the Atwoodian voice, I will raise questions related to how the poetic voice and its various modes of representation evolve throughout these volumes. Very much like the work of critics before me, my analysis can be considered as a supplement to an abundant and heterogeneous critical discourse. Like York, I use the term supplement in Jacques Derrida's sense: an addition, both necessary and optional, that signals to the never-completedness of prior critical texts, and that itself, can be considered as never to be fully completed (York, 1).

While exploring the Atwoodian poetic voice-print, I will also question what the term and its many associations represent for Atwood herself. As previously mentioned, Atwood plays with representations of what she calls "the voice" and these representations are connected to many different concepts (the muse, the artist's double personality, the "other self", the artist's calling or genius beckoning her back to work, or her many metamorphoses or poetic "disguises" which she uses to tell a story or to sing a song and finally her public persona). In her representation or personification of these concepts, Atwood systematically breaks free from all academic characterizations and distinctions between what literary critics refer to as "the voice", "the voice-print", "the speaker" and the "persona". Typically, a poem entitled "Voice" (TT 20-23) stages a persona which is the personification of the artist's gift. This persona (portrayed as a plant) is only one of the personae of the poem. The speaker of the poem is another persona speaking in the first person and referring to the voice-persona as an entity which belongs to the "I" of the poem, all the while existing independently. Therefore, when referring to Atwood's understanding or mentioning of the "voice", I will use inverted commas, or I will use the term voice-persona when the voice is incarnated as a persona. When using literary terms previously defined by critical analysis, I will not use any inverted commas. Finally, whenever referring to characteristics of Atwood's poetic voice, I will use Drury's expression of voice-print.

Turning to the many representations of the Atwoodian poetic voice, from the Sibyl, previously mentioned, to the many personifications or metaphors of the voice in her latest books of poetry, Atwood's split personae seem to navigate between two entities, one that does the living so to speak (that is the one referred

Introduction

to as "I" with "five / senses ribboned like birth- / day presents" (CG 49) and one that does the writing, and that is how I wish to refer to them in this volume, in order to distinguish these two entities. I will also refer to them using the many expressions that Atwood herself has used to portray the voice or the artist on the one hand or, on the other hand, "the thing that calls itself / I" (CG 50) – the "I" whose skin is "a sack of clever tricks" (CG 49) and who prefers to enjoy the presence of "a man danc[ing] / in my kitchen" rather than listening to her Sibyl who calls out: "I prophesy" (CG 50). As previously mentioned, the representation of Atwood's "voice" is far from being a static figure in her poetry: many poems describe the journey of "the voice", its tribulations and its near-death experiences. It is interesting to note that, more often than not, as the adventures of "the voice" unfold, "[t]he thing that calls itself / I" (CG 50) (the one that does the living) looks after the one who "calls to me with the many voices" (CG 50) (the one that does the writing), but it is not systematically the case. Indeed, Atwood also stages a tension between the two entities and the image that is perhaps best suited to illustrate the irreconcilable nature of these entities is the two-headed monster in *Two-Headed Poems*. The peace-making process is also a key element in the representation of "the voice", and it gives birth to many metaphors, such as the "The Woman Who Could Not Live With Her Faulty Heart" (THP 14-15) and "The Woman Makes Peace With Her Faulty Heart" (THP 86-87).

The initial analysis of the representations of the Atwoodian poetic voice will lead into a more personal interpretation of the voice in the second part of this volume. This subjective interpretation of Atwood's poetry has evolved over the years with every re-reading of her work. Critical comments have come to enrich my reading and the critical tools which I resort to here in order to show the originality of the Atwoodian voice are either philosophical tools focusing on vision, perception and reflection, or textual analysis tools which highlight the poetic quality of Atwood's work. I will draw on these tools to outline the philosophical and ideological stance of the Atwood "persona" which I will suggest exists as a permanent entity beyond the many guises of the Atwoodian representations of the poetic voice. In keeping with Atwood's own unanswered questions about the poetic voice, this personal interpretation will remain an open question and is to be considered as a possible lead in the exploration of the nature of the poetic voice and not as an absolute comment.

Since Atwood's poetic voice is not only present in her poetry, but also in her fiction, I will examine the resurfacing of the poetic voice in fiction. The many links between the poetic voice and the fictional voice have led critics to speculate as to what comes first in Atwood's writing. An analytical approach to her work in which volumes of poetry and fiction are examined chronologically will shed light on the relationship between the two forms of writing.

Finally, I will contrast the poetic voice to the voice-print of the living author and that of the author's public persona, each of which are also represented in Margaret Atwood's poetry. I will review Atwood's position on the subject of compromising with the market economy, based on a rich epitext as well as on *Negotiating with the Dead*. In an era of Internet communication, I will show how Atwood has learned to use technological progress on the Internet in order to speak in blog posts and in tweets, which contribute to the construction of her public persona. However my main aim is to show that Atwood's voice on the Internet is different but nevertheless coherent with the message of her artistic work and may go as far as providing a vivid illustration of some of the recurring themes of her poetry.

PART I

Representations and Stagings of a "Voice" in Margaret Atwood's Poetry

CHAPTER 1

Introducing Margaret Atwood's Poetic Voice

Commentators on Margaret Atwood's poetry have often remarked that the title poems of the different volumes convey the theme covered in her work. In a retrospective of Atwood's poetry, these titles can serve as points of departure and foci for a possible re-interpretation. Before highlighting the specificities of each volume, I wish to offer a brief commentary on Atwood's poetic stance.

Atwood's poetry has been labeled as either "autobiographical" or "mythopoeic" (Nischik 97), not to mention all the other labels previously mentioned ("feminist", "canadianist", etc.). The term "mythopoeic" refers to the "myth-making" quality of Atwood's writing as well as to her ability to revisit and subvert myths and cultural references, while the "autobiographical" label points to the highly personal tone of her "voice". However Frank Davey points out that "Atwood's recurrent use of personae […] means that the critic can never be sure that Atwood is speaking in her own voice (i.e. out of her own biography or beliefs) and wishes to be held responsible for the implications of a given statement or image." (Davey 15). Taking his cue from Atwood's poem "True Stories", Davey states that it is irrelevant whether the reader should interpret the poetic voice as stating Atwood's own voice or that of an "unsignalled persona" (Davey 15): as the persona of the poem "True Stories" advises: "Don't ask for the true story; / why do you need it? / […] / The true story is vicious / and multiple and untrue" (TS 3). The same comment applies to criticism, as Davey points out: "criticism of course, is not any more a 'true story' than is an Atwood poem or novel" (Davey 15). So why take any interest at all in the affinities between Atwood's poetry and her fiction and her own life as a person committed to the causes she chooses to support? These affinities can be seen as a sign of Atwood's capacity to explore, challenge, de-construct and re-construct her own world and the world around her. In the inventive craftsmanship with which she organizes a wide range of experiences as poems, it is the autobiographical *staging of a voice* which is of interest to the critic, not the degree of autobiography of the poem. Furthermore, as Sullivan indicates, Atwood is "fascinated by the bizarre fluidity of identity" (221) and, as Atwood's biographer, she notes:

> It almost seems as if we can get a fixed sense of who we are only momentarily, in our encounters with others; alone, we slide back into dark mystery that is ourselves. And for [Atwood] this might have been even more marked. She was such a keen observer and had such capacity to enter the minds of others that there must have been times when she worried whether she had a self. She once told Al Purdy: 'I am a different person (not even slightly but radically different) with each person I know. It is hard when two of them are in the same room. I feel as though I'm being pulled apart.' (Sullivan 221)

Thus, the "glue" that holds the volumes of poetry together is not the poet's autobiographical voice as such but the poet's skills in crafting a voice – or voices. This crafting is achieved through a number of techniques and through a distinctive tone. Indeed, Atwood's volumes of free verse poetry have been described as "both wryly lyric and blunt, savage in their ability to defy reader's expectations" (Wagner-Martin in York 71). The formal general characteristics of her poetry (leaving aside the prose poems, for the time being) are the following: no fixed stanza forms, no regular meter, no rhyme, a playful use of line breaks and punctuation and one (or, at times, several) continuous voice(s) informing the poem through the varying lengths of stanzas and lines[1]. The choice of form proves to be flexible enough to accommodate Atwood's wide range of topics and poetic images. Several of Atwood's poems are organized in the form of a sequence or a cycle. Poetic cycles provide Atwood with an appealing form which she can play with, giving her additional potential for variations and loops, for openness, structure and formal firmness.

Atwood's comments on the differences between writing poetry and writing fiction, help us to further explore questions of form. With a lyric poem, Atwood points out, "you look, and meditate, and put the rock back", while with fiction you "poke things with a stick to see what will happen." Atwood emphasizes that with both "there has to be something under the rock first [...] and this is where hope and despair [...] come into it" (Jarraway in Moss and Kozakewich 280).

If mapping out the themes in Atwood's poetry means looking "under the rock", for "hope and despair", we will take our cue from one of Atwood's poems in *The Door* and focus on darkness first:

> You wanted the hard news,
> the blows of hammers,

---

[1] For a more detailed analysis of form, we will later focus on the individual poems.

bodies slammed through air.
You wanted weaponry,
the glare of metal,
the cities toppled,
the dust ascending,
the leaden thud of judgment.
You wanted fire.

Despite my singed feathers
and this tattered scroll I haul around,
I'm not an angel.
I'm only a shadow of your desires.
I'm only a granter of wishes.
Now you have yours. (TD 79-80)

Fictions and poems, as Atwood underlines, respond to the reader's wishes (his wish for "hard news" and maybe his desire to understand darkness). The rhythmic pattern of this poem serves to underline the message concerning the reader's wishes hammered into the speaker's mind. The line breaks correspond either to a statement concerning the "you" (lines 1, 4 and 9: "You wanted the hard news", "You wanted weaponry", "You wanted fire") or to a list of things the "you" asked for: sensational events, a series of catastrophes ("the blows of hammers, / bodies slammed through air [...] / the glare of metal, / the cities toppled, / the dust ascending, / the leaden thud of judgment"). When the speaker finally reveals herself as a persona in the poem, she stages herself as a strange creature equipped with "singed feathers" and a "tattered scroll", but she claims she is not an angel. And, according to the reader's wishes, the non-angel but angel-like persona is there to deliver the "hard news", a task which is, according to the speaker in "Enough of these Discouragements" (TD 79-80), very much in keeping with the vocation of the poet. So we will start with Atwood's "hard news".

ATWOOD'S FREE VERSE POETRY VOLUMES

A brief chronological presentation of Atwood's poetry will provide an opportunity to explore many of the facets of Atwood's dark themes all the while focusing on the main themes and title poems. My corpus will include the free verse poetry volumes, leaving aside, for the time being, the volumes of short fiction or prose poems (*Murder in the Dark*, 1983; *Good Bones*, 1992; *Bottle*,

2004; *The Tent*, 2006). The free verse poetry volumes that Atwood has written to date are: *The Circle Game* (1967), *The Animals in That Country* (1968), *The Journals of Susanna Moodie* (1970), *Procedures for Underground* (1970), *Power Politics* (1971), *You Are Happy* (1974), *Two-Headed Poems* (1978), *True Stories* (1981), *Interlunar* (1984), *Morning in the Burned House* (1995), *The Door* (2007).

The Circle Game (1967)

The poem "The Circle Game" (which we will come back to for in-depth analysis) and many other poems in this volume combine elements from the personal, social, cultural and political spheres: for example, poems such as "The Circle Game" merge the narcissism of an antagonistic love relationship with wider thematic concerns. "This is a Photograph of Me" (CG 3) is the first of a number of poems about male/female relationships gone awry. This poem serves the function of introducing a landscape interpenetrated with "the human" – in this case, a woman's body, a metaphor central to Atwood's early poetry and prose.

The Animals in That Country (1968)

Throughout all of Atwood's volumes of poetry, nature holds a special place and it becomes particularly apparent with Atwood's volume published in 1968: *The Animals in That Country*. In this volume, nature is both threatened and threatening. It is threatened in the title poem, where the thrust of the poem is ecological, and it is threatening in other poems of that same volume like "Progressive Insanities of a Pioneer" (AC 36-39). In such poems, the external reality, or the outside world seems to be specifically devised to overwhelm and to crush the individual. "Progressive Insanities of a Pioneer" is about an "absence / of order" or an "unstructured / space […] a deluge". The fields themselves which, in darkness, "defend themselves with fences / in vain" (AC 37) eventually modulate into the unfamiliar chaos of nature. The lone and hapless self (a pioneer, a settler, a bus passenger) is all but eradicated. In the volume that follows *The Animals in That Country*, nature often resurfaces as a source of threat.

The Journals of Susanna Moodie[2] (1970)

This volume of Susanna Moodie's fictional "journals" is presented in the form of a sequence of poems. It is a seminal text in the history of the experience of early settlers in Canada. Atwood attempts to imagine and convey Susanna Moodie's feelings about her new life. The book is separated into three separate journals: Journal I, from 1832-1840, starting with her arrival in 1832 ; Journal II encompasses 1841-1870, narrating her adjustment to Canada, and Journal III continues on until 1969, as it includes a post-death narration where Susanna Moodie comments on twentieth-century Canada.

Through the embodiment of the anxieties and longings of a late nineteenth-century woman, *The Journals* are about the tensions between what Moodie ought to think and feel and what she actually does think and feel. In many comments to journalists about the volume, Atwood has highlighted her fascination with Moodie's double voice (CP 72) – a fascination which has inspired many more writers and artists to choose Moodie as a symbol for the Canadian psyche which Atwood has described as schizophrenic (CP 71-78).

Procedures for Underground (1970)

The title poem offers a descent into the underworld. The descent can be given many different symbolic significations. It speaks of resistance, resilience and regeneration. The personae of the title poem and other poems in this volume refuse to be dominated or absorbed: they seek to transcend their alienation. They perform acts of liberation which demonstrate the capacity to resist a male-dominated culture or to resist any condition of imprisonment. In the same way as Atwood's Moodie conjures her dual nature by becoming the national ghost, the persona of "Procedures for Underground", who "crosses over into the wilderness and becomes its voice" (Somacarrera in Moss and Kozakewich 291). As Cynthia Sugars points out, there are only two options: "to be engulfed within the landscape" or "to become the haunter of the landscape following this death" (Sugars in Moss and Kozakewich, 147). The first implies being "murdered as an intruder", the second means death of a different kind as the haunter "authenticate[s] the culture that imposed itself on the landscape." (Somacarrera in Moss and Kozakewich 291).

---

[2] Susanna Moodie was a nineteenth century British immigrant to the backwoods of Canada. She is also a writer and her autobiographical text provides a narrative context from which Atwood grapples with and negotiates the complex, nature of Canadian culture, identity, and art.

The crossing over to an underworld is the leitmotiv of *Procedures for Underground*, but so is the necessity and difficulty of agreeing to return from the underworld, as many of the poems in this volume and subsequent volumes underline ("Orpheus" and "Eurydice" in *Interlunar* for example).

Power Politics (1971)

The power games announced in "The Circle Game" are explored throughout Atwood's poetry with special variations on the love theme in *Power Politics*. An image worth noting is the sinister opening epigraph to this volume: "you fit into me / like a hook into an eye // a fish hook / an open eye." Thus, in keeping with the sinister despair of so many of the poems within that volume, one lyric in particular reads:

> Night seeps into us
> through the accidents we have
> inflicted upon each other
>
> Next time we commit,
> love, we ought to
> choose in advance what to kill. (PP 35)

Aggression between the sexes reaches back to *The Circle Game*, but also reaches forward to *You Are Happy*. However, Atwood avoids the feminist/political trap: she remains fascinated by subversiveness, but stays clear of the man-evil, woman-good dichotomy. Atwood is interested instead in the duality of the individual (and especially the female self), as underlined in a later volume, *Two-Headed Poems*. To encapsulate the message in *Power Politics*, the poem "Lying Here" is emblematic of the ambivalent position of the persona in this volume: she is both rebellious and filled with hope as regards to love[3].

---

[3] For example: "Lying here, everything in me / brittle and pushing you away / This is not something I / wanted, I tell you" (PP 52). However, in spite of its darkness, the sky of the poem which symbolizes the lovers' future, is "incredible" and "blue, each breath / a gift in the steep air" (PP 52). The journey takes place in a land that is not generous ("How hard even the boulders / find it to grow here" 52), but the persona's lover does have something to give her (his "freedom"), which she is hesitant to accept because it is both a "precipice" and a "joy" (52).

You Are Happy (1974)

In *You Are Happy*, the personae's search for identity and experience of wholeness is expressed in terms which are related to the personae's ordinary lives. "Is/Not" (YAH 74-76), "There is Only One of Everything" (92) and "Book of Ancestors" (94-96) express the belief that love can be achieved through the ordinary fellow-traveling of lovers. However, the sexual tension developed in *Power Politics* has all but vanished. A particularly relevant example in that respect is the "Circe/Mud" (46-70) sequence in which women are pictured with withered fists chained around their necks and Circe retaliates and exerts her power over men who bear the heads of eagles or the bodies of pigs.

Two-Headed Poems (1978)

The title of the collection refers to its central cycle of poems concerning Siamese twins. The twins dream of separation, and speak sometimes singularly, sometimes together within the poems. The tension of their desire for separation and their inescapable connection evokes the French-English tensions in Canada and Quebec separatism. These tensions are also evoked in the image of two deaf singers, an image which implies that neither English-speaking Canada nor French-speaking Quebec listens to each other. However, the metaphors of *Two-Headed Poems* can also be interpreted on a more personal level to refer to the tensions between two lovers or any dual entities.

Beyond the theme of a desire for separation, depression is one of the leitmotivs of *Two-Headed Poems*. The theme of depression is linked to images of biological decay: a heart that stops beating (THP 15), fading flowers (THP 55), contamination spreading (THP 74) and biological deterioration foreshadowing the end of an era (THP 89, 175).

True Stories (1981)

The collection is dedicated to Carolyn Forché, poet and human rights advocate. Atwood, as a member of Amnesty International, expresses her views regarding human rights in third-world nations both publicly and through poetry.

The poems of *True Stories* confront the nature of poetry and question poetry's effectiveness in relation to human rights advocacy. In exploring themes of atrocity, of war and torture, the volume diverges from Atwood's previous poetry and raises the question of whether poems such as "Notes Towards a Poem That Can Never Be Written" (TS 45-103) can indeed be defined as poems.

Several poems of *True Stories* deal with a very different subject: loss of love, sometimes against a backdrop of exotic landscape. Therefore, the dominant themes in the volume are those related to the obsession with the true story, political oppression, loss of love as well as the artificiality of both landscape and feelings.

Interlunar (1984)

The collection is divided into two sections: "Snake Poems" and "Interlunar". In the first section, the persona "Snake Woman" explores the animal motif of the snake. The second section deals with themes of darkness. It features several myths related from a female point of view. For example in the poems "The Robber Bridegroom" (I 62), "Orpheus (1)" (I 58-59), "Eurydice" (I 60-61), and "Letter from Persephone" (I 63-64).

Ambivalence and contrasts are key themes in *Interlunar* which commentators have duly noted. Emphasizing the possibility for rebirth[4] and the importance of transition[5], the volume points to the idea of "betweenness"[6] and the "acceptance of unacknowledged contraries" (Blott in McCombs 1988, 276). The poems in *Interlunar* can be linked to *Cat's Eye*, as both forms of writing explore the distinction between darkness and light[7] and both forms claim that "like cats, we need to make the most of the limited light we have." (Birch in Wilson 45) Indeed the narrator's last comments in *Cat's Eye* are: "It's old light, and there's not much of it. But it's enough to see by." (CE 421).

Interlunar marks the end of a regular and abundant flow of poetry which began in 1967. Eleven years will then elapse before the appearance of the next volume.

Morning in the Burned House (1995)

Morning in the Burned House is divided into four parts and displays many of the themes previously mentioned, including topics related to the Canadian landscape,

---

[4] See Wilson's comment on "death [which] makes possible the persona's descent and ultimate rebirth" (Wilson 1993 243).

[5] This transition is reminiscent of the very title of *Interlunar*, meaning "the period between old and new moons" (Wilson 1993 230).

[6] See Norfolk who explores the "[betweenness] which Atwood describes with accuracy and sympathy" Norfolk quoted by Hengen in her article entitled "Strange Visions: Atwood's Interlunar and Technopoetics" (in Wilson 45).

[7] See LeBihan who underscores the "impossibility of clear division between the light and dark" (LeBihan in Howells, Coral Ann and Lynette Hunter 1991, 105).

female-empowerment and torture, or themes related to both women and torture, as in poems such as "Helen of Troy Does Counter Dancing" (MBH 33-36) or "Sekhmet, The Lion-Headed Goddess of War, Violent Storms, Pestilence, and Recovery From Illness, Contemplates the Desert in The Metropolitan Museum of Art" (MBH 39-41). The retelling of myths such as those of Cressida, Helen of Troy, and a lion-headed goddess of war participate in the staging of the torture of women and their resistance.

Beyond the above-mentioned Atwoodian themes, *Morning in the Burned House* contains one distinctive subject matter: the fourth part of the volume is composed of a sequence of poems which was described by Spanckeren as "a memento mori, a skull on the desk, a look at death from a thousand angles" (Spanckeren in Wilson 106). This section explores the theme of aging and mortality, through the depiction and response to the poet's father's illness and decline.

Finally, the volume ends with the title poem "Morning in the Burned House" (MBH 126–127) which follows on from a poem in *Interlunar* "Burned House" (I 93–94). In "Morning in the Burned House", the persona's experience is one of temporal ubiquity: she inhabits two moments simultaneously in the past and in the present – and both moments are superimposed. The experience of ubiquity underlines the personae's capacity to endure and survive and to respond to a moment of sheer joy. This joy is expressed in a similar way in the poem "You Are Happy": it is not so much spelled out as evoked.

The Door (2007)

The Door demonstrates self-awareness on the part of the author, in many different areas. The poems of the volume confront themes of aging and facing death, as well as authorial fame and the efforts to produce writing. Other themes are explored in *The Door*, such as Atwood's last preoccupation with environmental issues, torture and war, and the relation of the personal and the political. From a structural point of view, *The Door* is divided into five sections. The first section explores an eclectic range of "autobiographical" themes such as personal loss of parents, cats or childhood with poems such as "Mourning for Cats" (TD 11) and "My Mother Dwindles" (TD 16-17). The second section explores the role of the poet with special emphasis on poems that I will refer to as "metafictional poems" or "poems for other writers and poets", such as "The Singer of Owls" (TD 43) which aims at comforting an author who did not get the prize he had hoped for. The third and fourth sections confront the horrors of contemporary life, all the while defending or mocking certain types of expectations and desires. The fifth section echoes Atwood's earlier collection, *You Are Happy*, in exploring the domestic relationship between lovers and a range of unexpected surprises and feelings such as the ones evoked in "You Heard the Man You Love" (TD 113).

As I complete this brief overview of Atwood's volumes of free verse poetry, I wish to underline the vastness of the themes covered and the incredible creativity and energy implied in such a prodigious output of poetry. I will often have the opportunity of highlighting further the continuous threads that run through Atwood's poetry and of establishing a link with other forms of writing, whether it be her fiction, her critical work or her comments to the media or on the internet. With the recent publication of Atwood's trilogy (*Oryx and Crake*, *The Year of the Flood*, *Maddaddam*), Margaret Atwood's extraordinary poetic achievement continues to recede in favour of her popular fictional voice. This volume therefore aims to rekindle interest in her achievements as a poet. I will focus on her poetry first and consider the many guises of Atwood's poetic voice. When the reader holds up a mirror to these varied representations of the poetic voice, what does he/she see?

PORTRAITS OF THE POETIC VOICE

Atwood offers a wide range of incarnations and representations of her poetic voice and, in spite of the many metamorphoses and playful handling of the term "voice", the concept behind the term gradually becomes familiar to the reader who recognizes it as typically Atwoodian. In analyzing both the concept of voice and its poetic representation, it is useful to turn to Atwood's epitext and mainly her essays. These essays do not provide a ready-made explanation of Atwood's poetical representation of the voice but they are – as one might expect – consistent with it. In metapoetry, poets inevitably begin with their understanding of concepts such as "voice", "inspiration", "creativity", etc., before turning these concepts into aesthetic material. The original ideas are by no means more significant than the fictional or aesthetic structures built around them. In Atwood's case, the final result of her work is a distinctive poetical version of her understanding of concepts such as "the voice", which are poetical constructions whose reality lies in a aesthetic vision rather than in the intellectual materials which gave rise to them. The concept of voice in Atwood's epitext is akin to that of the "creative geniuses" in Ancient Greece. Like the Greeks, Atwood represents the artist's gift as an independent entity – a character with a free spirit that comes to inhabit the writer or poet. In her portrayal and comments about this genius, Atwood calls it "voice" or "gift". While the poet or writer is not responsible for having that gift, he/she is responsible for nurturing it, looking after it as if it were a little genius in her care. This care-taking involves listening to the voice-persona, feeding it, following its journey to the underground, etc.

Romanticism has offered an understanding of the creative process which has become mainstream and which can be summarized as follows: instead of the genius being a separate entity which comes to inspire the poet (as in Ancient Greece), it is the poet herself who is the genius. This conception of the creative process places a great deal of responsibility on the artist who is solely accountable for the quality of his/her artistic creation. The romantic conception of creativity leaves aside what Atwood, in *Negotiating with the Dead*, calls the "wind" (79, 80) blowing through the artist. In this book-length essay, Atwood argues that the poet is not fully responsible for the quality of her work although she is responsible for persistently showing up at her writing table, on a daily basis, to do her work. Atwood shows that there are other forces at play in the creative process which she goes as far as to portray as voices from the dead. In her poetic work, Atwood expresses a similar idea through the personification of the artist's "other self" or "curio [in a bottle]" (TT 39) or "gift" or "voice" or "unconscious".

Indeed, Atwood personifies the creative genius and, while subjecting it to many metamorphoses, her poems also highlight a number of the genius's persistent traits or characteristics: the genius needs nurturing; it is demanding, sometimes overbearing. The "thing that calls itself I"(CG 50) has to learn to compromise with the genius. This requires sacrifices and renunciations on the part of the "I" – the one that cares about living rather than writing. As for the physical characteristics of the genius, he is frequently either old and wise or young and hungry – and in both cases, he cannot give without taking.

As images of the artist's personified gift are associated with other images (of the "other self" or the "unconscious" for example), many more questions arise concerning the poetic voice: for instance, is the other self to be equated with the poetic voice? Allowing for the other self or "Siamese Twin" (THP 59) to exist, making room for it to express itself, often implies resistance and combativeness or a discovery process and a journey. In Atwood's poetry, all of these concepts lead to further personification and metaphors. We may now examine examples of poems where Atwood's understanding of the creative process becomes apparent or when it raises further questions concerning the poet's identity. In the prose poem entitled "Voice" the speaker first proclaims the existence of a "voice" which belongs to the "I" of the poem: "I was given a voice. That's what people say about me. I cultivated my voice, because it would be a shame to waste such a gift." (TT 21) The poem then portrays the poetic voice in the form of a plant: "I pictured this voice as a hothouse plant, something luxuriant, with glossy foliage and the word tuberous in the name, and a musky scent at night." (TT 21) This representation of the voice as a plant is not uncommon in Atwood's poetry, although the animal representation is more frequent. The type of plant that is conjured up in this image is exotic, overwhelming and bold – with a tendency to grow faster than plants in moderate climates, an overpowering smell "at night", and described as "tuberous" – a qualification which evokes an excess of life.

Whether an animal or a plant, the voice has a life of its own. It grows and blooms: "I watched it climb up inside my neck like a vine" (TT 21), taking over the speaker of the poem by moving into strategic places, like her windpipe. The "I" of the poem is reminiscent of what the reader could call the "one that does the living" as opposed to Atwood's "thing that calls itself / I" (CG 50). The speaker considers the voice as a separate autonomous entity and watches as the voice develops and wanders off on a journey of her own: "What I saw was my voice, ballooning out in front of me like the translucent greenish membrane of a frog in full trill." (TT 22). The vegetable and animal imagery merge as the plant's "greenish membrane" is compared to a frog.

The shape of the poet's voice or other self is not always as clearly defined as in the poem quoted above. Sometimes the other self is not given a specific shape or sometimes it is concealed at first or hidden away in the most unexpected place. In "This Is a Photograph of Me" (CG 3), the persona is located in the center of a lake, "just under the surface", because "The photograph was taken / the day after I drowned." (CG 3). A mysterious piece of advice follows in the last stanza of the poem:

> It is difficult to say where
> precisely, or to say
> how large or small I am:
> the effect of water
> on light is a distortion
>
> but if you look long enough,
> eventually
> you will be able to see me.

The persona of the poem thus encourages the "you" of the poem (possibly the reader) to look for an image of a drowned "I" whose identity is lurking "just under the surface" of a lake. Clearly the persona seeks to define this image.

Although she outlines the background of the picture in great detail and although she goes as far as calling her own description a "photograph" in the very title of the poem, the image remains blurry. The first line of the poem breaks in mid-sentence "It is difficult to say where" and it breaks again in line 2 ("precisely, or to say"), as if to illustrate the very difficulty of finding and describing the drowned persona. The mysterious identity escapes the reader and the persona underlines that we need to "look long enough" in the hope that "eventually" something will become clear. The word "eventually" is isolated in a one-word line, pointing to the length of the searching and groping process in order to reveal the drowned persona.

Atwood's poetry is saturated with more blurred images, undefined entities that can be interpreted as the poet's other self or "voice". Furthermore, while the other self is sometimes referred to as the "voice", that is the artistic component of the persona – as in the poem "Voice" (TT 20-23) or the poem "A Voice" (AC 58-59) – it is not always the case. In many poems, Atwood chooses to focus on elements that she generally associates with a "voice", but that are not the "voice" itself. For example, Atwood plays with notions such as the capacity for creation, or word constructions or core material that the writer travels with, or the construction of identity. The notion of identity which is central to Atwood's work is staged in a wide range of metaphors. Whether Atwood refers to the identity of the poet, or the post-colonial identity, or both, the identity quest takes on many forms such as undertaking a journey or looking into the mirror.

In many of Atwood's poems, various insects and horrible creatures stand for the human capacity for creation. Creation starts with resistance ("a furtive insect, sly and primitive / the necessary cockroach / in the flesh / that nests in dust" in "A Meal", CG 28-29). The personification of the voice as an insect or some other kind of ugly creature is extremely meaningful in Atwood's imagery. Inevitably, the voice is incarnated in an ugly form, such as that of an insect or a wrinkled creature which is perfectly conscious of its own unattractive appearance. In "A Sibyl" (CG 48-50), the voice crouches in a jar on the window shelf. In "Bottle II" (TT 37-40), the voice takes on the form of an insect whose "fine and spidery fingertips" point to roads as "a process, not a location", the "trembling branchwork" of the future. The "arachnid state" of the voice accounts for its ability to crawl into the darkest corners and to see the world as roads which "are forking all the time". The voice thus brings the persona to change her outlook on life and to make use of the arachnid qualities bestowed upon her. As the personae of "A Sibyl" and "Bottle II" acknowledge the existence of the voice, they become two-headed creatures. They are composed of a "normal" persona and an insect-like personified voice. This imagery gives way to several beastly animal metaphors. Internal conflicts within the persona are metaphorized as a siamese creature in the opening quotation of *Two-Headed Poems*. The voice of "The shadow voice" (AC 7) takes on various visible animal-like forms which exist, speak and act autonomously.

In the same way, the speaker in "A Sibyl" (CG 48-50) sees herself as more than "The thing that calls itself / I" (CG 50), the speaker in "Bottle II" comprises a foreign entity. The speaker in "Bottle II" describes itself only in vague terms: it has cast away its past form: it used to be "young" and "beautiful" with "picturesque robes and exceptional talents" (TT 39) and has become "so tiny, so translucent, so wispy, so whispery" (TT 39). Even in Atwood's early poetry, written when Atwood was in her twenties, the persona portrays her voice-persona as a wrinkled and old spider-like figure. In both of the above quoted poems, the speaker realizes she is inhabited by two beings and she is asked to make more room for the sibilant "voice": gradually, this "voice" becomes more powerful. In "Bottle II", the "voice" stages itself not only as an unusual creature but also as a "curio". This "curio" seems quite innocent in the beginning of the prose poem, but it becomes a more significant figure in the last paragraph of the poem: "I am not a curio, my friend. Or rather I am a curio, but you'd have to say the curio, the best one of all. Only the very curious acquire curios like this." (TT 39). The persona who has earned the privilege of having been chosen by the "voice", also becomes a curio (perhaps with the potential to inspire other through her legacy of poems). The speaker acknowledges that they are two of a kind: "We are both the kind of person who takes the corks out of bottles. Not bottles of wine: bottles of sand." (TT 40). If one compares "A Sibyl", published in 1965, to "Bottle II", published thirty-two years later, one can not help but notice similarities and differences in the representation of the "voice" and its dwelling. The dwelling of the "voice" has evolved from an Ovaltine jar to a bottle of sand, thus blurring the contours of the voice-persona's home. The "voice" itself has become more blurry – from an insect to a curio whose shape is not specified. A muted curio at first – and then, when corks are taken out of sand bottles, the "voice" begins to speak. It enters into the speaker's space and starts to take over, like an insect crawling out of a corner.

CHAPTER 2

The Voice and the Underworld

THE EMERGENCE OF A POETIC VOICE

As previously mentioned Atwood's epitext can shed light on some of the concepts that the author plays with creatively and help us explore the relationship between the writer, and the emergence of a poetic voice. We may start by examining the location of what Atwood calls the voice in *Negotiating with the Dead*. Atwood claims the voice comes from the "invisible man", that is the writer who is both present and absent in the text: "[t]he writer is thus the original invisible man: not there at all but also very solidly there, at one and the same time [...] we can hear a voice" (ND 148). This allusion to the origin of the voice is in keeping with Drury's definition of the term voice, when quoting Carl Dennis: "For a poem to be convincing, the primary task of the writer is to construct a speaker whose company is worth keeping, who exhibits certain virtues that win the reader's sympathetic attention." (in Drury 343). Indeed, this conception of the voice, which completes the critical comments and quotes given in the introduction to this volume, is perhaps the closest of all to Atwood's. But Atwood adds another dimension which is present neither in Drury's definition nor in Dennis's. This dimension is encapsulated in the title of *Negotiating with the Dead* and further expanded in the last and eponymous chapter of this book. Atwood's "hypothesis is that not just some, but all writing of the narrative kind, and perhaps *all* writing, is motivated, deep down, by a fear of and a fascination with mortality – by a desire to make the risky trip to the Underworld, and to bring something or someone back from the dead." (156).

Indeed, Atwood's seems to set as a requirement for the emergence of the voice that the speaker undertake a journey to the underworld. Many poems, such as "Procedures for Underground" (PU 24-5), abundantly illustrate this motif of the underworld journey. Furthermore, in her epitext, Atwood highlights the connection between one's urge to write and the experience of one's mortality. She quotes Chekhov who, in a novel entitled *A Widow for One Year*, describes a character in melancholy mood, looking out onto the sea, thinking about his own mortality and suddenly overcome by the urge to "snatch [...] up a pencil [to] write his name on the first thing that comes handy" (in ND 157). This is only one

15

of the examples Atwood provides in order to illustrate how a "definite concern with [death] – an intimation of transience, of evanescence, and thus of mortality, [is] coupled with the urge to endite" (ND 158).

Seeking to explain the connection between an awareness of mortality and the urge to write, Atwood compares writing to other forms of art and underlines the specificity of writing, which is characterized by:

> [...] its apparent permanence, and the fact that it survives its own performance [...]. Other art forms can last and last – painting, sculpture, music – but they do not survive as voice. And [...] writing is writing down, and what is written down is a score for voice, and what the voice most often does – even in the majority of short lyric poems – is tell, if not a story, at least a mini-story. Something unfurls, something reveals itself. [...] There's a path [...] There's a plot. The voice moves through time, from one event to another, or from one perception to another, and things change, whether in the mind alone or the outside world (ND 158).

In other words, not only is writing a lasting art form, but it is also a "mini-story". If "[s]omething unfurls [and] something reveals itself" (ND 158) in the course of the creative process, finding one's own voice according to Atwood in *Negotiating with the Dead* is, as previously mentioned, connected to a journey which, more often than not, can be described as heroic. Heroic journeys, according to Atwood's epitext, require acknowledging the dead and "negotiating with the dead". For example, Atwood quotes "In Flanders Fields" by the Canadian poet John McCrae which she claims is the first "request-by-the-dead" poem that she ever was exposed to (ND 165) and then she goes on to give a series of examples where mythical and literary heroes request something from the dead. "Why do these heroes do it? Why take the chance?" (ND 167), Atwood asks before answering her own rhetorical question:

> Because the dead have some very precious and desirable things under their control, down there in their perilous realm, and among these are some things you yourself may want or need.
>
> What sort of things? To summarize: (1) riches; (2) knowledge; (3) the chance to battle an evil monster; (4) the loved and the lost. This list is not all-inclusive, but it includes the main aim of such journeys. (ND 168)

And so it is with the journeys of poets: "the poet, armed only with his poetry, enters the realm of the dead" (ND 172). Much like Atwood's poem "Euridice", and the Euridice described in *Negotiating with the Dead* who is "lost [...b]ut regained again. But lost again" (ND 172), the happy ending involves accepting a change. Atwood quotes Thomas Wolfe: "You can't go home again [...] but you can, sort of when you write about it." (173). "And so it is with all happy endings of all books, when you come to think about it." (173); and Atwood concludes: "A book is another country. You enter it, but then you must leave: like the Underworld, you can't live there." (ND 173).

Rilke, in his Sonnets to Orpheus, makes the underworld journey simply a precondition of being a poet. The journey must be undertaken, it is necessary. "The poet – for whom Orpheus is the exemplary model – is the one who can bring the knowledge held by the Underworld back to the land of the living, and who can then give us, the readers, the benefits of this knowledge." (ND 173-74). Describing Rilke's Sonnet 9 (Part I) on Orpheus, Atwood says: "This poet doesn't just visit the Other World. He partakes of it. He is double-natured, and can thus both eat the food of the dead and return to tell the tale" (ND 174). Atwood quotes Rilke[1]:

> And the world has to be twofold
> before any voice can be
> eternal and mild (ND 174)

It is this twofold world which makes the voice "eternal and mild", which Atwood's poems portray most convincingly, staging a speaker who is in contact with inspiring voices or creatures. These voices or creatures show the speaker the way to and back from the underworld. Whether it is portrayed in mythical terms as the kingdom of Hades in "Procedures for Underground" (PU 24-5), or whether it takes on the more practical form of a shelf, a bottle, a jar or a dark corner, the underworld – the true dwelling place of the inspiring creature(s) or voice(s) – is mysterious, possibly dangerous, it is not a recommended place for the speaker or reader to dwell in permanently. In "Procedures for Underground", it is a "country beneath the earth"; it "has a green sun" "and the rivers flow backwards" (24). In "A Sibyl" (CG 48-50), an unusual type of creative genius crouches in a jar. While this "jar" can be interpreted as a form of underworld, it also reminds the reader

---

[1] Virgil is usually assumed to be the first writer to make the underworld trip but Atwood proposes "a much earlier prototype for the subterranean adventurer as a writer – the Mesopotanian hero Gilgamesh" (ND 175).

that the dwelling place of the sibyl (or creative genius) is different from the one of the speaker of the poem. The word "creative genius" is not mentioned in "A Sibyl" (CG 48-50) but only implied, and the figure for this genius is first discovered among bottles accumulating on shelves:

> on my shelves the bottles
> accumulate
> my sibyl (every woman
> should have one) has chosen
> to live there (CG 48)

A special recommendation is given in parentheses: "(every woman / should have one)", a change of tone, perhaps a tongue-in-cheek comment mischievously added by the speaker. The sentence of this stanza is displayed in fragments resulting from the unexpected line breaks and parentheses which are frequent in Atwood's poetry. Although the stanza can be considered as one statement, the parenthesis makes an independent statement which is central to the poem (mainly stating the importance for the female reader to have a sibyl of her own). The line break in mid parenthesis creates anticipation, separating the subject "every woman" from the verb and object "should have one". Another separation between subject, verb and complement can be observed in the last lines of the stanza: "my sibyl [...] has chosen/ to live there". Atwood's playful use of meter and line breaks serves to generate different levels of anticipation and arrivals, to use Attridge's terminology: the questions that arise (such as: what should every woman have? Where is the "my sibyl" that the speaker alludes to? What is its hiding place? What is it doing? Why is it in a jar? etc.) reinforce the reader's interest in the sibyl. The poem partly answers the reader's questions but only partly because the speaker's treatment of these questions is both serious and playful. Also, some of the details in the poem are puzzling. For example, the one of the "jar" seems to imply that the Sibyl can be put into something that is easy to carry. Here Atwood's message mimics the tone of a TV commercial, which places special emphasis on the product's usefulness and convenient attributes – which is both essential and trivial to the main theme concerning independence and inspiration.

While the speaker in "A Sibyl" (CG 48-50) points to the genius (the artist's gift or voice) in a jar which corresponds to the Sibyl's own choice of dwelling, the voice in Atwood's poetry is not restricted to this one location: in "This Is a Photograph of Me" (CG 3), the voice is located in a lake, in a "Bottle II", it is a bottle, in "A Meal", a dark corner. Again, the tone of the speaker describing the home of the voice is either humorous or serious, or both. All of the above representations of the place where the voice resides correspond to Atwood's symbolic underworld, presented both humorously and seriously. The places and landscapes described contribute to the representation of the poetic voice in its natural habitat, so to speak, and these dwelling places of the voice may even come to replace the description of the voice itself, as, for example, in some of the previously quoted poems. In those instances, the places the voice resides in say as much about the voice as the description of the voice itself. As the speakers of the poem describe the dwelling place of the voice, these underworld locations partake in the very emergence of the poetic voice. The humorous tone of the poems often takes the reader by surprise and this may be interpreted as a direct result of the speaker's sense of mischievousness, connected with her ability to inhabit a twofold world, to use Rilke's expression. This twofold world is what Frank Davey calls the Atwoodian male and female space – a duality which is highly characteristic of the Atwoodian voice.

MALE AND FEMALE SPACE AND THE WORLD OF THE UNDERGROUND

Davey considers male and female space to be "[p]erhaps the most pervasive element in Margaret Atwood's poetry" (Davey 17). The male space is a space that asserts the priority of space over time. It is dominated by technology – measurements and instrumentation. The female space is characterized by its acceptance of time and natural processes and associated with organic elements. According to Davey, "[t]he Male is not merely inherited, defined by 'memories and procedures,' but in *The Circle Game* and after, is mathematical, imposes 'ruled squares on the green landscape' (CG 18)." (Davey 17). It is this enclosing male space which the pioneer of "Progressive Insanities of a Pioneer" in *The Animals in that Country* "attempts to 'impose...with shovels' on the Canadian landscape." (Davey 18). The landscape itself symbolizes female space and Davey further highlights the contrast to male space. It is "its Other – the 'girl' who must be fitted into the pastoral conventions, the 'green landscape' that must yield to chessboard pattern. Male space is substantial, ostensibly unchanging; female space is insubstantial, anonymous, subject to time, and often expressed as organic matter." (Davey 17).

Atwood's poetry resonates with examples of violence of male space against female space. For example, in *Power Politics*, male space is metallic and potentially lethal: "a fish hook" in a woman's "open eye" (PP 1). The idea of violence is expressed in the persona's characterization of the man and in the predictable, patterned relationship he seeks. The female space "replies to his phallic egocentric violence with its own anonymous and organic silence." (Davey 18).

Every poem in *Power Politics* is an argumentation of female resistance to the domination of male space. Coming back to our earlier example of "The Circle Game", we cannot help but notice that the appearance of the persona on the photograph is not, as we would expect, a spatial phenomenon; it takes place in time – "if you look / long enough, / eventually / you will be able to see me" (CG 3). With this photograph, the persona of the poem provides the reader with a form of self-portrait. She is one of the resistant females or the artist figures which are recurrent in Atwood's poetry: as she looks into the mirror, she tries to identify what makes her unique.

There are other examples of poems that use photographs with dissolving or fleeting subjects to argue about the artificiality of the time-fixing power of male space. In those poems (for example "Girl and Horse, 1928", PU 10 and "Camera", CG 45-46), the subject who evades and resists the "organized instant" is a woman. The poem "Camera" illustrates the time-fixing power of male space and female resistance in so far as the male subject is the photographer wishing to capture the instant by composing every element in the picture.

> you want to have it and so
> you arrange us:
>
> in front of a church, for perspective,
> you make me stop walking
> and compose me on the lawn;
>
> you insist
> that the clouds stop moving
> the wind stop swaying the church
> on its boggy foundations
> the sun hold still in the sky
>
> for your organized instant (CG 45)

The artificiality of the composition is emphasized by line breaks, word order and word choice. The highest level in the phrasing (to use Attridge's terminology[2]) comprises all three stanzas, from "you want", line 1 to "in the sky", line 10). The second level in the phrasing breaks the poem into three sections which correspond to the three stanzas, each making a statement about the schemes of the photographer. What the first two levels of scansion[3] show is that the onward movement of the lines is produced by the statement from line 1 to 10 whose implications gradually unfold in the two other statements embedded in the first. This movement is strengthened by the deep connection between the first and second level of phrasing – mainly as the final line ("for your organized instant") is preceded by a run-on line which begins in line 6. The insistence of the photographer of the poem seems all the more ridiculous that, without realizing it, he refuses the very essence of life: the movement of the clouds and the sun, and the poetic "swaying [of] the church / on its boggy foundations".

In the stanzas that follow the three above stanzas, the female subject however challenges the photographer's intention: "Camera man / how can I love your glass eye?" (CG 45). As the female subject describes in detail the uselessness of the photographer's enterprise, she also highlights his vulnerability: he is, himself, subject to temporality. The phrasal movement mirrors the construction of the beginning of the poem except that the reader is presented, not with what the photographer insists on having, but with what *there is*. The injunction "look again", addressed to a "you", located "wherever you partly are" is the turning point of the poem. The last six stanzas include the same images as the first

---

[2] This is how Attridge defines phrasing: "In our discussion of English verse forms in the foregoing chapters, we have frequently noticed the important part played by syntax and meaning in the movement of poetry. [...]
We call this dimension of the movement of poetry *phrasing*, a word which refers both to syntax and to meaning, and which in its form ("phrasing" rather than "phrases") indicates the *dynamic* nature of the phenomenon it refers to. Alternatively, we use the term *phrasal movement*, to remind us that this property of verse interacts constantly with [...] rhythmic movement. [...] A poem's phrasing is an important part of its varying sense of pace and onward impetus, and of its different degrees and types of pause and closure. Like meter and rhythm, phrasing is not something we *add* to language but something that is already part of what we know and do when we speak and understand a language." (Attridge 182). Attridge considers different levels of phrasing from the long unit of a full poem to shorter units which correspond to hierarchic units of the sentences within the poem: "Now a crucial fact about phrasing is that [...] it takes place over shorter and longer spans of the linguistic material *at the same time*. The movement within each sentence happens concurrently with the longer movement from one sentence to the next, and the same is true for shorter divisions." (Attridge 185).
[3] In *The Poetry Dictionary*, Drury defines scansion as the "marking of a poem [that] indicates its metrical structure and how it sounds" (Drury 273).

stanzas of the poem (the church, the speaker's clothes, the speaker herself, the landscape surrounding the church), but they are displayed differently, semantically, syntaxically and metrically:

> Wherever you partly are
> now, look again
> at your souvenir,
> your glossy square of paper
> before it dissolves completely:
>
> it is the last autumn
> the leaves have unravelled
>
> the pile of muddy rubble
> in the foreground, is the church
>
> the clothes I wore
> are scattered over the lawn
> my coat flaps in a bare tree
>
> there has been a hurricane
>
> that small black speck
> travelling towards the horizon
> at almost the speed of light
>
> is me (CG 45-46)

This poem serves the purpose of illustrating female resistance over male domination and it also provides us with yet another representation of the poetic voice: in the last stanza, the speaker has lost her shape as a persona and is merely "that small black speck / travelling towards the horizon / at almost the speed of light". The direct address, "look again", reinforced by the list of items which the speaker presents as very different from the way the photographer meticulously organized them contrasts with the effect of the monosyllables in the last line of the poem: the resistance of the speaker is encapsulated in those two simple words "is me": the "I" that dares speak her identity finally escapes the camera's attempt at capturing her.

The vanishing of the physical shape of the speaker coincides with the advent of a poetic voice, portrayed in its minimal form – a black speck –, evading male domination. The flight of the poetic voice taking place at the speed of light points to similarities between the voice and cosmic elements. This further enriches the imagery of the female space and its opposition to male space.

Having described both the female and male space, we may now come back to the dwelling place of the voice, which I have associated with Atwood's symbolic underground. The underground differs from female space although they have points in common: both the unpredictable elements and the possibility of withdrawal are characteristics of the female world or underground. But the underground world is presented as a refuge for the female subjects who, like the personae of *Power Politics*, find their identity rejected by a male subject or by a pragmatic, technological society.

In *Procedures for Underground*, Atwood offers a variety of uses for the underworld image to symbolize repression, the personal unconscious, the mythical underworld as well as the fertile natural world. There is a sense of danger in the underworld which we have previously highlighted in "Procedures for Underground". In "Delayed Message" (PU 19) the persona imagines her other self (possibly the voice), wearing the same "grey / skirt and purple sweater" (PU 19), "rising like an eyeless spirit from the lake to confront her" (Davey 110). Here the underground stands for repression and spiritual death. It may be the realm of an essential process but it is also a place where a human cannot live permanently: "It is dangerous because it is indifferent to human needs; as *Surfacing*'s narrator sees in the last words of that book, 'the trees surround...asking and giving nothing (192)'." (Davey 110)

The underground is present in the form of dreams which are recurrent in Atwood's poetry. Many of the poems in the volume entitled *The Journals of Susanna Moodie* for example, show Moodie's personal unconscious to be accessible through dreams. For instance, Moodie dreams of a deer hunter who claims he dies every time he kills, thus exposing the impossibility of wanting to dominate nature[4]. "The Creature of the Zodiac" (PU 29) offers another example of the importance of the unconscious. The poem sums up the difference between full control expressed by the persona in the day time ("In the daytime I am brave,[...] / I have everything under control", PU 29), and the unconscious

---

[4] In *The Journals of Susanna Moodie*, the deer hunter's death suggests crossing over into the wilderness and becoming one with nature. Sugars points to many other examples of characters crossing over into the wilderness in Atwood's novels and short stories. See Cynthia Sugars article entitled "'saying Boo to Colonialism': *Surfacing*, Tom Thomson, and the National Ghost" (Sugars in Moss and Kozakewich, 137-158).

surfacing at night: "But at night the constellations /emerge [...] / their teeth / grow longer for being starved" (PU 29). The world of the underground is a natural form – "constellations" oppose human "control". Much as Freudian psychology argues about the power of the repressed experience, Atwood's underground is populated by creatures whose teeth grow larger for being "starved" or ignored. According to Davey, "[t]he dream world is dangerous because it is unacknowledged by the waking life, not included within it." (Davey 111).

Remembering a dream, going underwater, entering a maze or traveling in darkness are recurrent images in both Atwood's fiction and poetry. These images represent the experience of traveling to Hades's underworld where the persona enters an instructive and yet dangerous rite of passage. This, very much like the narrator's plunge into the lake in *Surfacing*, has the power to transform the persona.

THE POWER OF THE UNDERWORLD

How is this transformation achieved? Whether it be the underworld itself, or creatures from the underworld, or the voice whispering to us from the underworld, this domain carries news from another and more fertile land, a more elemental land. Here the personae not only find a refuge from male domination, but they also learn new languages and are infused with new energy. Images of this fertility abound in Atwood's poetry, but most are highly ambiguous. For example, it is the "bush garden" of *The Journals of Susanna Moodie* from which strawberries come surging while everything planted "come[s] up in blood", or it is an eel caught in "Fishing for Eel Totems" (PU 68-69) and the persona, after eating the eel, claims:

> After that I could see
> for a time in the green country;
>
> I learned that the earliest language
> was not our syntax of chained pebbles
>
> but liquid, made
> by the first tribes, the fish
> people. (PU 98)

The very form of the poem illustrates the persona's new language. From the sonorities (the alliteration in the smooth fricative "first tribes, the fish"), to the images, syntax and phrasal movements, the poem displays a fluidity ("not our syntax of chained pebbles"), liquid sounds, short lines, liquid lines which are a sign of fluidity, as if something liquid were leaking into the text. The persona's enlightenment is the result of eating an eel who is killed and silenced and yet speaks to the persona in its mysterious way: "its long body whipped on the grass, reciting / all the letters of its alphabet" (PU 68). Just like the buffalo, described as a divinity – "the god of this place: brutal, zeus-faced" (PU 71), the sacred animal is threatened by extinction. The journey to the underworld restores a connection to these threatened animals and to the divine; on the journey, the persona eats a different type of food; this food provides a spiritual nourishment and an experience which becomes a gateway to hidden meaning. Davey notes that going under water in Atwood's work provides a similar experience to a journey to the underworld:

> Underwater, like the water that claims Susanna Moodie's son [...] is a mythic and instructive realm. Going under water in Atwood's writing usually means entering an instructive, ominous, and potentially transforming experience [...]. (Davey 111)

Davey provides examples from Atwood's fiction, including, on a comic level, the example of *Lady Oracle*'s mock suicide in Lake Ontario or Marian MacAlpin's baths in *The Edible Woman* in which she slowly gains insight concerning her destructive relationship with Peter. Howells points to several other examples in Atwood's fiction where characters go through a symbolic death by drowning as in *Surfacing*, with the narrator's plunge into the lake. Death, rebirth and greater power are also the subject of the poem entitled "Procedures for Underground" where the persona shares underground "procedures" which are the very fruit of her experience: indeed, she does not simply retrace an inward journey, but she offers the reader a guide (in the form of precise instructions to undertake this dangerous and risky journey to the kingdom of Hades) as well as the ultimate secret to be empowered by the journey to the underworld.

> Those who live there are always hungry;
>
> from them you can learn
> wisdom and great power (PU 24)

In this kingdom – the underworld of classical mythology – allusions to souls and to shadows which come to haunt the visitor abound. The relationship of the persona with the subterranean creatures leads her to "wisdom and great power" (PU 24). The poem stages a permanent opposition between two worlds or two components of the subject, illustrated by the tension between the form of the poem and its content: indeed, the regular structure of the stanzas contrasts with what is evoked in the poem – this strange underland landscape. While the construction of the poem (ten stanzas of three lines each) is regular (which is highly unusual in Atwood's poetry), the stress pattern may differ – which is a significant detail in itself: it may suggest a precision which matches expectations but which is not to be trusted. The subtitle of the poem itself – "(Northwest Coast)" indicated in brackets – is typical of Atwood's humour: it points to a geographical indication corresponding to a precise place on a map. This geographical indication is of course unnecessary in the case of a metaphorical journey. The poem begins with what Davey would call a familiar Atwood "mirror" image. It describes the underworld's logic:

> The country beneath the earth
> has a green sun
> and the rivers flow backwards; (24)

The line break after "The country beneath the earth" positions the subject at the head of the poem: it is this "country beneath the earth" which the speaker plans to describe to the "you" of the poem (and to the reader), in order to map out the areas of potential importance or danger. Visual points of reference no longer apply (the sun is green), and the underworld defies the logic of the "ordinary" world we live in: "the trees and rocks are the same / ... but shifted". The inhabitants of this world are "always hungry". They are from the world of the unconscious, and they hold power and wisdom. The animals are equally powerful and the reader is told to seek them out:

> You must look for tunnels, animals
> burrows or the cave in the sea
> guarded by the stone man (24)

The "stone man" remains mysterious, expressionless, neither helpful nor difficult. However, "those who were once your friends ... will be changed and dangerous" (24). The following stanzas of the poem explain to the reader how to prepare for the journey: unlike in the more practical poem "Provisions", the emphasis is placed on psychological preparation: "Resist [your former friends], be careful

/never to eat their food" (25). More recommendations follow, so as to say to the reader: proceed with care and caution, in order to discover the real nature of things. "Procedures for Underground" thus opens the gates to a hazardous journey to insight and self-knowledge. In the end, the fruits of the journey are promising:

> Afterwards, if you live, you will be able
>
> to see them when they prowl as winds,
> as thin sounds in our village. You will
> tell us their names, what they want, who
>
> has made them angry by forgetting them. (25)

The new stanza after "you will be able" creates anticipation as to the new powers given to the visitor of the underworld. The ability to see what the addressee of the poem previously could not is followed by an indication as to what the "you" will do. The line break after "you will" creates further anticipation. The unexpected line break separating subject from verb in "who / has made them angry by forgetting them" underlines the question concerning those whose names we do not know yet and who have been made angry by being cast into oblivion. The descent to the underworld will bring insight concerning the hunger and anger of "those who were once your friends", but the speaker further states "For this gift, as for all gifts, you must / suffer" (25) and:

> ... those from the underland
>
> will be always with you, whispering their
> complaints, beckoning you
> back down; while among us here
>
> you will walk wrapped in an invisible
> cloak. Few will seek your help
> with love, none without fear. (25)

Every line in the last two stanzas contains either a "you" or a "your" which is in opposition to one single "us" which stands for the underworld. What the "you" has the potential to achieve is underlined by this reiteration of the second person pronoun. The poem finishes with other people's perception of the "you" and the last run-on line serves to reinforce the manner in which these other people will seek help from the newly empowered "you".

The hazardous journey to gain insight and self-knowledge is portrayed not only as a necessary step to escape imprisonment, but also as a fruitful experience, potentially useful to others as well, and even enjoyable at times. These positive aspects are highlighted in Atwood's poetry to such an extent that the return journey sometimes seems difficult. In a series of three poems entitled "Orpheus I" (I 58-59), "Orpheus II"(I 78) and "Eurydice" (I 60-61) in *Interlunar* the Eurydice persona, present in all three poems, is reluctant to embark on a return journey, even if the refusal to return signifies death.

To conclude on Atwood's underworld, it is interesting to note that, while such importance is given to finding one's way to and back from the underworld, the theme of exploring the underworld, in Atwood's later poetry, gives way to a different type of journey which is less solitary and more about gaining an understanding of companionship as the speaker stages herself with a partner who becomes her fellow traveler.

CHAPTER 3

Representations of the Aging Voice-persona

TEMPORALITY AND ACCEPTANCE OF OLD AGE

We suggested earlier that the acceptance of temporality was a characteristic of female space as Atwood's early poems illustrate, from the time-fixing formal garden in *Double Persephone* to the shore by the a-temporal lake "This Is a Photograph of Me" (CG 3), and to the playground of "Girl and Horse, 1928" (PU 10). To quote Davey, Atwood's poems suggest that "[t]emporality lurks [...] under the deceptively solid surfaces of human creations." (20). We may wonder how Atwood's voice-persona itself is affected by temporality and whether it is possible to determine the age of the voice. In Atwood's first volumes of poetry, the voice-persona has already been described as old (as the "wrinkled" Sibyl previously mentioned), so how can she get any older? These rather simplistic questions pave the way for the analysis of some of Atwood's more recent poems in *Morning in the Burned House* and *The Tent*. In *The Tent*, Atwood chooses to stage the aging of the voice-persona. This enterprise allows her to establish a triangular relationship between the "voice" staged in the poem, the public persona of the author, and people's expectations of the authorial figure. Atwood also uses this opportunity to mock the media attention that she has received and continues to receive over the years. The persona of the prose poem "Voice" explains how her voice "was courted", how "bouquets were thrown to it" and "[m]oney was bestowed on it." (TT 22). The amount of attention paid to her voice increases as "[m]en [fall] on their knees before it" and "[a]pplause [flows] around it like flocks of red birds":

> Invitations to perform cascaded over us. All the best places wanted us and all at once, for, as people said – though not to me – my voice would thrive only for a certain term. Then, as voices do, it would begin to shrivel. Finally it would drop off, and I would be left alone, denuded – a dead shrub, a footnote.
>
> It's begun to happen, the shrivelling. Only I have noticed it so far. There's the barest pucker in my voice, the barest wrinkle. Fear has

entered me, a needleful of ether, constricting what in someone else would be my heart. (TT 22).

The intriguing first-person plural pronoun "us" of the prose poem refers to the voice-persona and to the speaker of the poem: together they form one single entity: a private individual with a special gift for words. By separating out the two elements of this entity and using the "us" pronoun as opposed to the "I" pronoun, Atwood reinforces the personification of the "voice": although the "voice" is neither incarnated as a plant nor as a sibyl, although it remains a shapeless creature, the voice-persona clearly has a form of physical presence which becomes all the more apparent as the poem takes on a poignant twist as the evening, both metaphorical and literal, grows near. The voice-persona "sits" in the hotel room with the speaker of the poem using the second person plural pronoun (we, us, our) to describe their situation:

> Now it's evening; the neon lights come on, excitement quickens in the streets. We sit in this hotel room, my voice and I; or rather in this hotel suite, because it's still nothing but the best for us. We're gathering our strength together. How much of my life do I have left? Left over, that is: my voice has used up most of it. I've given it all my love, but it's only a voice, it can never love me in return. (TT 22-23)

In spite of the "shrivelling" which has "begun to happen", the speaker of the poem still claims that the voice-persona is a superstar. But both the speaker and the voice-persona are aware of the ephemeral nature of their combined fame: yes, their celebrity life will be short-lived and there is nothing they can do to reverse the "shrivelling" process.

Moreover, the celebrity status of the voice-persona is described as something that will not give "in return". The speaker has devoted her professional life to *her* voice and has "given it all [her] love" but the voice-persona cannot love back. Unlike other areas of human activity which involve creating or nurturing human relationships (such as loving your partner or family, and caring for a close one in all sorts of different ways), writing is a solitary process and the work on one's craft will give nothing in return for the long hours of dedication. There is a certain bitterness when the speaker takes stock of the amount of time she has left and declares "my voice has used up most of it". Furthermore, the greediness of the voice-persona is emphasized as the persona declares: "it wants more, more and more, more of everything it's had so far. It won't let go of me easily." (TT 23).

In spite of the slight bitterness, it is the humour of the poem which predominates, as the speaker manages to mock not only the attention the voice-persona receives, but also the shrivelling process itself. In the staging of the aging voice-persona who still has the privilege of enjoying a hotel suite "because it's still nothing but the best for us", Atwood presents an ironic commentary of the poet who can foresee her own transformation and its effect on other people. Her use of the temporal marker "still" combined with the ironic comment on the hotel suite communicates a sense that the speaker anticipates a precipitous decline. Her ability to treat the subject with a great deal of humour indicates her readiness to accept this decline, although the speaker's comment also points to the impossibility of being fully prepared.

This ability is reminiscent of the "Miss July Grows Older" (MBH 21-23) persona in *Morning in the Burned House*. This poem takes aim at the conventions of calendars produced by magazines such as *Playboy*. Spoken by Miss July herself, now an older woman, the poem gives voice to a subject who is culturally portrayed as a silent figure. Miss July's voice however, like the one of the poem "Voice" of *The Tent*, is both humourous and deep in her acceptance of old age. The articulation of the poem is significant: Miss July first asks how much longer she can "get away / with being so fucking cute?" (MBH 21) and answers her own rhetorical question: "Not much longer. / The shoes with bows, the cunning underwear / with slogans on the crotch — Knock Here, / and so forth — will have to go, along with the cat suit." Miss July then wonders about her response to this: "After a while you forget / what you really look like. / You think your mouth is the size it was. / You pretend not to care." (MBH 21) From pretending not to care, to the acceptance of old age, the persona grows deeper. As the poem progresses, Miss July voices the concerns of all aging individuals. If, at first, the unlikely choice of Atwood's spokesperson both surprised and amused us readers, we gradually become attentive to the universal questions raised by Miss July: what becomes of the younger versions of ourselves? Miss July answers that these versions of ourselves do not "just disappear" but we learn to expand and appreciate things we used to overlook: "Though the vaporous cloud of chemicals that enveloped you / like a glowing eggshell, an incense, / doesn't disappear: it just gets larger / and takes in more." (MBH 23) Miss July who was once this playful creature with the knock here underwear, has grown out of sex "like a shrunk dress". New things become important such as: "The way the sun / moves through the hours" or "the smeared raindrops / on the window, buds / on the roadside weeds, the sheen / of spilled oil on a raw ditch / filling with muddy water." (MBH 23)

The lyricism of this stanza contrasts with the ironic tone of the rest of the poem. The metrics of the stanza mirror a kind of breathlessness which points to the persona's true awe: the line breaks are systematically preceded with what meets the persona's eyes and causes her to pause before she can describe further what she sees – "the sun", the "raindrops" or the "buds". Even the last image of an oil spill is beautiful as it shines while "filling with muddy water." The aging Miss July, like any aging reader, learns to appreciate the richness of these images which now stand out for her. As the persona herself points out, she has grown into her "common senses", those she shares with "whatever's listening." And now there is more to this older version of Miss July than meets the eye, as she playfully concludes, true to her humorous self: "Don't confuse me with my hen-leg elbows: / what you get is no longer / what you see." (MBH 23)

INVESTIGATION INTO AGING AND REPRESENTATIONS

The poems in *Morning in the Burned House*, *The Tent* and *Bottle* are part of an extended investigation into aging which Atwood undertakes from her earlier volumes of poetry. In a poem from the mid-eighties entitled "Aging Female Poet on Laundry Day" (SP 129), the speaker of the poem is focused on the body as she highlights the changes occurring in middle age, and imagines how this process will continue as she grows older:

> Whatever exists at the earth's center will get me
> sooner or later. Sooner. Than I think.
> Already it's dragging me down, already
> I become shorter, infinitesimally.
> The bones of my legs thicken – that's first –
> contract, like muscles.
> After that comes the frailty, a dry wind blowing
> inside my body,
> scouring me from within,
> as if I were
> a fossil, the soft parts eaten away.
> Soon I will turn to calcium. It starts with the heart. (SP 129)

The minute description of the biological transformation hinges upon scientific details – "The bones of my legs thicken – that's first – / contract, like muscles" – which are combined with poetic images: "After that comes the frailty, a dry wind blowing / inside my body / scouring me from within, as if I were / a fossil".

Atwood's fossil image plays upon a widespread cultural dread of old age. Scholars of aging reveal the ways in which our Western culture is heavily dominated and possibly haunted by negative views of aging. They stress the importance of reimagining our own and others' aging in new and more productive ways. For example, they rehabilitate relationships with the elderly which our Western Culture tends to push to the periphery of our lives. The cross-generational interactions enable us to anticipate rather than refuse the changes that we ourselves will go through as we grow older.

Pinkola's comment on aging runs counter to the dominant discourse which portrays aging as something to be repressed and possibly avoided:

> Though I myself find perils and challenges of age to be true, we must disavow the old prejudices about women and age. The true vision of the wise woman is one of bounty of love and age and wisdom. As she gathers years, like an ancient tree, she grows even more arms, even more flowers and fruits. She is more rooted, more vast, more sheltering – developing her callings to be throughout life, maiden mother, medium, crone, elder, healer, teacher, artist, knowing woman[1].

This comment, like the message in "Miss July [...]" (MBH 21-23) previously quoted, shows how we can learn to consider old age as an opportunity to expand and to "take [...] in more." (MBH 21-23) In the same vein as Pinkola, Atwood's poetry exposes our cultural fears about old age and provides a way of revisiting cultural imaginings. For example, many poems set up a comparison between the experience of old age and the ways in which our culture teaches us to consider middle and late life experience. Atwood's personae reflect back the culture we live in – a secular, post-modern culture of mass-mediated images, in which identity is reduced to appearance. But the speakers also express the desire to experience old age differently and this wish is best expressed in the last stanza of the fourth poem of "Five Poems for Grandmothers" (THP 33-40):

> Against the disappearance
> of outlines, against
> the disappearance of sounds,

---

[1] This quote is from a recorded commentary of Estés referring to her book: *Women who run with the wolves: myths and stories of the wild woman archetype* (1992). See press release entitled "Clarissa Pinkola Estés Releases Her Master Work as a Live Online Series from SoundsTrue.com" on (PRWEB) March 16, 2010:
http://www.prweb.com/releases/soundstrue/estes/prweb3732584.htm

> against the blurring of the ears
> and eyes, against small fears
> of the very old, the fear
> of mumbling, the fear of dying,
> the fear of falling downstairs,
> I make this charm
> from nothing but paper; which is good
> for exactly nothing. (THP 39)

The repetition of "against" strategically positioned either at the beginning, in the middle or at the end of the verse, precedes the main statement of the poem "I make this charm". However the "charm" which the speaker makes against all the negative consequences of old age is immediately undermined by the final statement: "which is good / for exactly nothing". Atwood positions this statement over the last two lines allowing for a positive anticipation beginning with "which is good" followed by a direct contradiction of that statement "for exactly nothing". This twist, achieved through the line break, is a hallmark of Atwood's poetry. When the twist is positioned at the end of the poem, as is the case in "Five Poems for Grandmothers", it becomes particularly significant: here it plainly states the speaker's helplessness against aging – in spite of all the charms made of paper, in other words in spite of the promise of immortality for the poet. The poet can, however, resist against the mass-mediated images of old age is the poem "Waiting". In this poem, old age is a "dark thing" that comes to envelope the "you" of the poem "in a damp enfolding, like the mildew/shroud on bread" (MBH 8). As Jamieson points out, in Atwood's poetry, age "is not simply a matter of how young we may feel ourselves to be, but it is conferred upon us by the judgments of others. The possibility of a painful disjunction between our own and the world's estimation of our age lies at the heart of Atwood's second stanza [of the poem "Waiting"]" (Jamieson 271). The poem "Waiting" (MBH 8-10) is precisely about this disjunction: the persona of the poem hid the aging process, not wishing to see it in herself:

> ... you thought it would hide
> in your closet, among the clothes you outgrew years ago,
> nesting in dustballs and fallen hair, shedding
> one of your fabricated skins
> after another and growing bigger,
> honing its teeth on your discarded

> cloth lives, and then it would pounce
> from the inside out, [...] (8)

Through the metaphor of age as just another item hidden in a closet "among the clothes you outgrew years ago", Atwood highlights society's expectations in terms of clothing, mainly the necessity to dress appropriately, according to one's age: as sociologists point out, disparities between age and costume are often perceived as confusing and sometimes even off-putting and frightening. Atwood plays on the notion of power that our society attributes to our "fabricated skins": they are "growing bigger" and "honing [their] teeth". This leads the speaker to express her fear of inadequacy when she declares that one of these "fabricated skins" will "pounce / from the inside out" (8). The item-in-the-closet metaphor is linked to the main theme of the poem: the "dark thing" which comes back and feels "strangely like home" because it reminds the persona of "fifty years ago" when "you realized for the first time / in your life that you would be old / some day, / you would some day be / as old as you are now" (MBH 9). As Sara Jamieson points out:

> Atwood does manage to deflate the impact of [...] judgments [concerning age] by suggesting a lack of proportion, equating age-anxiety with childhood terrors of imaginary monsters in the closet. Dismissing the fear of the clothes closet as one of several "melodramas" through which culture inculcates the fear of aging, the poem shifts into what initially seems a more realistic mode. Middle age turns out to be nothing like the speaker's imaginings: "Instead it is strangely like home" (8). Coming after the catalogue of horrors at the beginning of the poem, such familiarity might be expected to be reassuring, but this is not the case. Recognition of middle age turns out to be an eerie repetition of the moment in childhood "when you realized for the first time / in your life that you would be old some day [...]." (Jamieson 273)

And the poem concludes with the "dark thing" which is "nothing new" and therefore can be coped with:

> and the "dark thing" is here,
> and after all it is nothing new;
> it is only a memory after all:
> a memory of a fear,
> a yellowing paper child's fear

> you have long since forgotten
> and that has now come true. (MBH 10)

There are many poems in Atwood's poetry that stage this idea that becoming old is like coming home or coming into one's own, as in the case of Miss July who learns to see "whatever there is" (MBH 21). But coming home is not a place of comfort: from Miss July who pretends not to care about what she "really look[s] like" (MBH 21) to the speaker in "Waiting" (MBH 8-10) who laments her old "murky" body, Atwood stages old age as a "dark" home. This home conceals a "disturbing secret, the shocking recognition of a stranger as oneself, the surfacing of long-forgotten fears: all are characteristics of [Freud's] 'Uncanny'" (Jamieson 273).

The "uncanny"[2] is a Freudian concept of an instance where something can be familiar, yet foreign at the same time, resulting in a feeling of it being uncomfortably strange or uncomfortably familiar. Because the uncanny is familiar, yet strange, it often creates cognitive dissonance within the experiencing subject due to the paradoxical nature of being attracted to, yet repulsed by an object at the same time. This cognitive dissonance often leads to an outright rejection of the object, as one would rather reject than rationalize. Atwood's poetry however attempts a reconciliation between that which is both frightening and long familiar. In the poem "Waiting", the light which is "thick yellow" and the "yellowing paper" provide a link between past and present, and context for the return of "the dark thing". In this light, the old "murky" body is not totally strange. In the same way, "Shapechangers in Winter" (MBH 120-125) voices a recognition and acceptance of the middle-aged body. The poem is infused with a confidence that is absent from the other poems such as "Aging Female Poet on Laundry Day" (SP 129), "Five Poems for Grandmothers" (THP 33-40) and even "Waiting" (MBH 8-10).

Instead of merely staging the anxiety linked to aging, Atwood, in "Shapechangers in Winter", emphasizes continuities that allow us to make peace with the aging process. The poem acknowledges that there are times when a couple is bewildered when gazing at one another: they seem to be disguised, "you as a rumpled elephant – / hide suitcase with white fur, / me as a bramble bush" (MBH, 123). However, the speaker's humour leads to acceptance and this acceptance both enables, and is enabled by, the acceptance of aging of the persona's partner. The disguises of the couple – these "outer aliases" according to Jamieson's expression – serve another purpose: they invalidate the opposition

---

[2] The uncanny is from the German "Das Unheimliche" – the opposite of what is familiar.

between an outward aging appearance and an unchanging inner self. Indeed a certain form of continuity does not imply that the inner self is unchanging. Coral Ann Howells has said of this poem that it exposes as illusory any centring of the individual human subject. Atwood's conception of the self is therefore closer to Bruce Hood's in *The Self Illusion*. Bruce Hood dispels false ideas about the self as an "an integrated individual inhabiting a body" (Hood in Harris 1) and highlights the importance of distinguishing between the "I" and the "me":

> For most of us, the sense of our self is as an integrated individual inhabiting a body. I think it is helpful to distinguish between the two ways of thinking about the self that William James talked about. There is conscious awareness of the present moment that he called the "I," but there is also a self that reflects upon who we are in terms of our history, our current activities and our future plans. James called this aspect of the self, "me" which most of us would recognize as our personal identity—who we think we are. However, I think that both the "I" and the "me" are actually ever-changing narratives generated by our brain to provide a coherent framework to organize the output of all the factors that contribute to our thoughts and behaviors. (Hood in Harris 1).

The coherent framework manufactured by our brain which provides an illusory sense of the "I" – that is our "conscious awareness of the present moment" – and our "me" – that is the person we think we are – are essential to our mode of being: these narratives not only help us organize our thoughts and behaviors, but they also keep us from despair, as Hood argues that we need to tell ourselves stories to justify our own behaviour even to ourselves.

Like Hood, Atwood is aware of the tricks of memory and the art of self-fictionalization. In her writing, guises, "outer aliases", and illusions are presented as various aspects of identity quests that are not confined to middle age alone. In "Shapechangers in Winter", the speaker compares herself to a bramble bush and takes comfort in gentle self-mockery: "Well, the hair /was always difficult" (123). According to Jamieson:

> Refusing an interpretation of middle age as a catastrophic break with the past and with youth, Atwood instead emphasizes continuities that enable acceptance of the body as it ages as an integral part of the self. Her affirmation, "Yes. / It's still you," far from being a statement of faith in an inner identity that persists despite bodily changes, is rather an

> acceptance of change, including the changes of aging, as an essential component of selfhood. (Jamieson 274)

In "Shapechangers in Winter", continuity is expressed through the accumulation of many disguises, in spite of the fact that the speaker also emphasizes bodily changes: "Every cell in our bodies has renewed itself so many times since then, there's not much left, my love, of the originals" (MBH 123). This comment is infused with tenderness towards "my love" who sees and shares the persona's experience of aging. The couple's acceptance of their aging bodies is indeed clearly articulated through such addresses in the poem and through the speaker's emphasis on physical intimacy. Atwood points to new modes of companionship by staging a couple who values touching over seeing: "Taking hands, like children"; "the only common / sense that remains to us is touch" (MBH 125). Thus Atwood writes against a cultural portrayal of old age as unattractive and deprived of love and offers a new way of looking upon old age. For example, the speaker in "Shapechangers in Winter" fondly remembers youthful sexuality, but does not lament its loss because sexuality is taking on a new form in which humour is called for:

> Back then, I had many forms:
> the sliding in and out
> of my own slippery eelskin,
> and yours as well; we were each other's
> iridescent glove, the deft body
> all sleight-of-hand and illusion.
> Once we were lithe as pythons, quick
> and silvery as herring, and we still are, momentarily,
> except our knees hurt. (MBH 123)

The very structure of these lines mirrors regret framed by two statements starting with "Back then […]" and "Once […]". Beautiful images are weaved in to the memory of the "many forms" the speaker remembers: "my own slippery eelskin", "each other's / iridescent glove", "lithe as pythons". However the speaker does not give into nostalgia. The "quick and silvery" middle-aged lovers are still lovers although their "knees hurt" and they no longer share games of seduction and transformation. They are "content to huddle under the shed feathers of duck and goose, / as the wind pours like a river / we swim in by keeping still," (MBH 123). They share an intimacy that is different from the one they once had, but it is not diminished. Thus Atwood directly challenges the view according to which there is a contradiction between aging and sexuality and the value of aging sexuality is emphasized through the following image: "We're footprints / becoming limestones, [...] coal becoming diamond. Less / flexible, but more condensed;" (MBH 123). This idea of something more valuable and precious is conveyed in many images such as the "solstice" and "the year's threshold / and unlocking, where the past / lets go of and becomes the future" (124): it is "the "last full-blown moment" (MBH 123). Finally, at the end of the poem, Atwood once again represents the course of life in a way that stresses continuity over loss, with a special emphasis on touch. Touch becomes "the only common / sense" and it enables the couple to "hold on":

> But the trick is just to hold on
> through all appearances; and so we do,
> and yes, I know it's you;
> and that is what we will come to, sooner
> or later, when it's even darker
> than it is now, when the snow is colder,
> when it's darkest and coldest
> and candles are no longer any use to us
> and the visibility is zero: Yes.
> It's still you. It's still you. (125)

The end of the poem reads like a love declaration that the speaker whispers to a "you" who is getting older, like the speaker herself. Although the speaker describes an environment that is omnipresent – dark and cold – she affirms (all the more forcefully as the run-on line comes to close the poem): "Yes. / It's still you. It's still you". With this affirmation, the poem defies cultural taboos where attraction and sexuality are based on youthful images. But it achieves more than that: it maps out a new route into old age, where the use of touch is not only a key to physical intimacy but also a metaphor for human tinkering leading to a gradual understanding of ourselves. Acceptance of old age becomes an essential element of selfhood and the poem is an affirmation of identity and love, emblematic of Van Spanckeren's interpretation of *Morning in the Burned House*, a volume where Atwood encourages the reader to move from a "self-oriented mode to a more human vision" (Van Spanckeren in Wilson 106).

In Atwood's imagining of old age, touch is still available and it can be read "as an attempt to expose or even resist this particular form of cultural neglect of the elderly" (Jamieson in Moss and Kozakewich 275), although it seems equally possible to read it as an attempt to come to terms with old age – and this is always more difficult than we anticipate it to be: not only do we cringe at the prospect of aging, but it is often an idea that we do not even want to consider and that we tend to block out.

The question of aging inevitably leads to the question of identity. And we will now return to the major Atwoodian themes: the ones that characterize her voice-print. In the first chapter of this volume, the chronological presentation of Atwood's poetry offered a thematic approach to her successive volumes of poetry. One of the themes evoked in this first chapter in relation to self and identity is the question of assertiveness in the face of power, to which we will now turn our attention.

CHAPTER 4

Voices of the Powerful and the Powerless

VOICES OF ACCUSATION AND THE POLITICS OF POWER

As previously mentioned, every poem in *Power Politics* lets us hear a female voice resisting the domination of male space. The first poem in the volume significantly entitled "What Do You Want From Me" (49) expresses a cry of protest which resonates as the complaint of a wounded animal. Unlike the voice of a victim, the speaker formulating this complaint tries to gain control of the situation by addressing the "you" of the poem in an accusatory way (she hints at a triumphant Christlike figure and blames the latter for laying down the law). In contrast to "What Do You Want From Me" (49) and to most of the other poems in *Power Politics*, the last interrogation of "Lying Here" is perhaps the only one which radically moves away from the peremptory or accusatory tone of the beginning of the collection: "What do you see, I ask / my voice / absorbed by stone and outer / space / you are asleep, you see / what there is. Beside you / I bend and enter" (52). This interrogation points to the possibility of genuine communication between the lovers. In the same way, the persona's point of view seems to evolve in *Power Politics* and Cooley highlights the evolution in the volumes that follow:

> How much now, in subsequent poems, she opens to the world and invites it in. The imperatives fall away, the scoldings lie in abeyance, fears give way to love, the 'I' begins to lose its stranglehold and the 'you' becomes more prominent and honoured. (Cooley 89-90)

Indeed, in the volumes that follow Power Politics (mainly You Are Happy, Interlunar and Morning in the Burned House), love relationships are portrayed in different shades and lights. Atwood's conception of power which filters through her many poetic voices has often been compared to Michel Foucault's theories, as both poet and philosopher go against the traditionally defined conception of power as a social relation between two agents. These agents may usefully be called the "powerful" and the "powerless" and traditionally, power is defined as the first agent exercising his/her will on the unwilling second, dominating even silencing the voice of the other. Indeed, the aim of absolute power, Atwood explains, is "to silence the voice, to abolish the words, so that the only voices and words left are those of the ones in power" (SW 350). However, both Foucault and Atwood contest that power is based on a configuration dictated by the "powerful" only. Foucault's theories replace a unitary and compact conception of power with a dynamic model in which power is seen as a net of relations only existing in action: "Power in the substantive sense, 'le' pouvoir, doesn't exist. […] The idea that there is either located at – or emanating from – a given point something which is a 'power' seems to me based on a misguided analysis" (Foucault 198). The philosopher sees several main "hypotheses" in his new definition, of which I would like to highlight three:

1. That power is co-extensive with the social body.
2. That relations of power are interwoven with other kinds of relations (production, kinship, family, sexuality) for which they play at once a conditioning and a conditioned role. …
3. That there are no relations of power without resistances (Foucault 142).

Likewise, Atwood's poetry, fiction and epitext provide a commentary on power. According to Atwood, it is because of the partial or total cession of the concrete power that every individual holds, that the abuse of power occurs. Atwood's four victim positions[1] are relevant. These positions illustrate the possibility of change and emancipation from imprisonment to independence. The starting point of the liberation process is not to deny that the power structure exists, but on the contrary, to acknowledge it. As Atwood underlines: "We live surrounded by it: it pervades everything we are and do, invisible and soundless, like air" (in Somacarrera 292). However, Atwood questions the reality of power: "power after all is not real, not really there: people give it to each other" (in Somacarrera 292). She provides an illustration with the narrator of *Cat's Eye*: Elaine discovers she

---

[1] To Atwood, the central image of Canadian literature is the notion of survival. This notion is linked to a central character which is the victim. Atwood shows that the central image of the victim is not static: there are four "Victim Positions" (Surviv 36-39) which are clearly visible in Canadian literature. These positions are: position one: "[t]o deny the fact that you are a victim" (Surviv 36); position two: "[t]o acknowledge the fact that you are a victim" (Surviv 37) but to attribute it to a powerful force beyond human control (for instance God, fate, etc.) and therefore to resign yourself to your fate; position three: "[t]o acknowledge the fact that you are a victim but to refuse to accept the assumption that the role is inevitable" (Surviv 37-38); position four: "[t]o be a creative non-victim" (Surviv 38-39).

can escape her buddies by refusing to play this game: "It's like stepping off a cliff believing the air will hold you up. And it does." (CE 228).

Another characteristic of Atwood's approach to power is that she always stresses the connections between the political and the personal: "So many of the things we do in what we sadly think of as our personal lives are simply duplications of the external world of power games, power struggles" (in Somacarrera 292). For Atwood, war is the most obvious and visible form of the exercise of power, of men attempting to dominate each other. Foucault also sees power and war as concomitant terms: "power is a war, a war continued by other means" (Foucault 90). Atwood further explores the relationships between the atrocities of war and the power of words: "A word after a word / after a word is power" (TS 64), although the effectiveness of words is called into question by poems such as "Notes Towards a Poem Which Can Never Be Written" (TS 63-70), illustrating Atwood's previously quoted comment about absolute power aiming at "silenc[ing] *the voice*" (SW 350). According to Foucault, power relations prevail over language and meaning (Foucault 114), a view that is formulated poetically by Atwood in *Power Politics*: "Language, the fist / proclaims by squeezing / is for the weak only" (PP 31) and widely illustrated in her fiction. As Pilar Somacarrera points out, in her analysis of one of Atwood's novels, *Bodily Harm* mirrors Foucault's conception of power:

> The fictional portrait of this former British colony allows Atwood to lay bare the crudest dimensions of power: first, that power is ascription, as political leaders are given power at elections, but the elections can be manipulated. Second, that, following Foucault, the historical *raison d'etre* of political power is to be found in the economy [...].Third, that power is subject to inversions, or, to use Steven Lukes's terminology, "a principal in one relation may be a subaltern in another". (Somacarrera in Moss and Kozakewich 295)

Other fictional illustrations of Atwood's conception of power abound in Atwood's fiction, including Atwood's best-known novels, *The Handmaid's Tale* and *The Blind Assassin*. But to come back to the poetry, several of Atwood's poems in *True Stories* seek to lend a voice to those who are unable to speak out because their voices are suppressed. The voices of the tortured are silent and the persona of the poem takes over by describing the agonizing bodies of those tortured. For example, the persona in "Notes Towards a Poem Which Can Never Be Written" reports on how powerful agents impose their will on powerless and silent people whose only language is their "flayed body" hung and displayed like a flag:

> a flayed body untangled
> string by string and hung
> to the wall, an agonized banner
> displayed for the same reasons
> flags are. (259)

The minute description of the untangling of a "flayed body" that symbolizes all victims is followed by the metaphor of a banner and then a flag, both of which objectify the body. Power is thus staged as an anonymous agent which has the ability to enforce his/her will on the victim, and turn the victim into "an agonized banner" on display "like a flag". However, the poem moves beyond the view that the victim is powerless, by showing that everybody, including the victim who remains silent while being brutalized, holds some kind of power (if only the power to resist). Thus power does not correspond to a given distribution of roles, but rather it is something that is performed. In other words, acts of brutality and torture imply the presence of a victim and victimizer, but the victim may have her own strategy against the victimizer: refusing to conform, even if it implies unbearable sufferings. While many poems in *True Stories* focus on tortured bodies in totalitarian regimes, they also show that the silent voices display power by performing resistance. In other volumes, Atwood's poetry stages different situations of power. The highlighting of silent voices remains a useful poetic strategy, but Atwood does not limit herself to the portrayal of tortured bodies: she resorts to her strategy of guises, once again, in order to further explore the theme of power.

THE VOICES OF ANIMALS: FIGURES OF RESISTANCE

In Atwood's poetry, victims often take on the mask and the voice of animals. However, the animals are figures of resistance: they denounce the ordinary world in which victims are hunted and taken advantage of. Whether alarming the reader against possible dangers or leading the way to a creative space, animals such as those of "A Foundling" (AC 5) and "The Trappers" (AC 34-35) are signaled as trustworthy creatures, allies of the poetic voice. The animals are not only present through a description of the speaker: they also have a voice of their own. At times, it is the silent voice of the fossils or the cry of the victim or a voice from Atwood's underworld.

From these different symbolic orientations of the animal motif – the voice as the animal or the animals as allies of the voice – the reader can piece together an incredibly rich teaching which touches on a wide range of subjects including survival skills, artistic creation, voyages to the underworld, return journeys. As one maps out Atwood's thematic material, one finds animals included in every one of the authors' themes, and all sorts of possible artistic connotations are attached to the animal figures. Their voices and representations tie in with Atwood's life-long focus on animals and play on various symbolic orientations.

Atwood's childhood interest in animals is made apparent by one of her biographers, Rosemary Sullivan, who dug out a number of documents from the Atwood archives giving evidence of Atwood's early intertwining of woods and books. For example, Sullivan quotes an essay written by Margaret Atwood when she attended public school:

> [...] it is clear how precise her knowledge of woodlore was. She divided her twelve-page essay into chapters: chapter I was devoted to animal tracks; chapter II, to insects. She carefully illustrated her descriptions with drawings... "The tracks of the cotton rabbit always seem to be going in the opposite direction than they really are. This is due to the fact that he runs or jumps using his front legs as a 'lever' to swing his legs forward, and thus places the back legs in front of the front legs, (hard to describe, but it comes naturally to the cottontail)." (49-50)

Atwood's descriptions of animals in minute detail (greatly influenced by authors like Ellsworth Jaeger and Enerst Thompson Seton) reveal her capacity to draw on wildlife to nourish her imagination[2]. This is something Atwood herself readily admits in *Survival: a thematic guide to Canadian literature* and her theory extends to highlighting a possible link between animal stories in the Canadian literary heritage and the "Canadian psyche." She goes so far as to claim that these animal stories "provide a key to an important facet of the Canadian psyche." (Surviv 73). Atwood comments: "English animal stories are about 'social relations', American ones are about killing animals; Canadian ones are about animals *being* killed" (74) and she then raises the question: "If animals in literature are always symbols, and if Canadian animal stories present animals as

---

[2] This is achieved mainly through the victim pattern previously underlined and which many critics is clearly visible in Atwood's work: "Death [is frequently] suffered by humans (both genders); almost as often by animals and birds (the identification with victims crosses species lines); occasionally by the land, trees, gods." (McCombs in Nicholson 54).

victims, what trait in our national psyche do these animal victims symbolize?" (75) Atwood speculates that the Canadians' identification with animals is the "expression of a deep-seated cultural fear" (79). Her demonstration is inspired by Frye's comment in the *Bush Garden*, when asserting "the prevalence in Canada of animal stories, in which animals are closely assimilated to human behaviour and emotions." (Surviv 80), and Atwood adds that "the human behaviour and emotions in question are limited in range, being usually flight, fear and pain." (Surviv 80). Atwood's use of animal figures goes beyond her critical directions in that it does not merely follow the animal victim pattern described in *Survival*. In giving the animal voices, Atwood enriches the symbolic orientations of the animal motif. I will now give a few examples of voices which are part of a network of animal motifs which interact in a powerful and meaningful way.

I will start with the recurrent animal motifs in the early poetry and focus on the animals which are presented no differently from other organic components participating in the biological, geological and (ultimately) psychological transformation of the self. The animals are often present through synecdoche or through organic residues: their voice is silent. They speak without words. Their messages are cryptic. Atwood's first volumes of poetry offer possible illustrations: *The Circle Game, The Animals in That Country* and *The Journals of Susanna Moodie* include different modes of representation of the animal motif as well as different interpretational orientations. In several of the *Circle Game* poems, the animals are either living images inscribed in stone, water and air, or hybrid creatures constantly subject to metamorphosis or quasi-Darwinian regressions. In "The Settlers" and "The Explorers", animal bones constitute the organic material from which all living creatures draw their substance. In "The Settlers", animal bones grow flesh again and resurface in the form of trees, grass and seas:

> They dug us down
> into the solid granite
> where our bones grew flesh again,
> came up trees and
> grass.
>
> Still
> we are the salt
> seas that uphold these lands. (CG 81)

The speakers of the poem speak in unison as a "we": the animals' voices are a collective voice. Although they address the reader from the world of the dead, they are very much alive. The expression "dug us down" contrasts with "came up" and it is the *coming up again* that prevails in the poem. The prominent position of the adverb "still" which forms a one-syllable verse at the head of the stanza, affirms permanence and resilience.

Future generations of both animals and children feed on what remains of the former animals. Thus one generation leads to another. Each new generation tends to ignore the past (unconscious of "so many bluegreen centuries"), although, like the children with "green smiles", the new generation receives the earth as a gift. In "The Settlers", the natural heritage which offers itself up to the children is symbolized by the remains of two animal skeletons. The poem ends with the children running across the fields which stretch out in a gesture of generosity – the "open hands".

Atwood's ironic treatment of the explorers in the poem before last of *The Circle Game* suggests that all future generations will fail to understand the clues provided by "the two skeletons". The teachings of the animal skeletons is beyond anyone's understanding and both "settlers" and "explorers" need to learn to decipher the imprints of the earth and eventually integrate the ancestral element which reaches as far back as the formation of the world. This biological chain becomes tangible through a wide range of sensorial metaphors in *The Circle Game*. These metaphors are the very language of the animals although the images move beyond the animals themselves and become synecdoches (fossils, bones, almost-human shapes etc.).

In "After the Flood, We" (CG 4-5), animal fragments and residues melt into the landscape and provide the personae with tangible proof of both *her* and *their* integration into the biological chain. The intertwining themes of decay and re-creation become apparent in the final image of the poem:

> footsteps of the almost-born
> coming (slowly) behind us,
> not seeing
> the almost-human brutal faces forming
> (slowly)
> out of stone. (CG 5)

The adverb "slowly", between brackets, imposes a slowing down of the reading, a slowing down of the voice itself. This word, isolated on one line, whispers to the reader – the very sonorities of "slowly" (liquid l and a diphthong) protracts the whispering sound. This adverb repeated twice within the stanza provides a symmetry between the "almost-born" on the one hand and the "almost-human" on the other. Both are independently "coming" or "forming" "(slowly)", stemming from other natural elements and the scene thus highlights the motif of decay and rebirth. Another image of birth is to be found in "A Descent Through Carpet" (CG 15-17). In the final stanza of the poem, the persona's re-birth is conditioned to the collection of clues – remnants of animal-like ancestors – which allow her to acknowledge where she comes from.

>   my fisted
>   hand
>   my skin
>   holds
>
>   remnants of ancestors
>
>   fossil bones and fangs
>
>   acknowledgement:
>
>   I was born
>   dredged up from time (CG 17)

The display of the words of the poem into what appears to be two columns creates an opposition between "my fisted / hand" and "my skin" – the latter is associated with "remnants of ancestors" and "fossil bones and fangs". The explanation seems to lie in the last two lines which are displayed each in one of the two columns, giving the reader time to pause and reflect on the speaker's account of her Darwinian birth. The juxtaposition of the terms "fossil bones", "fangs" and "acknowledgement" underlines the importance of the mineral and animal heritage in a process of understanding evolution and creation which leads to creation and re-birth. The speaker of the poem is highly aware that she is the product of evolution and the recipient of a biological heritage: this heritage has been passed on and will continue to be passed on, making the speaker one element of the Darwinian chain which resurfaces when integrated by future generations.

Atwood's second volume of poetry *The Animals in That Country* further develops the motifs of *The Circle Game* and places a new emphasis on the animal-resistance and the animal-victim patterns. The eponymous poem "The Animals in That Country" (AC 2-3) presents the animals of "that country" in their allegorical form, as opposed to the ones of "this country" which are portrayed in their authentic form. In "that country", animals "have the faces of people" (AC 2) and are "fixed in their tapestry of manners" (AC 2), thus representing the voices of myths, fables and literary traditions[3]. Further allusions to myths and literary traditions are to be found in "Songs of the Transformed", where the transformations come full circle as Circe transforms men into animals – each song corresponds to one animal (the pig, the bull, the rat, the crow, the worm, the owl, the fox, the hen) – who speak like people or who take on human characteristics, as in fables.

Coming back to "The Animals in That Country" (AC 2-3), and moving on to the second half of the poem, the reader notices that the stanzas concerning "this country" follow a very different motif from that of the first half of the poem. In those last stanzas, the animals "have the faces of / animals":

> Their eyes
> flash once in car headlights
> and are gone.
>
> Their deaths are not elegant
>
> They have the faces of
> no-one. (AC 3)

The two-word line "Their eyes", strategically positioned at the head of the stanza "flash once" and then "are gone". These two verbs, placed at the beginning of the two lines (in the same position and following "Their eyes"), oppose one another, one signifying life, the other death; and this opposition points to the suddenness

---

[3] Atwood reverses Janet Frame's understanding of "this world" and "that world". In Frame's opposition of the terms, "this world" is the world of the imagination whereas "that world" is the world of everyday conformist life. However, both authors' imaginations are practical and grounded in the ordinary. As Sue Gillett points out, Frame's writing protects her from her shyness and social isolation but not in the sense of providing an escape into fantasy (Gillett senseofcinema.com 2000). For example, Frame describes her childhood imagination in the following terms: "it was not an escape in the sense of a removal from the unhappiness I felt over the sickness at home or from my own feeling of nowhereness in not having ordinary clothes to wear even to prove that I was a human being and there was a peopled world beyond home and school; there was no removal of myself and my life to another world; there was simply the other world's arrival into my world, the literature streaming through it like an array of beautiful ribbons through the branches of a green, growing tree, touching the leaves with unexpected light that was unlike the expected deserved habitual light of the sun and the seasons." (Frame 142).

of the animals' deaths. This is stated more directly and expanded to include the idea of a certain brutality in the last lines of the poem.

Here portrayed in their authentic form, the animals embody the author's theories on victimization and they also point to the desire to survive, emblematic of Canada's national identity. Nevertheless, survival only occurs at random, and there are many accidents and individual deaths. This is also apparent in other poems such as "A Foundling" (AC 5) and "The Trappers" (AC 34-35) where the animal figure becomes a victim.

Paradoxically, the symbolic orientation is reversed in *The Journals of Susanna Moodie*: "the animals" (63) stand for the survivor rather than the victim. Indeed, "the animals" seem to hold some mysterious secret that Moodie associates with all the necessary survival skills required by the settlers. Susanna Moodie realizes that she is "not ready / altogether to be moved into" and she is thus unable to retain their teachings:

> In time the animals
> arrived to inhabit me...
>
> ... I was not ready
> altogether to be moved into.
>
> ...I was
> (instantaneous)
> unlived in: they had gone.
>
> There was something they almost taught me
> I came away not having learned. (EF 63-64)

The poem is infused with regret as the persona (Moodie) realizes she has missed the opportunity of learning from the animals who had come to "inhabit" her and who suddenly – "(instantaneous)" – disappeared ("they had gone"). The last two lines of the poem express this regret clearly, as the persona departs from the bush. Throughout the poem, the emphasis is not merely on the animals' ability to survive in the bush (a hostile place for Moodie), but also on their teachings which go beyond survival skills.

SILENT VOICES AND "POTENT SIGNALS"

Although survival skills are important in Atwood's poetry, the questioning behind the very idea of our existence is even more so. And the animal voices provide us with clues as to where we come from, who we are, what we are trying to achieve, where our experience is taking us. This motif which is particularly apparent in *The Circle Game* – as I underlined in quoting "After the Flood, We" (CG 4-5) and "A Descent Through Carpet" (CG 15-17) – resurfaces in all of Atwood's later volumes of poetry. In "Notes from Various Pasts" (AC 10-11), for example, the persona is staged in the process of catching "messages / from a harsher level" in her fishing net: "[C]reatures of the most profound / ocean chasms are swimming / far under even the memory / of sun and tidal moon". Again, the voices are silent but the animals become "potent signals" for the persona who gradually translates them into words:

> The words lie washed ashore
> on the margins, mangled
> by the journey upwards to the bluegrey
> surface, the transition:
>
> these once-living
> and phosphorescent meanings
> fading in my hands
>
> I try to but can't decipher (AC 11)

Deciphering the meaning of the "once-living [words]" which lie washed ashore is not a skill that remains with the persona on a permanent basis; rather it is given to her in a fleeting moment which later simply attests to the existence of "potent signals" from animal and geological sources alike.

Survival and deciphering skills sometimes go so far as to take on a magic, supernatural or spiritual dimension. The motif is then closely related to the one which deifies animals. Both in *The Journals of Susanna Moodie* and *The Animals in That Country*, examples abound : in *The Journals of Susanna Moodie*, animal spirits come to haunt both external and internal space – "Departure from the Bush" (EF 63-64), "Dream 3: Night Bear Which Frightened the Cattle" (EF 72); in *The Animals in That Country*, the personae are puzzled by the presence of animal spirits identified either in their dreams or mind's eye – "Arctic Syndrome: Dream Fox" (AC 48-49), "Elegy for the Giant Tortoises" (AC 23). The very titles of these poems give the reader a clue as to how the animals speak to us: they convey their messages silently, through mysterious signs and "dream[s]". We, readers, are encouraged to communicate with them by addressing prayers and "[e]eleg[ies]" to them. The form of communication used with animals is the same as the one used with gods, thus illustrating Atwood's own comment about mythscapes in which "every animal ... speaks because the animals are also gods"

(Evain, Khandpur 76), but both Atwood's comments and poems also bring into question such mythologies, pointing to the subjective nature of any mythology.

Alternatively, as previously mentioned, the animals in Atwood's poetry are present sometimes only through synecdoche, mythical figures or various mysterious disguises. They may point to the story-telling voice, or to the silent artistic creation process. In "Siren Song" (YAH 38-39), the speaker is staged "squatting on an island / looking picturesque and mythical" in a "bird suit". Her voice is just a whisper: she is sharing a secret, the secret of her irresistible song – "the song that forces men / to leap overboard in squadrons / even though they see the beached skulls" (YAH 38). This secret is expressed in the last three stanzas of the poem (stanzas 7, 8 and 9):

> I will tell the secret to you,
> to you only to you.
> Come closer. This song
>
> is a cry for help: Help me!
> Only you, only you can,
> you are unique
>
> at last. Alas
> it is a boring song
> but it works every time. (YAH 39)

These stanzas express an irresistible secret which is to let out a cry for help; the speaker performs this action once again in stanzas 8 and 9. The secret whispered to the reader includes key words of seduction which are echoed in both stanzas "to you, / to you only to you" (stanza 7) and "Only you, only you can" (stanza 8). The poem then moves from the performance of the secret to an expression of regret ("Alas"): the speaker of the poem is tired of resorting to this bag of tricks (the bird-suit costume and the siren song), and she longs to cast away her disguise which is emblematic of the artificial nature of her discourse based on seduction and story-telling.

Another intriguing animal voice in Atwood's poetry can be found in poems which have been called "descent poems" by Atwoodian critics. These poems describe a journey to the underworld. This underworld which is staged mainly in the previously quoted poem "Procedures for Underground" (PU 24-5) is populated with creatures of all sorts. The voice of the speaker of the poem points to the animal figures who will potentially speak to the reader. But first, the reader needs to find the animals: "look for tunnels, animal / burrows or caves in the sea" because "from them you can learn / wisdom and great power, / if you can descend and return safely" (PU 24). The animal voices and whispers beckon the speaker to explore the underworld. They speak of journeys which lead to new discoveries but they also speak of safe returns.

On Circe's island, the animals are given a very different voice and a different role. They first represent the part of the story that Circe didn't have any control over: "It was not my fault, these animals / who once were lovers" (YAH 48), but later they represent the ruthless part of the story: "It's the animals I'm afraid of, they weren't part of the bargain, in fact you didn't mention them, they may transform themselves back into men." (YAH 68). Animals are the product of undesired magic in a "story" of which several versions exist. As they become components of a story, the unexpected or mutant voices and the silent stage props both fade into the background and represent the threat of a possible transformation.

Thus, in looking at the animal motif, it becomes apparent that Atwood's different symbolic orientations of their voices either echo each other, or clash against one another and yet release a set of axioms which are thought-provoking, puzzling, ambivalent, and ultimately meaningful. The animals are the guides the speakers of Atwood's poems can rely on to learn contradictory skills: mainly, the skill to both open herself up to those around her and to resist them ("Procedures for Underground" PU 24-5) in order to allow for her own complex identity to emerge. She needs to learn to feel her way forward, using both intuition and sensorial skills, as the poem "A Boat" (I 97-98) suggests. This animal-like reflex not only allows the speaker of "A Boat" to move forward, but it also provides the link to previous generations and the acknowledgement of one's own space and time. The connection to previous generations further sharpens the speaker's ability to see in the dark. The speaker has gained a new dimension, foreshadowed in *The Journals of Susanna Moodie*: she has allowed the animals to "move into" her: they are a silent presence within her which turn her into a complex animal figure herself: she becomes a sort of nyctalopic animal relying on the touch she goes by. Thus the speaker of the poem speaks of the importance of her silent guides who teach her a new form of power: "It is touch I go by" (I 97).

As we have seen in the first part of this volume, Atwood's poetry playfully stages a wide collection of voices. These voices range from the poetic voice herself (incarnated as a persona and referring to the creative gift or genius) to the voices of many creatures of all kinds, including animals. In several poems, the animals are metaphors for the process of resistance, survival and self-assertion and these processes are pre-conditions for the emergence of a voice. Through the many representations of the poetic voice, as well as the representations of its struggles and journey, we have not only explored Atwood's understanding of the concept of voice but we have also underlined recurrent themes associated with this concept.

In our exploration of the Atwoodian voice, we will now turn to Atwood's "voice-print" (Drury 343) – that is the poet's unique and identifiable voice, which is, as Drury mentions, as unique as a fingerprint. Atwood's ability to resort to a wide range of poetic voices is in itself a characteristic of her voice-print. But, more specifically, we need to explore the texture of these voices in order to determine what makes them unambiguously Atwoodian, whether they speak out individually or grouped together, as in a choir.

While the fingerprint analogy suggests an exact science, analyzing an author's voice-print involves a subjective interpretation of his/her work, and Atwood's particular voice-print is no exception. Furthermore, if Atwood's poetry has evolved and is still evolving over the years, so does the reader's perspective, with every re-reading of her work. In order to show the originality of the Atwoodian voice, the critic resorts to his/her experience of life as well as complementary readings that throws light on a given corpus. Therefore in our analysis of the Atwoodian voice it is possible to draw both on philosophical tools focusing on vision, perception and reflection, and textual analysis tools which highlight the poetic quality of Atwood's work. We will resort to these tools to conjure up a portrait of an Atwood "persona" characterized by a specific philosophical and ideological stance.

Our analysis of Atwood's "voice-print" will cover her poetical and fictional work, and sometimes we will refer to her critical work as well. We will start by echoing a question that Atwood herself raises when speaking about Canadian literature: is there such a thing as a Canadian voice? Does Atwood's own voice sound Canadian? As Atwood highlights the relationship between gaze and voice, she equally underlines the connection between the voice of an artist and the world he/she lives in. In doing so, she traces the movement of the poetic voice from the personal to the universal.

PART II

Identifying Margaret Atwood's Voice-print

CHAPTER 5

Atwood's Canadian Signature

In interpreting Atwood's poetic voice, one's perspective varies depending on where one stands. One may choose, at times, a close reading of a poem or, at other times, to move back and consider the whole of the Atwoodian corpus. To use Atwood's image in relation to a tree, "If you stand very close, you can see the molecules inside the tree. Move back, you see a green thing in the distance." (in Ingersoll 199-200). Even when considering one single poem, or stanza, several levels of interpretation are possible and all interpretations can co-exist. So, to start with, where do we position ourselves? What is there to see? I will begin with the Canadian context of the 1970s and then broaden the perspective both in time and space before focusing on the individual perspective.

As the author of *Survival* and many other critical articles and books, Atwood frequently raises the question: what is distinctive about Canadian literature? Her project is clearly related to raising her readers' cultural awareness. In *Survival*, she describes images and key patterns of plot and tries to determine a Canadian voice.

Significantly, Atwood's definition of Canadianness hinges on the concept of survival. Her comments include questions about cultural myths, such as the Canadian wilderness myth. If we turn to her fiction, her novels and short stories are full of references to the Canadian literary tradition of explorers' narratives, colonial life, survival manuals, and animal and wilderness stories. Atwood's fiction also contains references to the Canadian paintings of the Group of Seven. For example, in "Death by Landscape" in *Wilderness Tips*, the reference to the Group of Seven turns into a ghost story as the forest is presented as a territory which is empty of human figures though there are mysterious traces of them. Many critics have pointed out the influence of the Canadian wilderness, mainly the forests of northern Ontario and Quebec where Atwood spent her childhood and this would explain why she is so deeply impregnated with Canadian geography and cultural heritage. However, it would be a mistake to lock Atwood into the single label of "Canadian author" although she was active in raising awareness concerning the existence of a "Canadian psyche". Coral Ann Howells in her book entitled *Margaret Atwood*, comments that Atwood has indeed constructed her own version of the Canadian signature, out of "the dual context of lived experience and cultural tradition" (22), but it is a *changing* version of the

Canadian signature, one that she "writes and rewrites" and that becomes "*her distinctively Canadian signature*" [1] (22). I have already mentioned, in the introduction to this volume, Djwa's comment according to which Atwood changed from being "a Canadian poet" to an "international woman of letters" (in York 13-14). Indeed, although the "Canadian writer" label is still meaningful, Atwood's work is understood to be relevant beyond the Canadian context. For example, there are vivid representations of the wilderness in Atwood's poetry, but the imagery moves beyond the Canadian landscape into a network of metaphors built around the theory of Darwinian evolution. Atwood's poetic sequence of British immigrant Susanna Moodie provides us with yet another example of Atwood moving beyond the Canadian context. *The Journals* articulates Moodie's perspective which is highly ambivalent and described, in Atwood's terms, as an "inescapable doubleness of vision".

> We are all immigrants to this place even if we were born here: the country is too big for anyone to inhabit completely, and in the parts unknown to us we move in fear, exiles and invaders. This country is something that must be chosen-it is so easy to leave-and if we do choose it we are still choosing a violent duality.[2]

It is somewhat ironic that I should use one of Atwood's comments concerning the Canadian psyche to claim that Atwood's Moodie – often chosen as a symbol of the Canadian psyche – moves beyond the Canadian signature perspective. The very nature of what Atwood describes as an "inescapable doubleness of vision" applies not just to Canadian culture, identity and art, but to all who "move in fear, exiles and invaders". As interpretation "depends on where you stand", one can zoom in on the individual or zoom out to the world. Typically, the questioning is first egocentric and then extends to the universal. This is the experience that Atwood describes by quoting Joyce's protagonist, Stephen Dedalus, in *Survival* : "It begins with the personal, continues through the social or cultural or national and ends with 'The universe,' the universal." (15).

Atwood's own evolution as a critic is significant. Atwood started off attempting to define the Canadian voice and believing it was possible to do so, before moving beyond the questions of Canadian identity and voice (mainly addressing the question of literary creation in *Negotiating with the Dead*).

---

[1] Emphasis mine.
[2] This comment, extracted from Atwood's first edition of *The Journals of Susanna Moodie* (1970 62) was not included in the Eating Fire edition of the *Journals*. It was however included in the bilingual edition published by Bruno Doucey (trans Evain 2011).

However, Atwood stands by her early critical work, defending it whenever necessary[3], convinced that the central image of the victim highlighted in *Survival* is equivalent to the image of the island in British literature and to the frontier in American literature. In her book-length essay, Atwood claims that the Canadian voice (and identity) is indeed characterized by the symbol of survival (Surviv 32) expressed in the four "victim positions" previously mentioned. These four "victim positions" represent a scale of self-actualization which range from the unconscious victim to the creative individual (Surviv 36-42). In Atwood's four scenarios of the "victor/victim" relationship, the "victor" may or may not be another individual; for instance it can be the wilderness or other factors – external and internal – which oppress the victim (Surviv 36-42). *Survival* bears the influence of Northrop Frye's theory of "garrison mentality"[4] where Atwood turns Frye's concept into a critical tool (Pache in Reingard 122). As Pache points out, *Survival* also "reflects Atwood's strong fascination with literary archetypes" (Pache in Reingard 122)[5] inherited from Frye. In her later critical work, Atwood continues her exploration of the Canadian voice, for instance in lectures such as *Strange Things: The Malevolent North in Canadian Literature* (1995). Throughout her critical work, Atwood points not only to Frye but to numerous Canadian writers who articulate this notion of Canada's inferiority complex, or garrison mentality. These themes are interwoven with a historical and geographical experience of Canada. Indeed, the Canadian landscape perceived as inherently threatening, is, according to Atwood, a central element in Canadian writing. However, in the same way Frye had characterized Canada by the idea of vacancy, anticipating Birney's claim "it's only by our lack of ghosts we're haunted" (Birney 15-16), Atwood identifies the following paradox: the emptiness of the Canadian wilderness is the precise cause of its haunting effect, producing a voice made of silence, wind and void. This voice which, in Canadian literature,

---

[3] Atwood comments: "*Survival* was fun to attack. In fact it still is; most self-respecting professors of CanLit begin their courses, I'm told, with a short ritual sneer at it" (SW 105).
[4] Northrop Frye collected his disparate writings on Canadian writing and painting in *The Bush Garden: Essays on the Canadian Imagination* (1971). He coined the phrase "the Garrison Mentality", a theme that, to him, summarized Canadian Literature. Margaret Atwood elaborated on this idea in her book *Survival*.
[5] It is true that her contributions to the theorizing of Canadian identity has been much criticized, and it is even considered by many Canadian critics as outdated. See Laura Moss's article entitled "Margaret Atwood: Branding an Icon Abroad" (Moss in Moss and Tobi Kozakewich 28). The title of Walter Pache further illustrates the type of criticism that Atwood received: "A Certain Frivolity: Margaret Atwood's Literary Criticism" (Pache in Reingard 120-135). However, as Laura Moss, Walter Pache and many other critics underline *Survival* remains part of the standard introduction to Canadian literature in Canadian Studies programs internationally.

conveys a sense of threat also expresses the desire to survive and to move from the position of the victim to that of the creative individual. In her fiction, Atwood explores similar themes to the ones of her critical theories. Several of her works (for instance the poetry collection The *Journals of Susanna Moodie*, or novels from *Surfacing* to *Alias Grace* and *The Blind Assassin*), illustrate Linda Hutcheon's theory of "Historiographic Metafiction" (Howells in Moss and Kozakewich 111): in such works, Atwood considers the Canadian voice to be defined by a fear of nature deeply rooted in the Canadian psyche and made explicit through settler history.

Chapter 6

Gaze and Voice

Atwood's poem, "Spelling" (TS 63-64) stages the previously Joycean observation and shows the close relationship between gaze and voice: it is the gaze that directs the voice. The speaker of "Spelling" takes the example of her own daughter who is playing with letters and "learning to spell". As the persona's gaze shifts from her daughter to the outside world, her voice becomes infused with questions. Her relation to language changes because she shifts her gaze (moving backwards and forward, from her daughter to the outside world) and this broadening of her horizons leads her to experience the inadequacy of words. At the end of the poem the speaker returns to her home and comes to a Joycean conclusion as she describes the human experience and learning process which her daughter illustrates:

> How do we learn to spell?
> Blood, sky & the sun,
> your own name first,
> your first naming, your first name,
> your first word. (64)

This stanza is written in the form of a scientific observation – this is how we proceed: we start with ourselves and then we look to the outside. Learning to read and write is the very illustration of this: we learn to spell our name first and then the words "[b]lood, sky & the sun" – which can be interpreted as the human experience which includes suffering ("[b]lood"), as well as discoveries and joy ("sky & the sun"). While the poem states that, when learning to write, we start with our own name, the speaker's central claim concerns language as a whole: "[a] word after a word / after a word is power" (64) – a comment that applies both to the torture scene described in the fourth stanza ("the burning witch, / her mouth covered by leather / to strangle words", 64) and the feeling of powerlessness of the speaker who bears witness to this violence. The sixth stanza conveys the power of words – although the speaker claims to be at "the point where language falls away", that is at the point where her own voice seems to disappear because it is utterly inadequate:

> At the point where language falls away
> from the hot bones, at the point
> where the rock breaks open and darkness
> flows out of it like blood, at
> the melting point of granite
> when the bones know
> they are hollow & the word
> splits & doubles & speaks
> the truth & the body
> itself becomes a mouth.
>
> This is a metaphor.

When one's gaze focuses on oneself, it is easy to spell one's name and speak one's name. But if one dethrones oneself and reaches out to people who are subjected to unbearable suffering, "language falls away". However, the speaker's voice does not fail totally, in spite of her frustration with language. The voice speaks in metaphors to express "the truth & the body". These metaphors, which hinge on the main themes of the volume *True Stories*, bring together the concepts of body / mouth / word / power and the silent voice – not that of the speaker but that of the tortured man or woman. The power of poetry is to expose the practice of torture through words. It is the reader who then gives power to the poetic voice precisely as he reads that the speaker is experiencing the inadequacy of her voice and is therefore tempted to withdraw into silence.

To emphasize the relationship between the voice and the gaze, we may take a closer look at how the poem is constructed. Atwood uses a technique that film critics call the "dissolve" (Lewis 69). The "dissolve" technique is a special type of flashback where the disjunctive interruptions of the plot – transferring attention abruptly to a different locale and/or time-frame – is softened by a special type of transition: a close relationship between two scenes is suggested; thus, the "dissolve" technique superimposes a fade-out over a fade-in, momentarily fusing two images.

The "dissolve" technique is indeed the strategy that Atwood uses in her poem "Spelling": the persona's gaze moves from what is close to her (her daughter involved in play) to broader and more abstract interrogations. But it is only when the gaze moves back to the private sphere that the speaker becomes aware of her own thought process. It is only by recognizing the egocentric starting point of her thought process that she is able to dethrone herself and consider the larger picture. When observing her own eye movement, the speaker becomes aware of the changes that occur in her voice, mainly as she is suddenly confronted with the sight of torture and finds that words fail the poet.

Through the "dissolve" technique the poems of *True Stories* as well as the very organization of the volume, map out, with a great deal of lucidity the persona's experience which moves from considering herself first, to looking out at the world around her. Through observing the effects of her gaze shifting from the private sphere to the outside world, the speaker calls into question the effectiveness of language: the voice seeking to affirm the power of languages reaches the point where "the rock breaks open and darkness / flows out of it like blood" and where "the word [that] splits & doubles & speaks / the truth & the body". In other poems by Atwood, this movement – from the inside towards the outside, and vice-versa – is not always as explicit as in the poem "Spelling". Often – whether it is in *True Stories* or in other volumes – the origin of the movement is blurred, and the private and public spheres become one: it is up to the reader to disentangle and to interpret the different levels of reality. However, as the poem "Spelling" highlights, it is through *movement* that our gaze is made productive and one becomes aware of the fertile exchanges between the various spheres of reality. We are encouraged to scrutinize the world around us in a more in-depth manner and to question beyond the surface.

The idea of our gaze rooted in our experience of *seeing* which Atwood translates through the "dissolve" technique described in the above analysis of the poem "Spelling" establishes an extraordinary connection with Merleau-Ponty's concept of perception. Indeed, the Atwoodian speaker's voice is rooted in physical experience and speaks of the body experienced as organic material, capable of questioning her relationship with the world around her[1]. She gives

---

[1] Like other major phenomenologists, Merleau-Ponty believes in the foundational role of perception in order to understand the world as well as engage with it. At the core of his philosophy is his conception of the body as the primary site of knowing the world. This conception runs counter to the long philosophical tradition of placing consciousness as the source of knowledge. Merleau-Ponty claims that the body and that which is perceived cannot be disentangled from each other. It is his articulation of the primacy of embodiment which sets him apart from most phenomenologists towards what he calls "indirect ontology" or the ontology of "the flesh of the world" seen in his last uncomplete work, *The Visible and the Invisible*. Talor Carman and Mark Hansen state that, according to Merleau-Ponty's "indirect ontology", there is no "descent of a soul into a body, but rather the emergence of a life in its cradle, an instigated vision (vision suscitée). This is because there is an interiority of the body, an 'other side', for us invisible, of this visible" (Carman, Hansen 237). Similarly, the "lateral union" of humanity and animality calls for a "bottom-up" conception of perception which allows for an understanding of oneself as a product of evolution (Carman, Hansen 237). In other words, the soul does not descend into the body, but life itself stems from perception. As far as their conceptualization of experience is concerned, Atwood's wide range of speakers do have that much in common: their thought process is not based on abstraction, but is rooted in perception. Hence the following paradox: the typical Atwoodian voice, which by definition is only a voice and not a

voice to the "'bottom-up' conception of perception" and stages every experience as "the emergence of a life in its cradle, an instigated [...] vision" (Carman, Hansen 237). The speaker's thought process starts with her contact with the world – an interior or exterior reality that she is grounded in and on which she elaborates. In other words, the speaker focuses on things upon which her body has a "grip" – "la saisie du monde par son corps" (Merleau-Ponty 104). She establishes contact with the world through simple daily experiences or through deep emotional upheavals such as experiences of love and loss. The speaker's ability to be grounded in experience is not only a characteristic of the Atwoodian voice but it is reflected in the many poems in which the speaker's shifting gaze plays a significant role. The poem "Spelling" is a case in point as the speaker's gaze guides the voice and leads her to claim that we all "start with our own name first" and then we become capable of expanding in a Joycean manner. In this process, the Atwoodian voice speaks both of the inadequacy and the power of language, all the while struggling with the temptation to withdraw into silence.

The Merleau-Pontyan accent in Atwood's poetic voice is only one aspect of this voice. When reading the whole of Atwood's poetry, the poet's signature (or voice-print) appears to be highly recognizable through many types of echoes and similar characteristics. In order to capture the specificity of the Atwoodian signature, one must endeavour to discern between the solo voice and the polyphony, trying to understand the interplay of harmonies and dissonances. One can stipulate that the voice sings her personal truth – a truth based on the convictions and experience of the persona, although this so-called "truth" may be subject to interpretation.

---

physical entity, constantly refers to the physicality of things including the speakers' own bodies. In that respect, the speakers' experiences spring from what may be described as a Merleau-Pontyan perception of self.

CHAPTER 7

Trying to Capture the Atwoodian Voice-print

In 2007, when Reena Khandpur and I carried out a series of interviews with Atwood, our project was to ask the poet about her work, hoping to receive encouragement in our own interpretation of the work (although we were aware that any interpretation was an entirely subjective matter). In response to our questions, the author, with a great deal of humour, refused on several occasions to go into any kind of interpretation ("You're asking me to analyze my own individual poems and there's no point in me doing that. Other people will do that. That's for other people to do. May they have joy doing it." Evain, Khandpur 139). It is therefore important to underline the subjective nature of all commentaries (including the one of the present chapter). Whenever remarks made by the author during our conversations first published in 2006 as well as quotes from the extremely rich Atwoodian epitext will be included, they will serve the purpose providing supplementary comments, opening doors for possible interpretations. The reader will most probably consider Atwood's comments as insightful and sometimes pedagogical with regards to the understanding of both poetry and Canadian culture but they are no more than an additional light thrown on the corpus – and not the final word on the work itself.

The metaphor of the solo voice will be a recurrent leitmotiv in this section: we will try to demonstrate that this voice rises above the Atwoodian polyphony – which is characteristic of Atwood's voice-print. We will first map out how this polyphony is constructed and then show how the solo voice transcends the many voices of the choir. The musical metaphor can be extended from the solo voice to the other voices. Indeed, these voices can be seen as the different sections of a choir, not unlike the four traditional soprano, alto, tenor and bass sections.

As we have previously pointed out, Atwood sometimes gives her personae names resonant with intertextuality, often throwing an entirely different light on well-known figures or subverting them. The large range of masks includes many figures, from animal to literary or mythical figures. How does the soloist voice rise above their voices? It does so by taking on the role of a choir master, responsible for the staging and distribution of scores, the orchestration of the voices and the direction of the choir.

But the soloist-director also has a voice of her own which corresponds to a virtual subject that we will try to outline. This subject (a virtual subject, constructed by the reader upon reading the poem) will be called "Persona" with a capital P and the singers in the choir taking on the traits of well-known figures will be called the "masked singers". The Persona voices her emotions and ambivalences, in search of a deep reconciliation between two poles clearly mapped out: the desire to explore the underworld but also to return from the underworld into a world of so-called "normality" or everyday life.

The different sections of the choir and the masked singers resonate within the voice of the Persona: their song is about deep self-understanding and reconciliation – a difficult task, never fully accomplished and to be renewed constantly, which evokes the central metaphor of poems like "The Woman Who Could Not Live With Her Faulty Heart" (THP 14-15) and "The Woman Makes Peace With Her Faulty Heart" (THP 86-87). The speaker of the poem needs to accept her contradictory heartbeats as part of her human condition.

FOUR CHOIR SECTIONS

In the same way traditional choirs are composed of four sections, Atwood's poetry can be read on four different scores which critics clearly identify. The terms which are often used to characterize Atwood's poetry are the following: "about Canada poems" or "post-colonial poems"; "female-empowered poems; "descent poems"; and "metafictional poems" (this last category includes mainly the prose poems). The "about Canada" label, used by Atwood herself in the Ottawa interviews that Reena Khandpur and myself published in 2006 is similar to the "post-colonial" label which many critics often prefer. Atwood's label simply emphasizes the importance of Canada as a geographical entity and the label is used in connection with many geographical metaphors in Atwood's poetry which raise the question of identity. It is interesting to note that Atwood's geography bears the mark of a planetary evolution which unfolds over millions of years. The Canadian element in the "about Canada" label is invalidated because the scope of the poems is much larger than the national sphere and refers the reader to a broader sphere in which man questions his place within the universe (see "After the Flood, We" (CG 4) or the last three poems of *The Circle Game*).

The above labels are thus both useful and stereotypical. If critics have found it useful to read Atwood's poetry according to critical tools provided by the four categories – mainly the "post-colonial", "feminist", "metafictional" and "psychoanalytical" critical approaches – the originality of Atwood's signature lies in the poet's ability to superimpose themes referring to these four categories, allowing the four sections of the choir to sing simultaneously. The Atwoodian composition is like a counterpoint[1] where the different motifs or melodies in turn prevail, depending on one's critical angle.

When Atwood is asked about the poems in *The Circle Game* which are qualified as "about Canada poems" ("A Place: Fragments", "The Explorers", "The Settlers"), she shares a few ideas which inspired her at the moment of writing. For "Migration: CPR" (CG 51-55) – CPR being the acronym for "Canadian Pacific Railroad" – Atwood evokes the long train journeys that she undertook to promote her work throughout Canada. She also quotes *Survival* where she refers to James Joyce's hero and the following inscription in a geography book: "Stephen Deladus / Class of Elements / Clongowes Wood College / Sallins / County Kildare / Ireland / Europe / The World / The Universe" (Surviv 15). Atwood explains the superimposition of voices in her poetry by referring to the well-known phenomenon of self-perception in relation to world-perception: as underlined in my analysis of the poem "Spelling", one begins with the personal sphere and one moves into the social, cultural, national, world and universal spheres which are the very material that the writer can work with. The main Atwoodian themes – which can be gathered in key points such as identity quest, survival strategies and individual rebellion[2], reconciliation and quest for balance and peace – can be applied to the different spheres. In other words, each of the Atwoodian themes can refer to an individual, a social group, a given nation, the whole world or the universe itself. It is obviously a topical theme, in the late 1960s – the post-colonial decade when the centennial of the Confederation was celebrated and when Atwood's first volumes of poetry were published –, to defend a national identity in order to move beyond Canada's inferiority complex. That is how the personal and national levels are closely intertwined in Atwood's first volume, *The Circle Game*, with multiple images (taken from a range of fields including mythology, literature, folklore or science).

The eponymous poem in *The Circle Game* stages a cry of freedom: "I want the circle / broken" (CG 41), and this sequence of seven poems[3] actually constructs a network of images and correspondences that become a metaphor for

---

[1] A counterpoint is a melodic material that is added above or below an existing melody.
[2] These three themes are covered by Jagna Oltarzewska in *Témoignage, Identité, Survie : Stratégies féminines de lutte et d'émancipation dans l'œuvre romanesque de Margaret Atwood* (1999).
[3] McCombs comments on the "seven": "Seven is of course, a magic, centred number; many of *Circle*'s poems, from 'Photograph' on, are seven-part structures. And it should be noted that *Circle*'s northernmost 'A Place: Fragments', which was the concluding poem of 'Places, Migrations', is a seven-part sequence which follows, in its quest for identity, the nationalist painters called the Group of Seven."(in Nicholson 63)

the imprisonment from which the poetic voice tries to escape. The purpose of the poetic strategy is to denounce the closed circle and to stage a liberating affirmation which is encapsulated in the final outcry in the last poem. Two types of poems alternate: poems focusing on "children" (preceded by uneven numbers: i, iii, v, vii) and poems where the poetic voice addresses a "you" (preceded by even numbers: ii, iv, vi). In the seventh poem, the alternating movement within the sequence of poems is resolved with "children" and "you" equally present in the final metaphor that is reminiscent of the title of the poem "The Circle Game".

One can interpret the children holding hands in a circle as a social game, which functions according to a set of rules which are firmly established within a given group. In poems i and ii, the social and love games gradually merge into one, because of the recurrence of the images of the circle and the round. At the beginning of the sequence, the images express a form of tautology ("the whole point / for them / of going / round and round / is (faster / slower) / going round and round"). The children are inevitably part of this tautology because they are going around in a circle but also because of the reference to a popular song which creates this revolving dance: "We can only look beyond from where we've come, as our minds go round and round and round in the Circle Game". The reader can almost hear the song despite the fact that it is not quoted but simply referred to: it is highlighted by the refrain and accompanied by the images of the merry-go-round and the children singing. It is the song that enlightens the tautology: the social game is present from childhood onwards and thus children are trapped on a merry-go-round which keeps turning throughout all stages of life. This metaphor can also be interpreted as going beyond the individual time-line and extending to a temporal line which includes all generations, past and present. The children then become the symbol of humanity throughout time: they are the common point between past and present, the recurring element from one generation to the next – the social game itself encapsulated in the circular "round and round" movement. The reason the children are on the merry-go-round is for no other reason than to *go round and round*, as the poetic voice underlines in "The Circle Game". This second interpretation of the poem thus merges into the first, highlighting the absurdity of the movement which concerns any individual, social group or generation – and which all generations sing in unison.

We may now come back to the image of the unbroken, inescapable circle, present in each of the poems of the sequence. Whether the relationship is between children or lovers, it is inevitably symbolized by the closed circle of a joyless and idiotic round. The motif of the circle is used in the figurative sense as well: the speaker is located in a closed room, whose image is circumscribed by her partner's reflection or cartography. Many more images then enter into correspondence and come to enrich the interplay between children and lovers: war games, mirrors, geographical tracing or mapping. The lovers' relationship suggested here foreshadows the one staged in *Power Politics*. The lover, enwrapped in mirrors, is obsessed with his own reflection and neglects everything else: "You look past me, [...] watching / your own reflection somewhere / behind my head" (32). His negation of the speaker of the poem is stated in the games he plays (as with the children): "I notice how / all your word- / plays, [...] are now attempts to keep me / at a certain distance, [...] avoid / admitting I'm here" (34). The link with childhood behaviors is underlined in a couple of verses: "in childhood you were / a tracer of maps" (35).

Like a child tracing images, the lover in the poems is merely a copier, following the courses of the rivers on a map. He is a "memorizer / of names (to hold / these places / in their proper places)" (34). The parentheses are another means of enclosure, and they allow for the persona of the poem to speak with a slightly different voice – perhaps a more sarcastic and resentful voice. The lover imprisons the speaker of the poem in a definitive spot, against her will: "and I am fixed, stuck / down on the outspread map / of this room" (35). The network of images enables the reader to establish parallels between the different enclosing situations all the while creating an atmosphere of increasing rebellion which leads to the claustrophobic explosion in the last three stanzas. The sequence ends with an expression of anger which is also an outburst liberating the speaker's voice. It is a forceful and bold assertion emphasized by the first person pronoun and the verb of volition "want": the assertive voice of the persona thus finally emerges and she breaks free from the infamous closed circle.

The speaker's desire to leap into the unknown and to cross borders forms a leitmotiv in Atwood's poetry. Departure, change and resistance to imprisonment are themes which unfold and stem from the initial outcry. The strategic place of the speaker's outcry "I want the circle / broken" points both to the salutary nature and to the uncertainty of this liberation attempt.

The eponymous poem "The Circle Game" is only one example where the individual and collective spheres and voices are superimposed. Other motifs present in *The Circle Game* are connected with the idea of self-affirmation through a voice spoken into being and establishing the persona's identity. For instance Frank Davey's list of motifs include: "Technological Skin", "Mirrors", "The Gothic", "Refugees and Tourists", "Underground, Underwater", "The Maze", "Signposts / Totems" and "Metamorphosis" (Davey 93-127). The latter of these motifs – the metamorphosis – offers a relevant example of the superimposition between the individual and collective spheres. One of the variations of this motif is the image of decomposition in which decomposition is a source of regeneration (a metaphor which also works on the individual and collective level). These images are associated with a new beginning and the possibility of being nourished by a heritage which can only be received in a state of decomposition. In *The Circle Game*, "Pre-Amphibian" (62-63), "A Place: Fragments" (73-77), "The Explorers" (78-79), "The Settlers" (80-81) are a few examples of poems weaving metaphors stemming from the biological and evolutionary domains. Death holds the promise of new life although it does not take on the form of a resurrection in the Christian sense of the word. The new life is associated with a unique type of closeness with nature: an ability to perceive biological or psychological meaning in natural phenomena. This ability is provoked by deliberate or accidental acts, sometimes staged in a highly surreal environment of symbolic importance. The symbolic dimension is where individual experience becomes a collective one as in "After the Flood, We" (CG 4) where the couple in the poem stands for love relationships which are all capable of both destruction and reconstruction.

Another example of the superimposition between the group's and the individual's voices is to be found in "The Words Continue their Journey" (I 82-83). In this poem, the poet is staged as part of a lineage that connects the voices of all poets. This feeling of belonging to a group is central to the poem:

> Some days though I want, still,
> to be like other people;
> but then I go and talk with them,
> these people who are supposed to be
> other, and they are much like us,
> except that they lack the sort of thing
> we think of as a voice.
> [...]
> But look, I said us. (I 82)

The speaker of the poem alludes to the poets' unique gift without the arrogance one might associate with the recognition of such a gift. Although the "other people" are much like the poets, they "lack the sort of thing / we think of as a voice": the statement is expressed in a matter-of-fact manner and it does not place "poets" above "other people". The speaker of the poem finds herself referring to the poets as "us" in spite of the fact that it does not necessarily correspond to her preferred group of human beings ("But look, I said us. Though I may hate your guts / individually" I 82). Having stated this feeling of belonging to a group, she further elaborates on the idea of a group identity, in spite of differences within that given group:

> though I prefer to spend my time
> with dentists because I learn more,
> I spoke of us as *we*, I gathered us
> like the members of some doomed caravan (I 82)

The group of poets, encapsulated in a "we" and "us", is gathered in the last line of the stanza. The "doomed caravan" image is further developed in the poem and proves to be a metaphorical representation of the voice where the voice-persona sees itself not only individually but collectively. Of the many representations of the voice, it is perhaps the one where Atwood emphasizes most the sense of the poet belonging to a minority group undertaking a journey across the desert. However the idea of the journey itself is not reserved for poets alone; it is to be frequently encountered in the so-called "descent poems", such as "Procedures for Underground" (PU 24-25) or "Shadow Voice" (AC 7). These poems reveal an experience which can be that of a poet (and which Atwood comments on in *Negotiating with the Dead*) but which is also that of any individual wishing to gain a better understanding of him/herself and the human stuff we are made of. In spite of the highly personal tone of Atwood's poems – whether critics place them in the category of "about Canada poems", "female-empowered poems" or "descent poems" – Atwood's themes are universal, allowing for a range of voices to express themselves, echo each other, and raise fundamental questions about our identity and mode of being.

Now turning to the different voices in the choir, we may examine the range of characters that are staged in the many volumes of poetry. These characters exist only in a virtual form; the image of the virtuoso ventriloquist, fascinated by the interplay of voices and disguises comes to mind and completes or supersedes that of the choir master.

THE CHARACTERS AND THEIR SONGS

Atwood's talent as a ventriloquist leads to a metafictional reflection which is encapsulated in the poem previously quoted "Siren Song" (YAH 38). This poem stages a strategy of disguises which highlights the relationship between mask and voice. The speaker of the poem refers to the fatal voices of the sirens misleading the lost sailors. Then the speaker playfully promises the reader she will take off her disguise and expose her voice ("Shall I tell you the secret / and if I do, will you get me / out of this bird suit?, YAH 38). The analysis of the characters in Atwood's poetry will achieve a similar objective and establish a relationship between disguise and voice (or song), underlining the subtlety of the game and pointing to the position and interplay of characters and their music.

Among the gallery of personae, we notice certain recurring figures: animals, mythical characters, shamanic characters stemming from literature or popular culture, scientific and technological creations. All these characters play on various symbolic orientations. Consequently, the texture and the tone of their voices depends on what they stand for and on the reader's own interpretation. The metafictional prose poem "Bread" (MID 71-75) suggests that poetry starts with the exploration of possible symbolic orientations. It is this exploration which enriches the voice the reader hears (as well as the reader's own silent vocal performance upon reading the poem). This exploration implies stepping out of one's bubble and looking out at the world: "Put yourself into a different room, that's what the mind is for" (MID 72). The prose poem provides an exercise in five steps (and five poems): the speaker first asks the reader to imagine a piece of bread and adds that, in fact: "You don't have to imagine it, it's right here in the kitchen, on the bread board, in its plastic bag lying beside the bread knife." (MID 71). Then the speaker asks the reader to imagine a famine (poem 2), and then a prison (poem 3) and to explore the new meanings of "bread". Poem 4 looks at the meaning of bread in a German fairy-tale and finally, in poem 5, Atwood returns to the loaf of bread in the kitchen, on the bread board, and somehow this loaf is different, suggesting a transformation that occurs in the reader when he looks beyond his own small world. This seems to imply that it is the poet's role to help the reader "put [himself] into a different room" and see things – "I've somehow duped you into seeing" (MID 75), says the persona in the last lines of the poem.

A similar exploration, leading to an enrichment of the reader's perception of the poetic voice can be found in the "Snake poems" sequence and in the two poems "Landcrab" I&II (TS 12-15): both the "snake" and "landcrab" can be seen in a different light depending on context[4]. In her biography of Atwood, Rosemary Sullivan quotes a 1969 letter by Atwood to Eli Mandel, on the topic of what Mandel and Atwood call the symbolic and the real:

---

[4] To quote our conversation: "Q. In several of your poems, I get the impression that what you're saying is, that you pray to whatever is going to inspire you; that is, you can pray to snakes, you can pray to spirits. It really is a matter of personal choice or personal symbolic orientation.
A. Personal symbolic orientation is what it is. But you know, this is poetry, it's not a theological system..." (Evain, Khandpur 87)

> I suspect that some of the things in my poems which would be symbols for you are real things for me; or anyway real things which are themselves symbolic. I know that Frye says once you put a sheep in a poem it becomes a poetic sheep, a sheep-in-a-poem; not sure that I want that to happen. I think when I put a tree in a poem I want it to become a tree, which is a confusion between thing and word (Sullivan 224).

If, as underlined in "Bread", exploring the meaning of a "thing and word" and creating semantic associations becomes a necessity to understand the world we live in, it is also a game. The different symbolic orientations are enriched with a process of "theatricalization". For the theatrical effects, Atwood resorts to intertextuality (references to myths, literature and popular cultural). The voices of the Atwoodian characters can be enriched through theatricalization and through various possibilities of combining reading sequences, as the voices of the poem can be heard in the context of one poem, several poems or one complete volume. For example, the voice of the persona of Susanna Moodie is central to every one of the poems of *The Journals of Susanna Moodie*; the voice of Circe also occupies center stage in one given volume: "Circe/Mud Poems" (YAH 45-70). In the same way, one can imagine one single persona speaking throughout *Power Politics*. Several volumes offer a range of personae which are regrouped thematically: in *You Are Happy*, we notice that the sequence "Songs of the Transformed" (YAH 29-44) stages a series of animals who take turns in voicing their perspective on life. Other characters come on stage either on their own and for a one-off performance or for a series of interconnected performances or poems: "Speeches for Dr Frankenstein" (AC 42-47), "The Reincarnation of Captain Cook" (AC 61), "Cyclops" (42-43), "Projected slide of an Unknown Soldier" (PU 46 - 47), "Landcrab" I&II (TS 12-15).

It seems that Atwood enjoys giving her poetic voices masks and disguises that will help the reader hear and "see" a voice. Some famous figures whether mythical or literary, voice the triple Atwoodian emancipation theme previously mentioned. For example, in the second part of *Morning in the Burned House*, famous female figures hold center stage. Each of the personae lends her name to the title of the poem (out of eight poems, there is one exception only: "A Man Looks"). Whether the reader is in the presence of "Miss July [...]" (21-23), "Manet's Olympia" (24-25), "Daphne [...]"(26-27), "Ava Gardner [...]" (30-32), "Helen of Troy [...]" (33-36), or "Sekhmet [...]" (39-41), all of the poetic voices seem to have a definite connection with the speaker of "Gertrude Talks Back" (15-18) in *Good Bones*. In other words, even as Atwood's speakers are taking on different disguises and voices, they seem to have something in common. The voices are as recognizable to us as the Atwoodian voice, much like the voice of an actor playing different roles can be identified as one and the same voice.

The discourse of Atwood's personae is marked with tongue-in-cheek irony and a distinctive emancipation posture. Typically, in "Gertrude Talks Back" in *Good Bones*, the persona is staged as she defends herself, denounces, seeks vengeance or creates a scandal. This sequence of poems ends with the figure of an ambivalent lion. This persona is emblematic of several of the characteristics of Atwood's female personae, namely in her desire to empower ("I held power", 39), in her defiance of authority (she doesn't think much of the religious beliefs of her time) and her possession of a hidden truth.

In some poems, the Atwoodian personae tend to have more blurry forms. It is often the case with poems referred to as the "Descent poems" previously mentioned. In order to fully understand this term, it is useful to turn to the Atwoodian epitext – and mainly *Negotiating with the Dead* – where the author explains what she means by "The Dead": in Atwoodian vocabulary, "The Dead" is the world of the inner voice which speaks to the poet as in the poem "Shadow Voice" (AC 7). In order to differentiate this voice from the other Atwoodian voices, I will refer to this inner voice with a capital V. It is this voice which can be heard throughout Atwood's work from the first volume of poetry to the last published to date – *Bottle*. It is a voice that, in most poems, is not that of the speaker but rather a voice that speaks to the speaker. However in a couple of poems such as "Shadow Voice" (AC 7) for example, the Voice speaks in the first person and addresses the "you" of the poem as if whispering in her ear. The place where the Voice can be heard is often associated with the metaphor of the underworld, but not always, as can be seen in "Shadow Voice" where the main metaphor is that of a picnic.

Whether they belong to the literary, mythical or folkloric tradition – as in "Shadow Voice" (AC 7), "Returning from the dead", (PP 39), "Procedures for Underground" (PU 24-25), "Heart Test With An Echo Chamber" (I 86-87) "A Boat" (I 97-98), "Interlunar" (I 102-103), etc. – the Voices characterized with a capital V speak of their search for a deep reconciliation whereby they endeavor to enrich their inner lives by diving into the underworld and to make peace with the "every day" world, the world of normality and ordinary things.

These voices consider the places they inhabit as being in opposite and complementary locations. The underground world allows the speakers to escape from the "every day" world considered as limited: it is not a dwelling place in itself and the speakers can only visit this world but not remain there for very long.

This underworld presents many dangers. "Procedures for Underground" (PU 24-25) stages strange phenomena that the speaker is confronted with when descending into the underworld; and a short poem in *Power Politics* summarizes the difficulty of returning to the "every day" world:

> Returning from the dead
> used to be something I did well
>
> I began asking why
> I began forgetting how (PP 39)

These four lines express the speakers' temptation not to return to the "every day" world. Why not dwell in this hidden place that gradually becomes familiar? The speaker becomes attuned to the changed reference system highlighted in "Procedures for Underground". The land no longer seems foreign. The unusual becomes the new norm. The speaker finds herself perfectly at ease in her new surroundings. The "Shadow Voice" has managed to seduce the speaker thanks to promises of an intellectual life ("I give water, I give clean crusts / ...words / flowing in your veins / to keep you going", AC 7). The speakers of the two above poems (PP 39 and AC7) are not the only ones who are tempted to remain in the underworld. Atwood's Eurydice refuses Orpheus's help to come back to the world of the living: in the poem "Orpheus (1)", Eurydice reproaches Orpheus for the very help he provided in leading her back to the world of the living. She has absolutely no desire to follow him and Eurydice's obedience is only made possible because of a radical anesthesia:

> You walked in front of me,
> pulling me back out
> to the green light that had once
> grown fangs and killed me
>
> I was obedient, but
> numb, like an arm
> gone to sleep; the return
> to time was not my choice. (I 58)

The "green light" of the world of the living that had once been threatening to Eurydice is opposed to her own numbness which she compares to "an arm / gone to sleep". The line break creates a typical anticipation and twist. Because Eurydice has become aware of her own numbness in the world of the living, she claims that the return from the dead was "not her choice". In a second poem devoted to the myth of Orpheus, a voice – which is none other than the Voice of "Shadow Voice" – comes to warn Eurydice:

> He is here, come down to look for you.
> It is the song that calls you back,
> a song of joy and suffering
> equally a promise;
> that things will be different up there
> than they were last time. (I 60)

It is as if the Voice were beseeching Eurydice not to trust the promises that are made by the world of the living. Such a world cannot possibly satisfy Eurydice: her return among the living would inevitably be a huge disappointment. Indeed, the Voice claims that this world has not changed in her absence. Nothing has improved. There is nothing there to quench the thirst of the spirit.

In order to receive food and water for the spirit, one needs to go to the underworld where "water [and] clean crusts" (AC 7) are given freely. The Voice that speaks to Eurydice is like the echo of her own desire: Eurydice wants to send Orpheus back to the world of the living without her ("Go back, you whisper" I 61) and she wants to stay behind in the world of the dead. The Voice encourages Eurydice to listen to her own desire and helps her to see Orpheus for what he is: he is not a rescuer. The Voice warns Eurydice and, in substance she points out that Orpheus wants a female companion who will look after him, who will heal him when he is hurt, feed him when he is hungry: "…he wants to be fed again / by you. O handful of gauze, little / bandage", 61). Do not fall for this again, warns the Voice: "It is not through him / you will get your freedom." (61). This warning addressed to Eurydice reveals to the reader how tempting it is to remain in the world of the dead.

However, unlike the Eurydice of both of these poems, the voice of the Atwoodian choir master wants to come back to the world of the living. Her sojourns in the underground are fruitful but only temporary. Her desire to find her way back is constant, although the temptation expressed in "Returning from the Dead" (PP 39) is equally present. Many personae impersonate this desire to return to the everyday world after an underground experience – in *Morning in the Burned House*, as well as in the "Circe/Mud Poems" sequence of poems.

It is worth noticing that when the persona refuses to return from the underground, the poem takes on a slightly didactic twist, as if the reader could hear yet another voice singing independently from those of the personae staged in the poem. Indeed, it is hardly surprising that Atwood should choose to place those words of refusal of the everyday world in the mouth of Eurydice – it is precisely for the reader to come to the following conclusion and equation: to choose to dwell in the underground is to choose death. Thus, even when the persona who opts for the underground dwelling is the one speaking in the poem, the Atwoodian voice concealed behind the persona's voice conveys her message of warning. It is through this theatrical game that the choir master's voice is to be heard above those of the personae themselves.

To use a musical metaphor, the voice of the choir master does not follow the score of Eurydice's song, nor the one of the Voice which addresses Eurydice (the one that strangely resembles the inner voice of the "Shadow Voice" – hence the capital). The voice of the choir master sings its own musical score – a tune which runs counter to the melody sung by Eurydice herself. The poetic strategy informs the reader of the counter-melody. It is as if the choir master who directs the voices of the different personae were giving himself the right to make his own voice heard. This discreet voice of the choir master which completes the main melody, *in fine*, allows for the Atwoodian signature to emerge.

The voice of the choir master can now be heard more clearly, as it rises above all other voices. Indeed, the choir master is also a soloist, traveling freely within the four different superimposed sections of the choir, singing sometimes in harmony and sometimes in disharmony with the main melody. I have used the term counter-melody to evoke the idea of a tune which defines the song of the choir master but I still need to refine this definition. I will now try to establish the "profile" of this voice – and determine whether this enterprise is in fact possible. My wish is to highlight Atwood's original relationship with the world and the language of poetry.

THE VOICE OF THE CHOIR MASTER AS A SOLOIST

It may seem rather pointless to try to establish the psychological profile of a voice, while the very essence of a poetic voice is to exist only through its song. Indeed, the exercise suggested here goes against Maulpoix's comment according to which "the lyrical subject is a construction and does not exist as such" (in Rabaté 153). It is only a "potential I". In other words, the lyrical subject comes to life and establishes itself as a "poetic environment": "It is both an ever-changing project and a form of resonance ('a powerful echo' according to Hugo) which is inhabited by the most diverse emotions, the most changeable identities." (in Rabaté 150)[5].

---

[5] To quote Maulpoix, "le sujet lyrique s'effectue mais il n'existe pas" (in Rabaté 153). "Il est à la fois un être en perpétuel projet et en résonance ("écho sonore" eût dit Hugo) que

So, my attempt to establish the profile of a voice means that I am making the incongruous supposition of the existence of such a profile in spite of an absence of subject: I have nevertheless chosen to call this entity "Persona" with a capital "P". This artificial construction is motivated by the fact that Atwood's poetry bears the mark of a signature which I would like to characterize. I would like to embrace the whole of Atwood's poetry and underline the unity of her work.

It is not so much a question of proposing a personality profile which corresponds to that of the author, but simply of connecting the whole poetic production with a virtual construction made by an individual reader in order to show how this construction gives possible meaning to the polyphony of the poems. The process of constructing this Persona is an activity situated at the level of the reception of the work and it reflects the personal interpretation of an individual reader (who happens to be myself).

My approach is intuitive. It seems to me that the teaching of the poems strangely merges with what we find in the books of psychology addressing the issue of "exceptionally gifted" children. Atwood herself establishes a link between voice and gift when she claims: "I was given a voice. That's what people say about me. I cultivated my voice, because it would be a shame to waste such a gift." (TT 21) In the poem "The Words Continue their Journey" (I 82-83), Atwood alludes to this voice which is given to poets in a somewhat cryptic and elliptic way. While the gift of a voice characterizes all poets, does the questioning concerning this gift/voice contribute to the characterization of the Atwoodian voice? Can this special gift be compared to other types of gifts and singularities? The voice of the Atwoodian Persona conveys a message which is of value to those individuals who distinguish themselves by their sensibility and intelligence. We notice that the inflections of the Atwoodian Persona resemble those of an exceptional subject who has long experienced his/her difference in a painful way, and who is gradually becoming aware of the value of this difference and learns to assert him/herself serenely. The difficulty of expressing one's difference does not magically disappear upon realizing one's difference. But rather, a new type of challenge emerges: that of finding a unique personal balance which reflects the subject's psychological complexity. While isolation may appear as necessary and beneficial, the subject can only envisage withdrawing from the world temporarily. Because it is in the "ordinary" world that the Persona finds a certain social interaction and also the love which many of Atwood's personae long for (as in "A Sibyl", "On the Streets, Love" (CG 24-25) or in the love poems of *True Stories*).

---

traversent et sollicitent les émotions les plus diverses, voire les identités les plus changeantes." (in Rabaté 150)

It is in this world that the part of the speaker that she calls "The thing that calls itself / I" (CG 50) lives. Thus, in Atwood's poems, the Persona tries hard to integrate, if only momentarily, into this world which she cannot however totally identify with.

We may now explore further the comparison between the Persona and the gifted child. The gifted child is characterized by an unusual profile which allows him/her to live as someone who is both part of a given world and outside it. It is only through this ability of moving from an insider position to an outsider position that the gifted child can be reconciled with him/herself.

Many books have been written in order to help parents and teachers understand the "ordinary world" (the school, home and workplace environments) and the world of the gifted child. One of the fundamental characteristics of the gifted child – and of the poet – is a hypersensitivity that both possess. This quality is connected to many other characteristics, both intellectual and psychological. Giftedness engenders the following tension: on the one hand the subject tries to protect his/her difference and to cultivate it, on the other, he/she perceives his/her own emotionalism as a handicap and tries to be like everyone else and to forget his/her differences in order to experience a relief from isolation.

I will draw a parallel between Atwood's poetry and the situation of the gifted child who wishes to become reconciled with him/herself in three points: the first challenge is for the gifted child (or the Persona) to discover his/her own personality, and to understand both the strengths and weaknesses of such a personality; then, by integrating these opposite elements, it is necessary to think about the survival strategies which allow the gifted child (or the Persona) to learn to manage the complexity of his/her own voice and personality. Finally, the experience of moments of epiphanies, where the subject receives a clear-sightedness concerning him/herself and the world, allows him/her to celebrate an intimate reconciliation. This experience constitutes a point of reference which informs the subject about the possibility of such a reconciliation.

THE DISCOVERY OF A DIFFERENT PERSONALITY

In order to understand the uniqueness of an exceptionally gifted child – whether this gift is the gift of "a voice" (TT 21), or any other gift that sets the individual apart from other people –, one needs to consider the gifted person's singular mode of functioning: if we take for example, the exceptionally gifted child (who, like the Atwoodian voice, will be referred to here as "she"), she thinks and perceives the world differently from the so-called ordinary children. To use the Atwoodian image of "Shadow Voice", she is not a part of the picnic. She is singled by the "Shadow Voice" out to live on words ("I give water, I give clean crusts / ...words / flowing in your veins / to keep you going", AC 7), but she looks on with envy as other people take part in festivities from which she is excluded. Because of her calling, she can only remain on the outside of the picnic. The Voice (the internal voice of "Shadow Voice") shows her the wealth of experiences that comes from being different: mainly by pointing to the Persona's capacity to hear the very Voice others seem to ignore. But the Persona who should rejoice in having been chosen by the Voice appears to be overwhelmed by this gift which distinguishes her from others. This discouragement is staged in the prose poem "Bottle" (B 7-17) where the speaker rebels against the Voice who elected her. When the speaker finally agrees to accept the gift of the Voice, the latter disappears. In the same way, the exceptionally gifted subject does not wish to be different from other people and the acceptance of her peculiarity is the fruit of a difficult process where the meaning and use of her gift often escape her.

As for the hypersensitivity of the gifted child – which is more or less perceptible depending on the emotional maturity of the subject – it is both an asset and a handicap. It is an asset because of the sharpness of her perception which allows her to hear and understand her environment more clearly than "ordinary people". But this hypersensitivity is also a source of emotional pain. The Atwoodian Persona reflects these two aspects, as we will show through several examples which I will now present, beginning with poems expressing the delight of the speakers when making unique discoveries at various stages in life.

The poem "Bored" (MBH 91-92), which superimposes the timelines of childhood and old age, highlights the speaker's vivid curiosity, in spite of an acute sense of boredom. Even when the child of the poem imagines to lead such an uneventful life, she scrutinizes the details given within each moment. The speaker of the poem, when she becomes an adult looking back on her childhood, can clearly see the magnifying glass effect of her own childhood perceptions. This retrospective gaze allows her to restore every single detail of the perceived environment:

> ... It
> wasn't even boredom, it was looking
> looking hard and up close at the small
> details. Myopia. The worn gunwales,
> the intricate twill of the seat
> cover. The acid crimbs of loam, the granular
> pink rock, its igneous veins, the sea-fans
> of dry moss, [...] (MBH 91)

In this description, all the elements which enter the field of vision of the child seem to resurface: the materiality of the landscape, the character of her father – everything is evoked with a precision of vocabulary (highlighted by the list of "details" over five verses) which suggests the linguistic competence of an adult. While the precision of the observation comes from the child's perspective, the voice of the poem is that of the adult speaker. It is characterized by her ability to revisit these moments which she, as a child, had first considered as boring and she remarks that she would now know how to see their infinite wealth ("Now I wouldn't be bored. Now I would know too much. Now I would know" MBH 92). The nostalgia comes from the presentiment of her father's death – her father being the central figure of the poem – and from this feeling of immense gratitude when contemplating what she has inherited from her father. The disparity of age between father and daughter is irrelevant: the speaker establishes a filiation between the paternal marginality and her own. In these last moments of her father's life, the speaker who was once this child, enjoys a unique gift – an exceptional capacity for scrutiny[6] – which was passed on to her by her father. It is her feeling of joy – tinged with a sense of mourning to come – that is expressed here.

Several poems with very diverse themes reflect this awareness of a unique gift (the capacity to welcome the present moment and to give it new depth). As the speaker of this sequence of poems revisits her past experience, she celebrates her own gift. This celebration, both intimate and discreet, is contrary to an arrogant statement concerning her own identity and it becomes characteristic of her voice – a voice which is distinctive. Indeed, it is only the speaker herself who recognizes her gift and enjoys the pleasure of welcoming it fully – the rest of the world is not included in this private celebration. This comment also applies to the poem "The Healer" (I 39). This poem stages a persona – a healer – who has a unique gift and who is annoyed by the demands of his circle of acquaintances[7].

---

[6] Gifted children have an exceptional capacity for scrutiny and for spontaneously memorizing their observations. According to Siaud-Facchin, "[l]a sensibilité extrême à l'environnement provient d'une perception sensorielle exacerbée. L'enfant surdoué ressent le monde tous sens en éveil. Il dispose de capacités des organes des sens très supérieures et très performantes." (28). Gifted children also tend to have excessive emotional responses: "ses émotions en deviennent elles aussi exacerbées. L'enfant surdoué réagit à la moindre variation de son environnement et avec une intensité qui peut parfois paraître excessive. Ses capacités à voir d'infimes détails, à entendre le moindre murmure, à sentir l'odeur la plus fugace, à percevoir la plus petite variation de température [...] favorisent le déclenchement émotionnel bien plus tôt que chez les autres." (32)

[7] In the same way, Atwood's Circe grows impatient with people's demands: "People come from all over to consult me, bringing their limbs which have unaccountably fallen off, they don't know why, my front porch is waist deep in hands, bringing their blood hoarded in

To escape these demands, the healer flees the outside world, every Sunday, and indulges in a solitary meditation. The last stanza is infused with a serenity which reveals this contemplative gaze:

> Sundays ...
> ...I sit on the back porch
> ...and look out
> across the ragged fields at the real
> flowers, goldenrod and purple asters,
> the light spilling out of them
> unasked for and unused. (I 39)

The healer's message in this poem is perhaps that the type of happiness experienced by the healer is the only one worth experiencing. He needs to flee far from the incomprehension of his patients, far from their grotesque demands, far from his own arrogance and his ridiculous feeling of omnipotence. Although he makes extensive use of his gift and readily gives to his many patients, the perception of his gift is a private business. He allows himself to experience it when he turns to meditation on Sundays.

The speakers of several of the *You Are Happy* poems also express this capacity to live in the present moment. Ordinary life is transcended by becoming aware of the uniqueness of each and every moment ("There is Only One of Everything" 92, "Late August" 93, "Portfolio of Ancestors" 94-96, "Is / Not" 74-75). "There is Only One of Everything" as well as "Is / Not" depict a love relationship is which not exceptional ("there is nothing spectacular / to see and the weather is ordinary" 76). However, thanks to the inspired gaze of the speaker, the ordinary nature of the couple's relationship is transformed into something exceptional. This particular gift, which consists of turning simple things into a sheer miracle, is associated with a unique sensitivity which the Atwoodian voice displays. Many poets and common people have this sensitivity and therefore, although I am underlining this characteristic, I do not consider it to be totally unique.

Atwood herself tends to emphasize her belonging to a group – that of the poets. Indeed, while some of the *You Are Happy* poems previously quoted offer

---

pickle jars, bringing their fears about their hearts, which they either can or can't hear at night. They offer me their pain, hoping in return for a word, a word, any word from those they have assaulted daily, with shovels, axes, electric saws, the silent ones, the ones they accused of being silent because they would not speak in the received language. / I spent my days with my head pressed to the earth, to the stones, to shrubs, collecting the few muted syllables left over; in the evenings I dispense them, a letter at a time, trying to be fair, to the clamouring suppliants..." (YAH 49).

illustrations of the capacity of the speaker to attribute poetic value to the ordinary things of life, the poem "The Words Continue their Journey" (I 82-83), previously quoted, offers an analytical comment on the gift of the poet, by exploring the concept of "difference". Although the very idea of a difference between "these [other] people" and "us" is challenged, the speaker of the poem comes to recognize that she belongs to a group – that of the poets – who differs from other people by the gift of "a voice": "these people who are supposed to be / other, and they are much like us, / except that they lack the sort of thing / we think of as a voice." (I 82)

However the speaker of "The Words Continue their Journey" shows the clear-sightedness of the Atwoodian position with regards to this particular notion of a "gift". The superiority complex that the poet could be entitled to feel in relation to his/her gift, is mocked by typically Atwoodian humour:

> We tell ourselves they are fainter
> than we are, less defined,
> that they are what we are defining,
> that we are doing them a favour,
> which makes us feel better.
> They are less elegant about pain than we are. (I 82)

Like the persona in "The Healer" ("Such arrogance, to have expected miracle. / What was it anyway I thought flowed through me?" I 39), the speaker mocks the representation she has made of her own talent. Indeed, she points out that to become aware of one's gift inevitably leads to a sort of self-proclamation or self-justification which can bring about a ridiculous feeling of superiority. So, the speaker catches herself *in flagrante delicto* of a smugness which she is quick to denounce with irony. Having refuted her own obnoxious condescension, the speaker nevertheless reaffirms her belonging to a group: "But look, I said *us* [...] I gathered us / like the members of some doomed caravan" (I 82).

The fact is there is an undeniable difference between the speaker and "these [other] people". It is not that the speaker herself is the only one to have a special gift since the persona belongs to a group clearly identified as the one of "poets". However, the mission of the poet is a distinct one, though in no way superior to that of other human beings. Indeed, the poet's mission is similar to that of all people who bravely follow their calling. The title of the poem, "The Words Continue their Journey" resonates in the last stanza in a surprising way: the caravan of the poets is moving forward – a caravan which makes slow and laborious progress, and which is comparable to the immense human procession.

> and we're no more doomed really than anyone, as we go
> together, through this moon terrain
> where everything is dry and perishing and so
> vivid, into the dunes, vanishing out of sight,
> vanishing out of the sight of each other,
> vanishing even out of our own sight,
> looking for water. (I 83)

It is hardly surprising that the poem should end with this image of the caravan "looking for water" and with the repetition of the word "vanishing" in the last two lines – as if the voice itself were disappearing with the poem coming to an end. Like all groups of seekers whatever their profession, the caravan of poets experiences the trials, tribulations and death experience of the human race. Thus the suffering and the difficulties of the poet are not to be considered as a unique phenomenon. In the previously quoted poems, as well as in several of the poems of *True Stories* (in particular "Note Towards a Poem That Can Never Be Written" TS 45-103), the speaker's awareness that she equally belongs to one larger group – the human race itself – prevails.

However, moving beyond the universal character of human suffering underlined in *True Stories*, I now wish to turn to the poems which focus on the singular suffering expressed by the Atwoodian voice throughout the course of her volumes of poetry. These volumes, which are published over a time-span of nearly fifty years, evoke, more or less directly, various stages of maturity of the speaker. Indeed, the reader eventually recognizes clearly this undertone of chronic depression which runs through Atwood's poetry. Depending on the volume, the expressed suffering will take on a slightly different tone, which seems to correspond to the various stages of life. The youthful voice of *The Circle Game* is confused by the depressive assaults; that of *True Stories* and *Two-Headed Poems* focuses on deciphering the origin of her own feelings – *True Stories* is strongly tinted with a sense of loss of love and *Two-Headed Poems* seems torn between the two poles of the speaker's life (private, public or professional). Finally, the voice of *Morning in the Burned House* – "Sad Child" – speaks of the desire to overcome a chronic depression which the speaker recognizes has been present since childhood.

Indeed, the depression motif, which is particularly developed in *Two-Headed Poems*, undergoes a transformation in *Morning in the Burned House*: the anxiety experienced by the speaker produces a different effect: instead of destroying the speaker and leading her to express a desire to commit suicide (as in "The Woman Who Could Not Live With Her Faulty Heart", THP 14-15, "Marsh, Hawk", THP 88-89, etc.), the voice we hear is soothing. The speaker contemplates her own anxiety with self-mockery: it is as if she were divided in half, and one half addresses the other half:

> You're sad because you're sad.
> It's psychic. It's the age. It's chemical.
> Go see a shrink or take a pill,
> or hug your sadness like an eyeless doll
> you need to sleep. (MBH 4)

In spite of the teasing tone of the first stanza, emphasized by the tautology of the first line and tertiary rhythm of the second line, the speaker's compassion infuses the poem. Indeed, far from making fun of the anxiety of the speaker's younger or more depressed self, addressed as "you", the speaker in the poem comforts her other self, not unlike the way "A Shadow Voice" (AC 7) enlightens the "you" of the poem as to the cause of her sadness. However the speaker of "A Sad Child" (MBH 4-5), contrary to that of "A Shadow Voice", does not advocate social withdrawal or abstinence in love. The speaker simply traces the origin of all sorrows to "Your sadness, your shadow, / whatever it was that was done to you / the day of the lawn party" (MBH 4) and shows the other self that her melancholy is not new, that she is not alone in experiencing suffering – it is the lot of humanity as a whole:

> I am not the favourite child
>
> My darling, when it comes
> right down to it...
>
> none of us is;
> or else we all are. (MBH 4-5)

The final twist in the last two verses "none of us is; / or else we all are" points at the two sides of the same coin and hints at the possibility of considering the bright side (we are all favourite children). Furthermore, the shrinking of the lines and the words themselves (reduced to monosyllables) seems to illustrate how the speaker manages to let go of her sadness and accept things for what they are. In the first part of *Morning in the Burned House*, namely in the poems "In the Secular Night" (6-7), "Waiting" (8-10), and "February" (11-12), the speaker responds to the persona's sadness in the poem. The comfort brought by the speaker stems from an in-depth understanding of the feelings experienced by the persona: the speaker expresses kindness and patience for the recurring fragility of the persona of the poem (addressed as "you"). The very notion of suffering becomes something to be considered as a separate entity – a fictional companion like the beloved doll which the voice suggests squeezing against one's heart ("hug your sadness like an eyeless doll / you need to sleep" 4).

This sequence of poems in *Morning in the Burned House* thus offers a defense strategy in the face of suffering which allows humour to be woven into compassion. This tactic is exactly the one recommended by psychologists specialized in counseling gifted children – not that this strategy is uniquely for gifted children but, to them, it becomes a skill which they need to learn to develop at a very early age in order to cope with a school system which often proves to be ill-suited to their particular needs[8]. For them, it is a question of survival, as their personalities and talents can be more easily crushed when they experience a difference between themselves and their peers, without having any insight into the cause of this difference. Indeed, Fiaud-Sacchin explains why humour is a key strategy for emotional management: humour is a compromise between emotional control through cognitive tools and emotional management. Humour allows us to put feelings in a bearable shape. Humour nuances affects without eliminating them. Thanks to humour, the emotional world remains active but is kept at bay. But humour also supposes complex intellectual skills because it is a subtle alchemy between:

- a transformation of a situation achieved through an intellectual operation,
- a sensible manipulation of the emotional weight of the situation,
- creativity.

Only a good balance between these three ingredients gives humour its comical dimension and allows it to work as a defense mechanism[9].

Indeed, the humour expressed by Atwood's speakers – a humour widely illustrated in the volumes of poetry – enables the staging of both an expression of affect and a withdrawal achieved by the intervention of intelligence. Atwood's poetry also stages another defense strategy often used by gifted children: the defense through cognition. This strategy, often criticized by therapists because of

---

[8] According to Fiaud-Sacchin, for most gifted children, relationships with peers are equally problematic. Interestingly enough, a child's social difficulties is one of the main themes in *Cat's Eye*. Atwood's main protagonist in *Cat's Eye*, Elaine, is helpless, as her so called best friends bully her. One must note however that Elaine, who is clearly very bright and who becomes a talented artist, is never described as "gifted" – Atwood's novel was set at a time when this label was not used.

[9] This summarises Fiaud-Sacchin's main points in her chapter concerning the importance of humour for gifed children (Fiaud-Sacchin 57).

its inevitable excesses, is also denounced in Atwood's poetry. This defense tactic consists of taking away all emotion from a given situation and removing the emotional sting to keep fears at bay. For the exceptionally gifted child such a strategy seems necessary when the latter notices that she spends a large part of her energy fighting against an emotional surplus[10]. However, this strategy may lead her to the renunciation of a part of herself. Indeed, if the subject refuses to express the emotional side of its identity and to focus only on the intellect, she deprives herself of her own resources, personality and voice. This defense strategy through cognition can lead to a cleavage within the subject which is precisely the leitmotiv of the *Two-Headed Poems* volume.

Rather than agreeing to this type of cleavage, Atwood's poetry points to the danger of cognitive defense strategies and leads the way towards a place of regeneration. The Atwoodian approach implies a complete disorientation and an inevitable fall into darkness. It means entering a place where it becomes necessary to question and wonder. The Persona learns to find new points of reference in the underground world and to turn this world into a known place. Several poems (in *Interlunar* in particular) stage this progressive process of learning as well as the building of a new brand of trust.

> It is touch I go by,
> the boat like a hand feeling
> through shoals and among
> dead trees [...]
> This is how I learned to steer
> through darkness by no stars. (I 97-98)

The speaker's identification with the boat which is feeling its way "through shoals" leads to the final statement in the last two lines. The grammatical construction starting with "this is how" emphasizes the darkness and absence of stars at the end of the poem. However the last but one line encapsulates the speaker's skill (steering in the dark) with the verb "steer" strategically placed at

---

[10] This is how Siaud-Facchin describes the way a gifted child fights against emotional surplus: "L'énergie que consacre l'enfant dans sa défense contre les émotions est comparable à l'édification d'une digue pour contenir un océan déchaîné. La force des vagues vient régulièrement produire des brèches dans cet édifice. Et il lui faut sans relâche réparer, consolider pour lutter contre les forces de la nature. Avec, constante, cette crainte que tout s'effondre et d'être emporté par les flots... La défense par la cognition est un mécanisme efficace car il permet de soustraire toute marque affective à une situation, de désactiver la charge émotionnelle, de mettre à distance les angoisses. Mais, son risque majeur est un appauvrissement et une rigidification de la vie psychique. Tout ce qui relève de la pulsion des affects, de l'émotion est abrasé, dénié. Cela peut alors conduire à un repli sur soi, à la construction d'une personnalité désaffectivée [...]" (Siaud-Facchin, 56).

the end of the line and counterbalancing the darkness in the two lines that immediately follow.

The same experimentation with the speaker learning to steer is staged in "Interlunar" (I 102-103) where the voice which addresses "you" incites "you" to discover the light beyond darkness.

> Trust me. This darkness
> is a place you can enter and be
> as safe in as you are anywhere;
> you can put one foot in front of the other
> and believe the sides of your eyes.
> Memorize it. You will know it
> again in your own time.
> When the appearances of things have left you,
> you will still have this darkness.
> Something of your own you can carry with you.
>
> We have come to the edge:
> the lake gives off its hush;
> in the outer night there is a barred owl
> calling, like a moth
> against the ear, from the far shore
> which is invisible.
> The lake, vast and dimensionless,
> doubles everything, the stars,
> the boulders, itself, even the darkness
> that you can walk so long in
> it becomes light. (I 103)

The last two stanzas of this poem which are balanced in length (they have roughly the same amount of words and lines) leave the reader with two images of equal weight: the first gives the reader advice on how to enter darkness and nevertheless feel safe; the second describes the darkness in such a way that it becomes a landscape that the reader is no longer afraid of. It is a lake in the wilderness which "doubles everything", even the darkness itself – it is a space "that you can walk so long in / it becomes light". Whether it is to navigate or to walk in this darkness, the Persona realizes that she needs her intuition to guide her. This predominance of what the psychologists call the right brain, asserts itself quite clearly when the subject agrees to enter the world where another self is present. It is as if, following the example of the gifted child who has long remained in ignorance of her own faculties, the Persona suddenly discovers a singular world to which only *she* has access. Thus the Atwoodian speakers assert the importance of a journey to the underground world all the while underlining the necessity of returning to the ordinary world. Furthermore, the personae know how to play with the various components of their identity – very much like the speakers and personae of the previously quoted poems "A Sibyl" or of "Manet's Olympia".

The mischievous persona of "Manet's Olympia" displays an attitude that both disturbs and provokes a circle of acquaintances and perhaps the reader himself. In spite of a deep happiness stemming from a successful reconciliation between two aspects of her personality, the persona of this poem comes up against obstacles which are no longer internal but external: she needs to manage the surrounding hostility, ignore attitudes of contempt and put-downs, and find the courage to assert her identity and voice. The Persona, who has experienced internal reconciliation, eventually finds a way of dealing with such hostilities. Whether these hostilities are expressed in a comic mode ("Manet's Olympia") or with gravity ("Spell for the Director of Protocol" PU 45), Atwood's poems highlight the power of subversive strategies.

Like an individual who decides not to renounce his giftedness, the Atwoodian Persona establishes a way of being and thinking which is uniquely hers and where both weaknesses and strengths are acknowledged and accepted. Indeed, it is her unique giftedness that allows her to hear the Voice, but it is also this giftedness which renders her emotionally vulnerable in a way that is often expressed in the poems tinged with a depressive atmosphere. In the same way the gifted child has to learn to recognize that he "is not capable of thinking without emotional intervention" ("[Il] ne *sait pas* penser sans ingérence affective", Siaud-Facchin 82), the Atwoodian Persona reaches a stage of clear-sightedness about herself which allows her to welcome her specific way of functioning. She sets up diverse strategies which all converge coherently in the possibility of developing each of the facets of her identity. This enterprise is similar to the Nietzschean approach which aims at moving beyond value judgments in order to evaluate each enterprise according to the fruits it yields (Nietzsche 1974).

The Persona is constantly trying to establish the right balance: whether it is in undertaking a journey towards the underground world and finding the motivation to return towards the ordinary world; or whether it is in remaining attentive to the calling of the Voice without isolating herself from love and social relations or rejecting the put-downs of an intolerant environment or a repressive system; or, better still, in patiently enduring the assaults of depression and finding the road back to humour.

The peculiarity of the Atwoodian Persona is to demonstrate a unique clear-sightedness and to enlighten the reader as to what is worth fighting for. Far from all false humility and arrogance, far from imprisonment and pointless emancipation, the Persona is in search of a point of equilibrium where she is allowed to develop the faculties described as a gift – not that these faculties are judged in any way superior to that of others (any superiority complex is mocked), but these faculties are identified as different and belonging to her as well as to the well-known lineage of poets. Even in the face of discouraging demands on the part of "other people" (I 39, 82), Atwood's personae move forward "into the dunes" (I 83), "looking for water" (I 83), pausing along the way like the healer who takes time off and meditates every Sunday. It is thus a question not only of welcoming, but also of being filled with delight when experiencing these singular faculties, finding the means to protect them, to develop them, and to renew them. Finally, this approach leads to a very humble, intimate celebration of a gift by which the poet's offering is transmitted to each one of us, "fellow / traveler" (YAH 74) and readers. Through the transmission of this offering we enter a perception of the world which is the one of the persona of "Interlunar": one grows so accustomed to darkness that it "becomes light" (I 83).

The specificities of the Atwoodian poetic voice have led us to explore the symbolic orientations of "a voice" (TT 21) as well as the interior dialogues of Atwood's speakers. While to be given "a voice" (TT 21) means to be offered a gift, this voice (which needs to be "cultivated [...] because it would be a shame to waste such a gift", TT 21) also becomes a metaphor for any other type of talent or singularity. Whether Atwood's speakers seem to be in full possession of their gift as in the poem "The Healer", or whether they are struggling to fight off depression, they experience coming into contact with a Voice that heals and comforts – a voice which gives them insight into what causes the difference between themselves and the world around them, a voice that allows them to walk through darkness, to celebrate their own uniqueness (and voice).

Having explored the specificities and symbolic orientations of a voice in Atwood's poetry, we may turn to an exploration of the links between Atwood's poetic and fictional voices, in order to highlight the similarities and differences of message and tone. For this task, it will be useful to come back to the chronological approach of the first part of this volume and to include the novels in our sequential list of the poetry volumes.

CHAPTER 8

The Voices of a Two-headed Opus

When asked to explain the differences between poetry and fiction in laymen's terms, Atwood explains that it is "partly a matter of wavelengths, […] in a poem, everything is very condensed, so the waves are very short, the things that are rhythmically connected are quite close together. In a short story, they're a bit further apart and in a novel the waves are [very far apart]" [1]. John Stuart Mill's critical comments on the subject are not unlike Atwood's in the sense that he highlights both differences and connections between prose and poetry, focusing on the differences first:

> [T]here is a radical distinction between the interest felt in a story as such, and the interest excited by poetry; for the one is derived from incident, the other from the representation of feeling. In one, the source of the emotion excited is the exhibition of a state or states of human sensibility; in the other, of a series of states of mere outward circumstances. (Mill in Wasson, 357)

The description of "outward circumstances" requires the use of wavelengths which are much larger than the tight wavelengths for "the exhibition of a state or states of human sensibility". Fredman, having established, through his reference to Mill, a major distinction between poetry and fiction, explains how fiction can provide a context in which poetry becomes "authorized", that is a context in which it becomes understandable or interpretable to the reader:

> […] in the absence of an embracing cultural tradition, the prose statements perform an important duty by authorizing the poetry. An awareness of this crucial quality of the prose is absolutely essential for reading American poetry. There is a theatrical quality to the prose that creates a mise-en-scène for the poetry, a context in which the poem can be performed. When readers isolate a particular American poem and

---

[1] Video of Margaret Atwood on "Big Think" (Miller 2011), posted on https://www.facebook.com/MargaretAtwoodAuthor.

> debate whether it "works," they often miss the "work" of American poetry. Reading a poem by Charles Olson for the first time, for example, many readers complain about stylistic infelicities, such as ungainliness or corniness, and wonder how this apparently awkward poet merits such high regard among his partisans. A significant portion of the answer lies in Olson's prose essays, which prepare his readers not by engaging in some sort of special pleading for his poetry but by creating such a powerful staging for it that his poetry gains a context in which it can become affecting and convincing work. (Fredman 3)

The creation of fiction as a "powerful staging" in which poetry does not necessarily imply that fiction should precede poetry: the understanding of fiction may pave the way for the understanding of poetry, but that says nothing of the order in which the author creates fiction and poetry. The two types of writing simply represent two facets of an author's work – two facets best illustrated by Atwood's two-headed creature image. It is worth noting that the metaphor contained in the title of Atwood's volume of poetry, *Two-Headed Poems*, is not only central to the eponymous poem and to the volume of poetry itself, but it also resurfaces in all of Atwood's work from her very first book of poetry to the later novels. The two-headed epithet can be used to describe Atwood's work not only because each book of fiction or poetry is based upon a principle of duality, but also because the two modes of writing themselves are like the two heads and the two voices of one body.

A parallel reading of Atwood's prose and poetry suggests that links between the two voices are of a different nature at the beginning of her career and in her later work. My study will therefore focus on three periods (1967–1972; 1973–1995; and 1996–2003) when Atwood's poetic output gradually decreases while her production of fiction continues to grow. It has often been commented that themes and aesthetic characteristics filter through from Atwood's poetry into her novels and vice versa, but these capillary links remain a somewhat vague notion. When Atwood herself was asked to comment on the relationships between these two modes of writing in her work, she said, "Each volume of poetry is a seed planted for the next novel" (in Evain and Khandpur 107). Indeed, when one given novel and the volume of poetry which precedes it are brought together, the result is a "twoheaded prodigy" (CG 48). As one contemplates this unusual creature, one may wonder whether the poetry head always leads and whether it truly breaks new ground for the fiction head to discover. In other words the question is whether the poetry voice comes first and whether it actually enriches the fiction voice that follows.

This metaphor of Atwood's work as a "twoheaded prodigy" – speaking with two voices – can also be considered in its plural form: it is possible to juxtapose a series of separate "twoheaded prodigies" and duets, each composed of a volume of poetry and a book of fiction, which may vary according to thematic perspectives, but which, if examined as part of a chronological sequence, are still an indicator of the progress of Atwood's work. For example, one may create a link between *Procedures for Underground* and the novel *Lady Oracle*, as the poem "Procedures for Underground" is an invitation to discover an underground world which Joan descends into in *Lady Oracle* when she experiments with automatic writing. However, *Lady Oracle* may also be connected to the prose poems in *Murder in Dark* as their metafictional content is a condensed version of the teachings of *Lady Oracle*. The poetry is an extremely dynamic head in the Atwood corpus, but the experience of the fictional head does feed back into the later poetry mainly by stimulating its metafictional dimension.

THE RESURFACING OF THE POETIC VOICE IN FICTION (1967—1972)

When examining Atwood's early publications, it is possible to determine what her fictional voices owe to her poetic voices. Frank Davey's previously mentioned work on Atwood's leitmotivs provides an ideal starting point as Davey shows that the typical Atwood vocabulary includes the following expressions: "technological skins" (Davey 93), "mirrors" (Davey 94), "the gothic" (Davey 98), "refugees and tourists" (Davey 104), "underground, underwater" (Davey 109), "the maze" (Davey 114), "metamorphosis" (Davey 120), "signposts/totems" (Davey 121), giving birth to a voice which is both erudite and sophisticated, characterized by the speaker's ability to move freely between different domains and to construct images where these different fields collide and/or converge. All of the images which are present in *The Circle Game* then resurface in the fiction. Just like Atwood's first volumes of poetry, her two first novels explicitly stage female acts of liberation which demonstrate the capacity to resist a male-dominated culture. The characters of *Surfacing* and *The Edible Woman* translate into narrative form the experience of *The Circle Game* speakers. The general pattern of both novels mimics the movement of many of *The Circle Game* poems as the protagonists descend into the underworld to avoid being dominated or absorbed and then transcend their alienation.

Atwood's speakers and protagonists gain greater power when they begin to integrate the ancestral element which reaches as far back as the formation of the world (*The Circle Game* is saturated with cosmological imagery which resurfaces in the novels). As the speakers and protagonists learn to decipher the imprints of the earth, they are overwhelmed by a feeling of continuity: each creature is part of a biological chain which becomes tangible through all of our senses. It is through bodily perceptions that the speakers and protagonists recognize their multiple heritage, and they deliberately set out to become members of the human race through symbolic actions which are performed by *the body* itself (in *Surfacing* for example, the narrator decides to bear fruit and to become pregnant). Their voices become impregnated with a Darwinian conception of the biological experience. Both in the poetry and the novels, the individual melts into the landscape in order to gain tangible proof of his or her identity. The subject is thus mapped out as a biological entity signified by the recurring metaphors of the "body as landscape." The metaphors imply both that the body is a result of biological evolution, and that the sensorial body gains a sense of identity by connecting to the past, by sucking in the "salt" of "living" ancestors and by performing sensorial actions through which the individual willingly becomes part of the biological chain.

While this body-centred imagery resonates from the poetry to the novels, further parallels can be drawn between the two forms of writing, as a direct link can be established between scenes from the novels and the poems from *The Circle Game*. The poetry nourishes the fiction, as demonstrated by the following examples: the symbolic value of running away from the camera is at the heart of the poem "Camera" (CG 45-46) and mirrors Marian's flight in *The Edible Woman* as well as the unnamed character's resistance to David's shooting of Anna in *Surfacing*. The poem "A Meal" (CG 28–29) precedes the restaurant scene in *The Edible Woman*. Like the persona in the poem, Marian resents the cutting of the food, this cool butchering act, reduced to its purely biological significance, transforming it into a "diagram" or "a china bowl" (CG 28–29). The conversation between the two fiancés in the novel echoes the one in the poem which equally revolves around the subject of safety and control. Furthermore, Marian's resistance to the patriarchal values that Peter stands for resembles that of the "furtive insect" which "is hiding / [...] sly and primitive / the necessary cockroach / in the flesh / that nests in dust" (CG 28–29). This insect has the capacity to resist the temptation of love. Like the speakers in *Power Politics*, "[t]heir attitudes differ", or like the sibyl in *The Circle Game*, the insect feeds "on other peoples' leavings" (CG 28) and "gorges on a few/unintentional/spilled crumbs of love" (CG 29). The function of that insect is to rescue "the thing that calls itself / I" (CG 50) from the inevitable loss of identity resulting from a lover's submission, and to bring out the subject's prophetic voice. Atwood's novels taking their cue from the poems, show the dangers of a lack of self-affirmation. Both poetic and fictional voices provide leads for the subject's identity quest and empowerment.

In *Surfacing*, empowering the sibylline voice implies a descent into Atwood's underground world. When the female subject descends into the underground world, she becomes one with nature and fully integrates the heritage of "the drowned mothers" or "the forest" and the city, "wide and silent [...] lying lost, undersea" (CG 4). This heritage is an indispensable part of the regeneration process. In "After the Flood, We," the mineral and biological heritage allows for new faces to emerge (CG 5). Stone becomes bone in the poem "The Explorers" (CG 78–79) as two skeletons wait to be discovered, while in "The Settlers," they become the nourishing substance for future generations (CG 81). In *Surfacing* a similar metamorphosis is observed by the narrator (167) who also seeks to participate in the regeneration process in order to become whole.

Atwood's first five volumes of poetry place special emphasis on the symbolism of metamorphosis. The symbols are drawn mainly from images of quasi-Darwinian regressions and mythical figures such as Proteus. At the end of Atwood's first period, in her sixth volume of poetry, *You Are Happy*, the speakers' search for identity and experience of wholeness is expressed in terms which are related to ordinary daily situations that take on a symbolic value. In the last sequence of the volume, the lovers are one another's equals and relish the present moment as they realize that "There is Only One of Everything" (YAH 92). The female subject then experiences a new form of love which no longer cripples her but, on the contrary, allows her to discover her own potential and materialize an expanded identity where the two components (the sibyl and "the thing that calls itself / I") cohabit harmoniously. It is this process of metamorphosis which empowers the voice and which, in the case of love, allows the speaker/protagonist to transform a relationship.

Lady Oracle offers an ironic twist to the perfect balance found in the third sequence of *You Are Happy*. Joan longs for both an intense and ordinary life. When she mocks other women's expectations, she realizes that their fantasy lives are not much different from her own – bordering on absolute submission to male domination which then results in a total absence of identity and individual voice. Nevertheless, she finds her "own arrangement [...] more satisfactory" (LO 216) because she knows better than to "demand all things of just one man" (LO 216). The irony of Joan's discourse becomes increasingly apparent as her growing dissatisfaction is revealed: "It was true I had two lives, but on off days I felt that neither of them was completely real" (LO 216). Indeed, it is only because she has two lives and two voices – including a voice as a romance novel writer – that she is able to explore the question of identities. Because of Joan's many mistakes (which account for the mess in her life – encapsulated in the last sentence of the novel) the reader is sceptical about her capacity for harmony, that is finding a "completely real [voice]" (LO 216). The novel thus offers a comic treatment of the themes of the last sequence of the *You Are Happy* volume. Although Atwood's heroine can only make a mess of things, the speakers in poems such as "Is/Not", "There is Only One of Everything," and "Book of Ancestors" express the belief that wholeness occurs when the humble and ordinary fellow-traveling of lovers is transcended in love. However, Atwood's seventh volume of poetry once again emphasizes the conflict of the two heads and voices, giving each voice new symbolic meanings as the poems move from the personal level to the social and political levels. *Two-Headed Poems*' superimposition of themes can be observed in *Life Before Man*, the novel that succeeds it. According to McCombs, *Two-Headed Poems* marks the transition from Atwood's "Stage I Closed, Divided, Mirroring World" to Atwood's "Stage II Realistic, Open World" (McCombs 1988, 69).

BEYOND THE VOICE OF THE "PARALYSED ARTIST" (1972—1983)

The patterns of Atwood's early production shift focus and are extended from 1972 onwards. In the novels following *Lady Oracle*, the voice of the "paralyzed artist" (to use Atwood's expression in the ninth chapter of *Survival*) grows older and more present, as if Atwood's heroines were moving on to a different stage of life and as if they were discovering a more ordinary and yet more complicated and demanding world around them. This complexity is not only the result of greater importance given to political and social issues, but it is also linked to a more realistic type of novel writing conferring more mature voices to the narrators of these novels. Depression is one of the leitmotivs of both *Two-Headed Poems* and the novel *Life Before Man* where it is linked to imagery in which biological decay dominates: the heart is caught up in its contradiction and stops beating (THP 15), flowers which are emblematic of the domestic sphere simply fade away (THP 55), contamination spreads (THP 74; LBM 238), and biological deterioration foreshadows the end of an era (THP 89, 175; LBM 238). Language itself fails, as words become biological material subjected to violence. Elliptic strategies become more sophisticated, staging the voices' withdrawal into silence.

Now moving on to the next "twoheaded prodigy" composed of *True Stories* and the novel *Bodily Harm* both published in 1981, there are many common themes to be found in the voices of the two books. The dominant themes are those related to the obsession with the true story, political oppression, artificiality of both landscape and feelings and, finally, loss of love.

The heroine of *Bodily Harm*, Rennie, oscillates between anger and feelings of helplessness and depression like those expressed by the personae in "Late Night" (TS 20), "Hotel" (TS 23), "Earth" (TS 76-77), "Last Poem" (TS 47-75) or "Variation on the Word *Love*" (TS 82-83). Although Rennie dwells on her past and on her own pain, feeling her wounds as she feels her scar after her mastectomy, she resists the temptation to "regurgitate," (Barthes 191) defined by Barthes as "loquèle" that is "le flux de paroles à travers lequel le sujet argumente inlassablement dans sa tête les effets d'une blessure" (Barthes 1977, 191). Rennie's remembrance does not lead to repetition. It is not an endless replaying of the past. In the same way as the speaker of the poem "Rain" moves beyond pain, Rennie discovers a breathing space which helps her overcome her past traumas and experience sexual pleasure: "she enters her body again and there's a moment of pain, incarnation, [...] she's grateful, he's touching her, she can still be touched" (BH 204).

In both the novel and the poem, this "breathing space" is a state of grace: "This much will have to do, this much is enough" (BH 204), "a pause [...] a day after a day [...] a breathing space" (TS 89). The subject's voice is characterized by this gratitude and a cry of joy: "the rain / throwing itself down out of the / bluegrey sky, clear joy" (TS 89) and "he's touching her, she can still be touched" (BH 204).

These are only a few examples of the echoes between *Two-Headed Poems*, *Life Before Man*, *Bodily Harm*, and *True Stories*. Many symbols including the ones previously underlined (the circle game, the mirror, in *Circle Game*, the hand in *True Stories*, or the heart in *Two-Headed Poems*) are not only recurring images in the poetry but they also resurface in fiction[2]. The fertilizing power of poetry is ascertained over and over again in the many themes and images carried over from poetry to fiction. In the third period of Atwood's work a different type of relationship between poetry and fiction prevails and the corpus enters a new phase.

THE DYNAMICS OF METAFICTION AND THE CONFESSIONAL VOICE (1983 ONWARDS)

From 1983 onwards, the principles of the predominance of poetic output and the thematic unity which characterized the first two periods give way to a gathering

---

[2] The symbol of the hand resurfaces in *Bodily Harm*, the heart in *Life Before Man*, etc.

together of themes and previously explored forms, a combination that opens the door onto a new creative voice. I wish to focus on the metafictional aspects of the third period (mainly in *Murder in Dark* and *Good Bones*) before moving on to Atwood's last two volumes of poetry *Morning in the Burned House* in relation to the fiction of that period.

Murder in the Dark marks a turning point in the corpus as Atwood embarks on a new genre of writing. The ambiguity of the new form is underlined by the subtitle of *Murder in the Dark*: "Short Fictions and Prose Poems." Each piece in the volume seems to be both a piece of short fiction and a prose poem, allowing the reader to discover a hybrid form and voice.

The filtering through of Atwood's previous work into *Murder in the Dark* is multi-faceted, but I will focus on a couple of elements only, starting with the example of "Women's Novel." The poem "Women's Novel" (MID 57-62) and the novel *Lady Oracle* both parody and pastiche low-brow literature[3]. In *Lady Oracle* the element of pastiche stems from the imitation of the voices of the "historical romances" genre (LO 156), as Joan, the narrator, is a writer of such novels, while the parodic note is derived from a process of exaggeration. In much the same way, "Women's Novel" also uses parody and pastiche and intertwines metafictional commentaries alongside these techniques. The other common factor between *Lady Oracle* and "Women's Novel" is that both the novel and the prose poem work on the principle of an internal mirror in which the speaker or the heroine contemplates her multi-faceted image. Like Joan (who uses two voices in *Lady Oracle*, as the writer of "costume gothics," as well as a consumer of the genre because she is hooked on the very plots she creates), the speaker of "Women's Novel" takes on the three distinct roles of writer, consumer of the genre and protagonist, interweaving the voices of all three in her highly metafictional prose poem. The reader of "Women's Novel" is also included in this multi-faceted mirror game, as he/she recognizes his/her own image in Joan's triple role. It is as if "Women's Novel" were a miniature construction of the mechanics of *Lady Oracle*, highlighting a set of techniques as well as an underlying ideological discourse.

Unlike "Women's Novel," "Happy Endings" does not refer to any particular genre, but it points to the components of the story and sends back to the reader a

---

[3] Genette's definitions are the following: "[La parodie – ou travestissement, transposition – est] tout texte dérivé d'un texte antérieur par [...] transformation ou par... imitation" (40); le pastiche (ou charge, forge): "Le pasticheur se saisit d'un style [...] et ce style lui dicte son texte" (40). The difference between a parodie and a pastiche is that the parody is based on a text (which is transformed and potentially transposed into a different style), whereas the pastiche is based on a specific style.

reflected image of his/her own credulity as well as an addiction to the narrator's voice in romance novels. This mirror game then leads to the rejection of stories constructed according to such recipes:

> That's about all that can be said for plots, which anyway are just one thing after another, a what and a what and a what.
>
> Now try How and Why. (MID 70)

Combinatory dexterity is not enough. What the speaker finds of greater interest revolves around the questions of "How and Why" – a "How and Why" which we discover through the different perspectives and voices within the text. Readers qualified as the "true connoisseur" (MID 70) will equally appreciate the effort put into working with these questions related to the art of narration.

Many of the prose poems in *Good Bones* also deal with metafictional issues. "Gertrude Talks Back," "Unpopular Gals," "The Little Red Hen Tells All" (GB 11-14), "There Was Once" (GB 19-24), "Bad News" (GB 9-10), and "Let Us Now Praise Stupid Women" (GB 31-38) are all poems which participate in the deconstruction of clichés and voice arrangements. In order to underline cultural stereotypes, they subvert the ingredients and techniques of literary genres such as the fairy tale and popular novels. Atwood draws on her experience of novel writing to create prose poems which encapsulate the tensions between genres of writing. She also weaves in ironic comments on readers' expectations and habits. This ironic metafictional voice is also present in the novel *Alias Grace* where the reader's voyeurism is mirrored in the following comment:

> Confess, confess. Let me forgive and pity. Let me get up a Petition for you. Tell me all.
> And then what did he do? Oh shocking. And then what?
> The left hand or the right?
> How far up exactly?
> Show me where. (AG 39)

While the narrator's voice in romance novels has the ability to turn the reader into a confidante, the Atwoodian voice both reveals and mocks this dynamic bordering on voyeurism, as the accumulation of questions in the above quote underlines. In the novel *The Robber Bride* the three protagonists' eagerness to be chosen by Zenia as her confidante is equally emblematic of the reader's own desire to be the narrator's bosom friend. In *The Handmaid's Tale* the narrator's power as a storyteller stems from this same narrative strategy of bringing the reader into her confidence. The mechanics and the power of confessional discourses are exposed in the previously quoted poem "Siren Song" which, as we have shown, stages a voice-persona echoed by her own ironical discourse.

Atwood's novels published after "Siren Song" are clearly constructed on the self-reflective and ironical dynamics of a confession addressed to the reader, which is in keeping not only with the teachings of the poem but also with its double-voiced discourse. One also notices that the prose poems in *Murder in the Dark* and *Good Bones* parody the functioning of such a dynamic, thereby reformulating the main teaching of "Siren Song" and further emphasizing the reader's cheap infatuation with any voice which speaks of his uniqueness: "you are unique / at last" (YAH 39).

To complete our overview of Atwood's third period of poetic work, one needs to consider *Morning in the Burned House*, which is the author's last published volume. *Morning in the Burned House* is divided into five parts. The last two parts are composed of two unique sets of poems on mourning (this theme feeds back into the short story *Labrador Fiasco* published one year later) and the first three parts allow typical Atwoodian themes to resurface (depression, in the first and third part of the volume, female identity, mainly in the second part). In the poems touching on female-empowerment, *The Circle Game* themes are revisited and further developed with a supplementary ironical twist. The use of irony in these poems leads to the assertion of an expanded identity made up of two distinct components. The poems thus stage the reconciliation between the two heads of the persona, all the while mocking traditional views which claim that this reconciliation is either impossible or undesirable. Indeed, the voices of the first three parts of *Morning in the Burned House* denounce the female icon as a male construct. They refuse to conform; they reject the domination of their lover and thus move beyond the Atwoodian victim position[4]. The rebellious victim whose voice is not unlike that of the paralyzed artist trying to achieve self-affirmation ultimately breaks free and integrates the two components of her extended identity, denouncing the passivity of her lover(s). The symbolic representations of the speakers in *Morning in the Burned House* draw on a store

---

[4] Even in the third period, Atwood's novels owe a great deal to her poetry. Let us mention a couple of images or themes which can be directly traced back to the early volumes of poetry. In *Alias Grace* the opening of the novel (5) is reminiscent of the poem "Visit to Toronto, with Companions" in *The Journals of Susanna Moodie*. In *The Blind Assassin*, the Sibyl figure (42) much resembles the one in *The Circle Game*. And *Oryx and Crake* offers an ironic reversal of the Frankenstein theme, such as the one presented in "Speeches for Dr Frankenstein" in *The Animals in That Country*.

of typically Atwoodian imagery: mythical, biological, technological, gothic, and literary, all of which assert the plural identity of the personae. The vitality and confidence which some of the personae display stem from the successful reconciliation of the different components of an expanded identity, and this reconciliation is expressed through bodily metaphors and through the personae adopting a playful tone, mocking the voyeur, the lover or the potential manipulator.

Finally, the experience of having a double voice takes on a new meaning in the two poems "Burned House" (I 93–94) and "Morning in the Burned House" (MBH 126–127). It then becomes an experience of temporal ubiquity in which the speakers inhabit two moments simultaneously: past and present are superimposed. The body itself becomes double: "including the body I had then, / including the body I have now" (MBH 127). This amounts to a form of resistance to time which speaks both of permanence and change. The personae spell out the inevitable movement from life to death ("this house has long been over," MBH 127) which is further underlined by the titles of the two poems. However, at the same time, the personae underline their ability to endure and survive. The experience of ubiquity becomes a moment of sheer joy: the subject experiences life as a gift for which no justification is needed. It is no longer a matter of saying: I exist because…, but simply: I exist.

In Atwood's first two periods of creative activity, the influence of the author's poetry on her novels is made apparent when the following two-headed prodigies are considered: *The Circle Game* / *The Edible Woman*, *The Circle Game* / *Surfacing*. The early work (from *The Circle Game* to *Power Politics*) actually filters through all of the novels, and Atwoodian themes and ideologies become clearly recognizable when the author's body of work is considered as a whole.

The systematic alternation between poetry and novel writing, observed in Atwood's first period, is even more visible in the second period (three volumes of poetry in 1974, 1978, and 1981 and three novels in 1976, 1979, and 1981), as if the author had drawn on the poetic activity in order to renew her artistic potential. *Lady Oracle* offers an ironical treatment of the achievement of harmony between the sexes suggested in the last poems of *You Are Happy*. *Life Before Man* echoes themes and images from *Two-Headed Poems*, mainly Siamese duality, spatialization of depression, and suicidal impulses, while the themes of political oppression and loss of love are explored in *True Stories* and then in *Bodily Harm*.

The first two periods of Atwood's work thus illustrate her own comment about the importance of poetry: "If you think of language as a series of concentric circles, poetry is right at the centre. It's where precision takes place. It's where that use of language takes place that can extend a word yet have it be precise" (in Ingersoll, 169).

A chronological approach to Atwood's work clearly reveals that the dynamics of writing start with the poetry. The poetry not only leads to the creation of a body of work (a dozen books of poetry and three volumes of prose poems) with distinctive qualities in itself, but the poetic linguistic work is also later transformed into an organic material from which the novels are shaped.

During the third period, a close examination of the corpus suggests a different process of creation. The principles of alternation, predominance of poetic output and thematic unity which characterised the first two periods give way to a mixing of themes and forms that allows for the metafictional games of the prose poems. Finally, in Atwood's last volume of poetry, the two-headed characteristic of the female-empowered poems becomes a cry of victory over cultural and social entrapments.

If much of the innovation in Atwood's artistic creation finds its origin in the poetry, one may suggest that the fecundity of poetry is not an exclusively Atwoodian characteristic, but rather, inherent in the very nature of poetry itself. Poetry plays on the tension between form and content. Yet, as a result of this tension, poetry does not give any straight-forward answer: it remains a source of questioning and wonder for the reader which contrasts with the continuity of prose. The reader is expected to play a more active role in interpreting both the graphic and the textual form of the poem[5] and exploring the relationship between the two. According to Donoghue, there are two types of readers in poetry: "[Epireaders] read or interpret – the same act – in the hope of going through the words to something that the words both reveal and hide ... [they] say to poems: I want to hear you. Graphireaders say: I want to see what I can do, stimulated by your insignia" (in Bradford 151-52). Bradford, using Donoghue's terminology, explains that "[The lines] work as a kind of 'score' for vocal performance, observing that when 'read aloud,' the change of [line and rhythm] ... signals a change of emphasis" (33). The active part played by the reader results in the undertaking of a vocal performance – if only a silent one in the mind of the

---

[5] According to Donoghue, there are two types of readers in poetry: "[Epireaders] read or interpret – the same act – in the hope of going through the words to something that the words both reveal and hide ... [they] say to poems: I want to hear you. Graphireaders say: I want to see what I can do, stimulated by your insignia" (quoted by Bradford 151– 52). Bradford, using Donoghue's terminology, explains that "[The lines] work as a kind of 'score' for vocal performance, observing that when 'read aloud,' the change of [line and rhythm] ... signals a change of emphasis" (33).

reader. In this vocal performance, the reader experiences the contradictions and opposite states of mind and feeling. Ultimately, this exercise of internalizing and acting out the poetic voices shows the reader the importance of exploration and searching for balance. Through working on Atwood's poetry, we learn to grow attentive to a polyphony of voices, to a wide range of emotions and to various degrees of perception, leading us to a better understanding of ourselves and others. We learn to identify themes and build networks of images, all of which, as Fredman would say, exhibit "a state or states of human sensibility" (in Fredman 357). We learn to accept opposite a wide range of moods and feelings all the while resisting the temptation to numb out the negative. We learn to embrace our vulnerability, very much in keeping with Brené Brown's research on vulnerability [6] (Brown 2010). We learn to develop humour as a defense mechanism as well as a source of pure enjoyment. And thus, like the two-headed beings of "A Sibyl," "Shadow Voice," "Miss July Grows Older" or "Manet's Olympia," we learn to listen, to listen carefully, and to integrate the different components of our extended identity.

Having focused on representations of Atwood's poetic voice, as well as its power to infuse fiction, we may now contrast the poetic voice with the "living author's" voice and with the voice of the author's public persona. Many authors take an interest in metafictional themes, turning the very balancing of their creative voice, their personal and their public speaking voice into material for their fiction. As Vanessa Guignery points out "contemporary writers often insert self-reflexive asides in their novels, commenting on their writing process as they go along, thus no longer hiding the hand that writes or the voice that speaks, but exposing them."[7] Furthermore many authors indulge in public appearances (as well as in comments concerning these promotional activities) because public appearances are considered as a part that needs to be played to promote the work (and, at times, they can be experienced as a very welcome break from the tedious exercise of writing). Whether, they enjoy it or not, it seems that there is a great deal of pressure for authors to take part in promotional events. Consequently, young authors who are impatient to be noticed and to come into the spotlight may

---

[6] In her book on imperfection, social researcher Brené Brown explores the concept of vulnerability, linking it to positive qualities such as authenticity, self-compassion, or a resilient spirit, intuition, meaningful work, and even laughter.

[7] Vanessa Guignery further comments: "In some extreme cases, a double of the author even appears in his own fiction as, for example, in John Fowles's *The French Lieutenant's Woman* when the writer sits in the same compartment as his character, or in Martin Amis's *Money* when Amis meets the narrator. Far from being erased or deemed dead, the author is thus very much alive and his voice is distinctly to be heard." (2013, 2).

feel a greater urgency to develop a voice as a public speaker than a distinctive and original creative voice. How does Atwood negotiate this balance between time devoted to the development of her public speaker voice and creative voice? How does she advise younger generations of writers? How does she use these themes in her fiction and poetry? Both her creative writing and epitext provide a rich basis for our critical analysis.

Part III

The Poetic Voice and the Voices of the "Living Author" and of the Author's Public Persona

CHAPTER 9

The Need for Different Voices

When an author concentrates both on producing his work and defending it, each activity requires a different type of voice. The promotional voice is not under the same aesthetic obligation as the artist's voice. For example, unlike several other writers and many amateurs, Atwood has not embraced the idea of poetry on Twitter and she does not set her social media voice an artistic objective. My point therefore is to highlight the different types of voices that Atwood has crafted. Indeed, I do not think that Atwood has crafted a *poetic* social media voice, and I do not wish to show that the voice-print of her poetry voice can be linked to her social media voice (or vice-versa), although the thematic links between the two voices are worth underlining – mainly when Atwood deals with the theme of artistic creation, either in an artistic form or in an epitextual form. How Atwood adapts herself to the constraints of small-scale expression in a social media such as Twitter is not to be related to her ability to craft a concise and powerful poetic voice, but only to her skills for non-artistic work as a promoter of events or ideas. Indeed, Atwood does not provide a new poetic model for the use of social media, nor does she express the desire to explore this avenue in the future. However, she does display an ability to use the media extensively and effectively, all the while protecting the creative sphere and artistic voice from the danger of being "sucked into the Twittersphere like Alice down the rabbit hole" (NYRblog March 29, 2010). Atwood fully demonstrates her understanding of the different language forms on the Internet by adopting different voices depending on the media. While the uniqueness and authenticity of a poet's voice in poetry may be identifiable with the author's voice-print, the question of the voice-print does not seem to be as relevant when dealing with Atwood's voice in a media where she does not claim to have any aesthetic ambition.

As far as the Atwoodian reader is concerned, one could go as far as to say that Atwood's social media voice could be handled by a different person (a sister, cousin, friend or agent) and it would not be a great loss to us, the readers. Atwood does have a journalistic skill for us to enjoy, but it is not to be placed in the same category of skills as her artistic talent as a fiction or poetry writer. If Atwood were to give up her social media activity, the loss in terms of cross-fertilization would perhaps be greater to Atwood herself than to the reader. It seems that Atwood uses the social media opportunity to be fully connected to today's world and it provides her with valuable material which sometimes nurtures her artistic work or gives her a break from the solitude of her writing. I will try to highlight how Atwood uses and plays with this type of material.

It is also interesting to note that, in her handling of different voices and skills, Atwood resembles great multi-talented writers such as Shakespeare. Shakespeare's influences include mundane works (lurid ballads, murder pamphlets and scandalous broadsides) as well as classics. In the same way Shakespeare liked to include elements of the changing society around him and was not afraid to mix them into classical heritage, Atwood turns to a wide range of material from classics (Shakespeare's work included) and intertextual sources (fairy tales, gothic writing and images) to comic books, pulp fiction, gossipy news items, advertising and social media. Shakespeare was also gifted for business and most certainly had a "business voice" of which all traces are lost (apart from the fact that we do know that Shakespeare did not make a fortune from his plays, but he did make a considerable amount of money from his business investments allowing him to return to Stratford-upon-Avon and purchase the second-most-expensive home in town). Atwood is equally capable of displaying a set of skills which are separate from her writing skills.

Atwood is thus a multi-talented individual, equipped with an attentive ear and eye allowing her to play with a wide range of voices; she is fully aware of the aesthetic constraints required by her artistic work – which she claims should not exclude a sense of "fun" as well as "seriousness". The way she pursues her various promotional or business activities provides us with an example of how writers can achieve the balance they seek in the different fields of their lives. This is a subject that Atwood has widely commented on, using both her poetic voice and her journalistic or social media voice. And I will try to underline how her sharp observation of our consumer society, with its inevitable consumption and image-building pressure, fuel her multi-faceted discourse.

Thus, contrasting the poetic voice with the "living author's" voice and with the voice of the author's public persona leads us to raise many questions. As we have seen in the first chapters of this book, the persona of the poet and that of the author as "the one that does the living" (as opposed to Atwood's "thing that calls itself / I", CG 50) are often present in Margaret Atwood's poetry. These representations provide the reader with clues as to where the author is situated in relation to her work. How does Atwood's fiction and epitext provide additional commentaries on the subject?

My purpose will be to examine Atwood's rich epitext including her critical work and essays such as *Negotiating with the Dead*, in order to review the author's position on how to balance living and writing. Atwood's thoughts on the subject include a reflection on how to compromise with the market economy. I will also look at the dynamics of image construction and show how Atwood has turned these dynamics into material for fiction writing.

Finally, in an era of Internet communication and new publishing opportunities, the writer needs to renegotiate the balance between artistic work and promotional work. In the last section of this volume, I will therefore focus on how Atwood has explored new publishing tools in order to comment on publishing strategies and experiment with a wide range of Internet voices.

CHAPTER 10

The Celebrity Culture, Atwood and Hyde

Since the end of the twentieth century, writers have become part of our celebrity culture. The publishing industry as a whole (from publishers to booksellers) expects the writer to play a major part in promoting his/her work. Publishers themselves *know* that people are interested in writers, especially successful ones. Some publishers go as far as to say that many readers are more interested in the writers than the writing itself[1]. Many authors seem to enjoy making public appearances and yet they know that the promotion of their work is often carried out at the expense of the writing itself. Doris Lessing deplored:

> Writers sadly joke that having written a book, we then have to sell it. This is no joke. It took three and a half months of my life – of writing time – to "promote" *Under My Skin* in Britain and in America, in Holland and Ireland and France. [...] The obsession with the autobiographical element in a writer's work here reaches its fulfilment: having seen Shelley plain, what need to read the work? (Lessing 97-98).

However, as most industry players point out, authors' tours are a necessary condition of the business of books. Doris Lessing nevertheless makes fun of the author-signing sessions and mainly of the personalized messages writers are requested to include (such as "For Marie" or "For Bobbie", followed by "Happy birthday" or "Merry Christmas"):

> The writer who has begun with a fierce concern for the honour of literature, and who might even once have refused insane messages, since she has never heard of Marie, Bobbie, and the rest, is broken down by the demand, will do anything to put an end to this miserable business. [...] A couple of summers ago there was a joke going around the Oxford

---

[1] See Douglas Gibson's book entitled *Stories about Storytellers Publishing Alice Munro, Robertson Davies, Alistair MacLeod, Pierre Trudeau, and Others*, mainly Gibson's comments in relation to the audience's perception of Alice Munro (343-362).

students: I have the only unsigned copy of... How can anyone possibly value these signatures? (Lessing 97-98)

The author-signing sessions provide good material for jokes on talk shows about fiction and they also provide good material for fiction itself. Because we live in a world in which both the new celebrity culture and the marketplace prevail, it is hardly surprising that most media outlets tend to "privilege the person over the work, the catchy anecdote over the literary discussion, and focus on the most recent publication that needs to be promoted without considering the larger picture" (Guignery 2013, 2-3). When collaborating with promotional activities, Atwood is only too familiar with the efforts put into making her public speaking voice available. Because these efforts take the writer away from developing a creative voice, one may question the value of pressurizing the author to put more time and effort into public speaking. Atwood recognizes both the strain and the temptation to be part of the celebrity culture and raises the question of how "guilty [a writer] should [...] feel about [the promotion of] his art?" (ND 93). In *Negotiating with the Dead*, she reports humorously:

> I can still hear the sneer in the tone of the Parisian intellectual who asked me, 'Is it true you write the *bestsellers*?' 'Not on purpose,' I replied somewhat coyly. Also somewhat defensively, for I knew these equations as well as he did [...]. (ND 68)

In that same volume, Atwood clearly states that a writer's artistic value is neither related to the "money factor" nor to the author's availability for public speaking. This may seem a little obvious, and yet both critics and authors are "well acquainted with both kinds of snobbery: that which ascribes value to a book because it makes lots of money, and that which ascribes value to a book because it doesn't" (69). Going beyond such simplistic judgments implies addressing a number of issues, which are at the heart of the series of conferences given by Atwood at the University of Cambridge in 2000. *Negotiating with the Dead* covers a number of points, including the author's personal writing experience and other writers' experiences which have helped Atwood map out the difficulties of the activity of writing in a commercial context.

Negotiating with the Dead was not Atwood's first opportunity of questioning the writer's position in a post-modern commercial culture. Atwood's critical work contains a number of texts addressing contextual issues that include the politics and economics of literature. *Second Words* (1982) contains texts, published prior to *Survival*, that focus on the author's experience of developing a voice for public speaking and becoming a public figure. Atwood comments on the necessity of dealing with both promotional obligations and the demands of the mass media. Other texts include comments on the publishing world and on the power of the distribution system. In *Negotiating with the Dead*, Atwood's critical angle, format, and tone are different from those in her earlier essays and comments. Atwood chooses to raise her voice – that of an experience writer – in support of younger writers, which is revealed not only by her dedication "for others" but also by her allusion to "Reena, a thirty-four-year-old woman who has been writing since the age of six and throwing it all into a waste basket, but who thinks she may now be almost ready to begin" (*Negotiating with the Dead*, xix).

Atwood's motive for coming to the rescue of young writers is not simply that she fears they are in danger of being overlooked by university or mainstream critics (as she has done on a number of occasions in the past): Atwood also feels the need to protect their talents from the surrounding commercial pressure. In targeting a generation of younger artists, Atwood's approach is both analytical and slightly provocative (in her easily recognizable style) and it issues out a rather alarming warning to those ignorant of context. Atwood realizes that, when she started out in the sixties, it was probably easier to become a writer, even though publishing activity was limited in Canada and already under the threat of being dominated by the American commercial approach. Back then, writers who placed hope in the Canadian market and industry made their contributions to the expansion of publishing houses and managed to create for themselves the situation they sought. Today, writers face an even more difficult situation than the generation of the sixties: the challenge is no longer to bring about the golden age of Canadian literature but to retain it. Although Atwood underlines the prevailing commercial pressure on the one hand, and, on the other hand, the various mythologies that every writer needs to come to terms with, the tone of *Negotiating with the Dead* is encouraging and stimulating for young writers. It is obvious that the changes of context do not affect Atwood's fundamental belief that the artist's role in any society remains essential and that, more than ever, writers need to be concerned more with developing their creative voice rather than promoting their work through their public speaking voice.

Atwood's position on the subject of compromising with the market economy is made clear not only by her latest book and various critical essays from the 1970s onwards but also, in an indirect way, by the portrayal of our market-driven society and image-based culture in her novels. Atwood turns the issues of media constructions and the dynamics of marketing art into a material that examines the problems of the modern artist. Not that Atwood claims to offer ready-made solutions and ways of dealing with these problems, but her purpose is to make them visible to the society whose problems they are.

The crafting of the writer's creative voice also hinges upon a question of balance. Atwood's literary and commercial success clearly demonstrates that she never loses sight of the fundamental aesthetic obligation the writer is under, but she does deliberately set out to hook the reader in some way: "You've got to give the reader a reason to read on, apart from your delightful prose." Also, Atwood underlines the entertainment value of literary voices: "A lot is trying to keep oneself amused, isn't it?" (Ingersoll 213). Nevertheless, she adds: "Writing is play in the same way that playing the piano is play. Just because something's fun doesn't mean it isn't serious" (Ingersoll 236). Atwood is fully conscious that the writer depends on the reader's willingness to buy the book (and amusement from the book is therefore desirable). Therefore it is in the writer's interest to craft a creative voice which is likely to be commercially successful (in order for the writer to earn a living from his art). Because the book also needs to be marketed professionally, Atwood fully endorses Lewis Hyde's theories on commercializing art both in her review of his book, *The Gift* in 1999 and in her series of conferences in Cambridge in 2000. On the jacket of Hyde's book, Atwood's comment clearly indicates that the dilemma articulated by Hyde lies at the heart of all artistic activities: how can the artist keep himself alive, in both the physical sense (earning a living) and spiritual sense (expressing his talent) in the world of money "when the essential part of what [he does] cannot be bought or sold?"

Hyde's observations help us understand Atwood's own position in *Negotiating with the Dead*: there is no shame in having a creative voice with commercial potential. Furthermore, "[w]ithin certain limits, gift wealth may be rationalized and market wealth may be eroticized" (Hyde 274) – the subtitle of Hyde's work, *Imagination and the Erotic Life of Property,* holds the key to this theory. The "gift wealth" is defined as the artistic element that springs from an act of love and that is therefore considered priceless. As Atwood rephrases, it is "the part of any poem or novel that [...] doesn't derive its value from the realm of market exchange" (ND 69). The realm of gift has a mode of operating which is often discussed superficially, in various authors' interviews. Atwood herself contributes to the elaboration of myths about creativity which the media eagerly perpetuates. Although Atwood often emphasizes that artistic creation starts with discipline and hard work, she quotes writers like D. H. Laurence: "Not I, not I, but the wind that blows through me" (79), and Rilke: "A nothing-breath. A ripple in the god. A wind" (80); she often resorts to metaphors and images in order to describe the setting in which a voice arises – solitude, receptiveness, to start with.

The image of the prophet fighting with the angel lends artistic creation a religious overtone to which Atwood alludes again and again. In *Second Words*, Atwood resorts to the struggle between Jacob and the angel to illustrate the concept of the "daily battle with words, language itself" (SW 203): "[...] the encounter with language in which each side is equally active, for what writer has not felt the language taking him over at times, blocking him at others? We all hope for the blessing; we all hope finally to speak our names. And, we hope that if we receive the blessing it will not be for ourselves alone" (SW 348). In *Negotiating with the Dead*, Atwood uses the term "grace" to describe Hyde's gift:

> [T]he realm of gift [...] has altogether different modes of operating. A gift is not weighted and measured, nor can it be bought. It can't be expected or demanded; rather it is granted, or else not. In theological terms it's a grace, proceeding from the fullness of being. One can pray for it, but one's prayer will not therefore be answered. If this were so there would never be any writer's block (ND 69).

According to Hyde's definition, the gift sphere and market society correspond to two different modes of logic: the logic of love (Eros) and the logic of reason (Logos). The tension between the two is unavoidable. When Hyde first started researching the subject, he underlined "an irreconcilable conflict between the gift exchange and the market," and, as a consequence, he claimed that "the artist must suffer a constant tension between the gift sphere [...] and the market society [...]" (Hyde 273). This common analysis produces many of the mythologies Atwood ironically denounces in *Negotiating with the Dead* (such as "the fasting artist," sacrificed at "the altar of art," 82).

Hyde describes his own evolution as regards the "irreconcilable conflict between the gift exchange and the market" stated above. His examination leads him to dismiss the notions of sacrifice that are so often associated with artistic dedication. As a result of his research (carried out in different cultural contexts), Hyde demonstrates that although the gift of a voice stands in danger of being destroyed by the market place, the poles of the dichotomy are not necessarily as strongly opposed as he first believed them to be. Similarly, Atwood's religious respect for artistic creation and her high expectations in terms of literary accomplishments do not rule out her understanding of how to deal with context. She realizes, as does Lewis Hyde, that there is little to be gained from being at war with the market. But since our society tends to overemphasize the market and deny the gift economy to which artistic activity belongs, the artist needs to find workable methods to protect the gift economy. Hyde's advice to the artist is the following: "First the artist allows himself to step outside the gift economy that is the primary commerce of his art and make some peace with the market [...]. [T]he artist who wishes neither to lose his gift nor to starve his belly reserves a protected gift-sphere in which the work is created, but once the work is made he allows himself some contact with the market" (Hyde 274-275).

This two-step process ties in with Atwood's approach and accounts for her active participation in her publisher's marketing efforts once the writing has been accomplished. Hyde goes on to give advice on how contact with the market should be made. Hyde suggests the recruitment of an agent to deal with the financial and promotional aspects. Doing so helps the artist minimise time spent on marketing his work and it also contributes to maintaining, in Atwood's words, a "firm division in his soul" between the two realms (ND 70). Protecting the gift sphere means concentrating on the development of a creative voice first and allowing the finished goods to be marketed second, all the while in pursuit of perfect artistic expression. In *Negotiating with the Dead*, Atwood not only reformulates the conclusions of Hyde's work but also adds advice based on her own experience. In doing so, she both creates the mythical Atwood her audience is longing to hear about *and* gives the potential writer valuable advice on how to proceed.

Atwood's introduction to the Cambridge conferences focuses on how it *feels* to write, which is probably what most young writers need to recognize first. Atwood links the experience of writing to classical and biblical myths: the writer, like Persephone, delves into the world of the dead and then tries to "illuminate [darkness], and [...] bring something back out to the light." Atwood adds: "[*Negotiating with the Dead*] is about that kind of darkness and that kind of desire" (ND xxiv) – the very underworld experience which, according to Atwood's poetry and fiction, is a precondition for the emergence of a poetic voice. The main emphasis is not on "how to compromise with the market economy" because, although she fully endorses Hyde's work, she is aware of the fact that, for each writer, contexts differ. The message that comes across to the reader is the importance of cultivating an authentic writing experience and total independence from market demands. The public response may be very negative (and ignore artistic accomplishment, thus discouraging the writer) or on the contrary very positive (and turn the artist into a superstar, thus distracting him from his main purpose). The ability to remain independent is characteristic of Atwood, as she demonstrates on a number of occasions: "My reader's responses to my work interest me, but I don't 'draw' upon them. The response comes after the book gets published; by the time I get the responses, I'm thinking about something new" (in Ingersoll 235).

The challenge to create "something new" and, time after time, to return to the crafting of her creative voice, protects Atwood from the danger of feeding on the public's response. Nevertheless, having reached superstar status, Atwood needs to deal with pressure from the media and that in itself, she claims, is an art – but of a different kind. On many occasions, Atwood has been treated as a superstar, and played the part elegantly. Her appearance on stage in a silver dress after the premiere of *The Handmaid's Tale* at the *Berlinade* triggered standing ovations, as did her appearances at the Sorbonne, or in Cambridge, or in the various Booker Prize celebrations, or in the famous "Atwood as goalie" video which has gone viral since it was originally aired on January 31, 2005.

Atwood willingly becomes a generous public figure going beyond the audience's expectations and amusing both herself and the audience in playing cleverly with various dress codes (she likes to point out the "influence of wardrobe choices" – a matter not "all that frivolous," taken up by "earnest [ideological] commentators " (*Negotiating with the Dead*, 107). She is now among the most sought-after interview stars; and, as Susanne Becker has pointed out, "her ease with public appearances has cemented her fame. Margaret Atwood and the media is thus a story of the tension between the possibility and the curse of such celebrity; between using the media and being used" (in Nischik 30).

Although Atwood seems to control much of the media imagery and although she can afford to be very selective and careful in her dealings with the media, she also has experience of having to defend her image; some of the articles in *Second Words* were written in response to the many attacks she received from 1972 to 1976 (mainly in relation to *Survival*). Nevertheless, Atwood knows that she cannot totally control her image, nor the reception of her voice and the inevitable destructive gossip. Her only defense is indifference and humour: "People who attack me for having curly hair, breast feeding and making public appearances I can't do much about" (SW 14). As Becker points out: "Her ironic response to attacks and projections has turned into ironic anticipation" (Becker in Nischik, 38). Atwood remembers a time, at the very beginning of her career, when she felt helpless when attacked; furthermore, her promotional efforts were tedious and did not always pay off (as captured, for instance, in such works as her short story "Lives of the Poets" in *Dancing Girls*). She also remembers, with humour, when she was sent off by Jack McClelland to a book signing of *The Edible Woman* in the Hudson's Bay men's underwear department (King 139). Today Atwood is very much at ease in public appearances: her public speaking voice has evolved out of sheer necessity. It is neither a fake voice, nor a disguised voice, but through her dealing with promotional events, she has learned to craft her public speaking voice. Her experience therefore encompasses both struggling for attention and being in the spotlight. In both cases, she insists upon the artificiality of the exercise: "Interviews are an art form in themselves. As such, they're fictional and arranged" (in Ingersoll 191).

In order to master the art of fictionalising oneself, Atwood distances herself from her own public speaking voice and from her projected image which she sees as a double that escapes her: "[The Margaret who's] the person on the big billboard [...] is sort of like a twin who looks exactly like you, who is running around out of control. A lot of it is mythology" (Viner *The Guardian*, September 16, 2000, 27). For the benefit of promoting her work, Atwood cleverly contributes to her own mythologization and in *Negotiating with the Dead,* she does so by relating entertaining anecdotes about herself; she also analyses with great lucidity the myth-building force of her physical characteristics (her curly hair for example and her "wild and dishevelled [...] slightly crazed look – the right look [...] for a female poet," 64) and various happenings of her life (her childhood in the wilderness, motherhood, etc.). These physical and historical characteristics participate in the fictionalising of a voice. And why shouldn't Atwood develop that skill? Fictionalising her own voice is an art that she has learnt to master extremely well and, as most university critics will agree, this has not been achieved at the expense of her literary standards.

As Atwood herself has replied in response to polemical charges revolving around her critical work: "People often have difficulty handling somebody who does more than one thing. That's their problem. It's not a difficulty for me" (in Twigg 226). Atwood has demonstrated her ability to master more than one voice. Her artistic accomplishments also include visual art and, as far as her critical work goes, she once remarked upon being a "good amateur plumber" (in Ingersoll 208). Self-mythologization is simply yet another one of Atwood's skills – one that she obviously considers to be minor in comparison to her writing but she nevertheless recognizes her own ability to deal with media attention. Slipping effortlessly into a promotional role while maintaining a critical distance is a useful skill for any young writer to learn, implying as well a refusal to be locked into a specific role, image and voice. The ability not to be distracted by the construction of one's image and the capacity to build up the necessary concentration for artistic excellence remain central to any serious writing activity. But such concentration may be increasingly difficult to achieve. Book trade conditions have worsened, and authors need to devote more time and energy to negotiating advances. Multimillion dollar deals are struck for such authors as Danielle Steel and Stephen King, whilst others do not receive any advance at all (Mogel 15). Either way, these business concerns increasingly preoccupy many authors[2].

The book industry situation used to be different in Canada and in the US. As Atwood has pointed out, in Canada, in the sixties all new books being published would get critical attention, whereas in the States there were already "so many writers that it [was] impossible for anybody to keep up with them" (in Ingersoll 35). But as Canadian publishers are struggling to retain independence from the States, their mode of operating has become more cost-driven and profit-oriented. Publicists have to "hype" and to endeavor to find other forms of publicity to promote authors. As American editor Gerald Howard underlines:

> The successful marketing of literary fiction depends upon a collaboration between the writer, the publisher and the mass media. Publisher and writer have a common interest, and the media have been very eager to collaborate with them for their own reasons [...] They all have an inexhaustible appetite for raw material; discussion and gossip about books and writers is a cheap source of raw material (in Gross 63).

Back in 1959, Roland Barthes, in his article criticising panel discussions, warned authors against such practices, claiming it was impossible for an author to concentrate both on producing his work and defending it – each activity requiring a different type of voice. The danger of doing both has clearly been underlined by Hyde and Atwood. But both authors have a practical approach to promoting artistic work as a means of earning money. Both indicate that "writers too must eat" (ND 64), and both rebel against the idea of the "fasting artist's [body] [...] at the foot of the altar of art" (ND 82). Atwood has no intention of playing the part of "the doomed female artist" (ND 89) – a myth that she claims "still [has] power" (ND 90) – and she proves herself to be perfectly at ease in the cultivating

---

[2] Book life cycles, too, are becoming shorter and shorter. According to an industry analyst, Albert Greco, "90% perhaps as many as 95% of the books published are stone cold dead by the end of their first year of life" (Greco, 204-205), not to mention the hundreds of thousands of self-published books today which are, in effect, stillborn; and no other American consumer industry produces more than 50 000 different, relatively-low priced products each year, each with its own personality requiring individual recognition from the market. Greco's analysis dates back to the end of the XXth century. With the advent of self-publishing, the situation has got worse with so many writers seeking visibility. The effect of Globalization on the book industry is the same as on many other industries: when markets go global, so do commercial practices and US models prevail.

of different voices depending on the work at hand. Her ability to construct a powerful authorial public speaking voice and to enjoy such fictional constructions – "[Atwood] plays up to the scary identity that has been constructed for her and by her [...]. She likes her doubles" (Viner 27) – only demonstrates that this is one of her many minor arts – one that she knows to be extremely useful for the promotion of her work.

The ability to distance oneself from one's double and to recognize one's limits in the construction of one's image and public voice probably ranks as the most important skill involved in self-promotion. If it weren't for this ability, the other skills mentioned earlier would only lead the writer astray. Managing public appearances, successfully playing with dress codes, using one's wit to come up with cutting comments and anecdotes, responding to interviewers with unsettling repartees, walking a fine line between cultivating one's mystery (protecting one's privacy in the process) and revealing small details which are emblematic of one's original personality – all of these skills have contributed a great deal to Atwood's image and public voice (not to mention the sheer energy involved in accepting interviews and author's tours). Nevertheless, Atwood also demonstrates her capacity to stand back and let her agents and editors handle the promotional work while she simply locks herself away and deals with her writing (on various occasions she has lived abroad for a year to get the writing done), and that is where she demonstrates her unconditional commitment to her work.

Another dimension of the Atwood-media relationship is the author's ability to turn both the dynamics of image-building and voice crafting into material for her fiction. Taking examples from her novels (*Alias Grace, Cat's Eye, The Robber Bride, The Edible Woman, Life Before Man, Lady Oracle, Surfacing*) and short stories, I will show that the image-building and market relationship theme is built into a reflective and entertaining component of her work.

CHAPTER 11

The Atwood-Media Relationship Reflected in Fiction

In her fiction, Atwood stages the problematic situation of the artist in a commercial society – his or her struggle to affirm an authentic creative voice all the while compromising with the market economy. When dealing with this complex matter of the relationship between voice and the artistic/wealth economy, she invites the reader to reflect on three points: the importance of voice and image; the question of representation (the gap between reality and perception); and the commercial context where the logic of consumption revolves around social signifiers which encourage or stifle different types of voices.

In her latest novel, *The Blind Assassin*, for example, Atwood presents the importance of image, appearances and constructed voices as recurrent themes. Richard acts according to the necessities of his political image. He constructs lies for the press when his sister-in-law Laura, runs into trouble (when she runs away from home, when she gets pregnant, etc.) or when his wife leaves him. His success in deceiving the public is clearly a question of power. The press cannot risk opposing his version of events. As both his financial and political power decline, so does his control of media constructions. His public voice is revealed as fake when his true identity is brought to light. Having highlighted the power of the media, *The Blind Assassin* also, incidentally, points to the problem of the author's image and demonstrates how readers often confuse the voice of the narrator with that of the author. Atwood often calls attention to this confusion in her interviews: "People have a habit of identifying the author with the narrator [...] I do it myself when I'm reading a book – I catch myself saying, I wonder if that really happened to her [...] It's because we're human beings [...] You catch yourself in the act, you know it's not real, but you do it anyway, because that's what humans do" (Viner 23). When Atwood is the victim of such identifications, she responds with humour and, as some journalists report, with firmness and determination: "Margaret Atwood would like to clear a few things up from the start. She is not a murderer (this in spite of writing as a murderer in *Alias Grace*). She was not bullied to within an inch of her existence by her childhood best friend (unlike the narrator of *Cat's Eye*). She is not about to steal your man (*The Robber Bride*), she does not have an eating disorder (*The Edible Woman*), and she is not a woman whose lover committed suicide (*Life Before Man*), or a woman searching for her lost father (*Surfacing*)." (Viner 18)

By thus making readers' speculations sound ridiculous and by pointing out the incompatibility of her various heroines' characteristics, Atwood anticipates all the usual criticism based on the author-character identification. She reminds the reader, before agreeing to embark on the interview, that fiction is *not* reality and the voice of the narrator is *not* her voice. In *The Blind Assassin*, Atwood manages to teach the reader a lesson by pulling a trick on him. She leads the reader on to believe that Laura's novel (also entitled *The Blind Assassin*) bears some resemblance to her life. But, as the novel progresses, the reader begins to doubt: is it Laura's voice that the reader hears when reading her story? Can the reader assume there is a direct link between the voices of the novel and of the novel within the novel? And, finally, one last question emerges: is Laura really the author of *The Blind Assassin*? The final disclosure – that Iris is the author of the book signed Laura Chase – sheds light on the author of the fictional novel, Iris; but it does not reveal much about Laura's mystery – thus illustrating one of the quotations at the beginning of the novel: "The world is a flame burning in a dark glass."

This comment also applies to *Alias Grace* where secrecy, speculation, and image are so closely entwined (Becker in Nischik 37). Atwood exposes the incredible curiosity and greediness of society – the need to know, the irresistible attraction of confessions, of hearing the author's own voice, the public's gullibility for ready-made images and hollow constructions or deceptive models. Her novels map out all different kinds of responses to society's curiosity and greediness. Grace's response is a silent amusement ("I think of all the things that have been written about me [...] And I wonder, how can I be all of these different things at once?" (AG 23). In *Cat's Eye*, Elaine is fed up with being reduced to a role model for female artists. She actually enjoys going against the expectations of a feminist journalist who wants her to be the voice of feminism, claiming female independence. The journalist asks, "So you don't feel it's sort of demeaning to be propped up by a man?" In response, Elaine simply points out: "Women prop up men all the time [...]. What's wrong with a little reverse propping?" (CE 89). Elaine can tell from looking at the journalist that she's a great disappointment to her: "[The journalist's] voice is getting farther and farther away, I can hardly hear her. But I see her, very clearly: the ribbing on the fine neck of her sweater, the fine hairs on her cheek, the shine of a button. What I hear is what she isn't saying. *Your clothes are stupid. Your art is crap. Sit up straight and don't answer back"* (CE 91). The journalist's voice seems to echo Elaine's inner voice – a silent voice but nevertheless a powerful voice which has been shaped by the criticism and mockery Elaine has been subjected to in her youth.

In spite of the reproaches she hears (those of the journalist and those of her own inner voice), Elaine refuses to respond to expectations. It is plain to the reader that she will not get a very good review from the journalist if she does not. She tries to answer the following interviewer's question truthfully: "Why do you paint?" Elaine replies: "Why does anyone do anything?" (CE 91) – which is obviously the last thing this particular journalist wants to hear. The voice of practically any made-up feminist answer would have given the interviewer more satisfaction. On the contrary, in *Lady Oracle*, it is when Joan leaves behind her desire to craft a voice that pleases that she manages to create a unique authorial voice for herself. She equally scares off the interviewer (a young boastful macho – another stereotype) when she reveals her automatic writing experiments, but the public's response to the radio interview is surprisingly very positive. As luck would have it, Joan is turned into an inspired original figure, much more successful than she imagined she would be. This incident illustrates Atwood's comment about her own luck with the public: "I did not expect a large readership when I began writing, but that doesn't mean either that I write for a 'mass audience.' It means I'm one of the few literary writers who get lucky in their lifetimes" (in Ingersoll 235). The luck factor is beyond any writer's or publisher's control although it is always possible to try to analyze it retrospectively and underline which sociological trends have contributed to an author's successful voice.

As famous artists, both Elaine and Joan encounter very different implications of artistic fame, which also include negative responses to their work. At a party, Joan defends herself against what Atwood calls a "sexual compliment-put-down" (SW 199) and demonstrates her capacity to deal with attacks directly (LO 266). Elaine, whenever possible, avoids managing her relationship with the public directly. As if following Lewis Hyde's advice, she relies on her agent, Charna, for the promotion of her work and recognizes that she needs Charna's professional skills and voice. Charna knows exactly how to handle Elaine's public appearances: "Now Charna hustles me in mauve leather, clanking with ersatz gold. She whisks me back into the back office: she doesn't want me dangling around in the empty gallery, at loose ends while the first revellers trickle in, she doesn't want me looking unsuccessful and too eager. She will make an entrance with me, later, when the noise level is high enough" (CE 410). Charna is in control: she gives Elaine expert advice on how to behave, how to make an entrance. Because Charna is associated with Elaine's image, her mode of dressing is carefully thought through, resulting in the choice of "mauve leather" and jewellery of "ersatz gold" ("wardrobe choices" again!). The message to the reader is that wardrobe choices affect the crafting of image and voice. Whether the voice is artistic or promotional, there needs to be a definite coherence between dress and voice. Both the reader and Elaine cannot help noticing and appreciating the professionalism of Charna's approach. Elaine herself has a hard time deciding on what to buy and wear for such events – as revealed in the scene in chapter 8, thus illustrating the self-doubt which is characteristic of Elaine's narrative voice.

Elaine's capacity to stand back and assess image constructions is particularly visible on one occasion: a middle-aged puritan fanatically disapproves of Elaine's work and throws a bottle of ink on one of her paintings. Elaine understands that this gesture of hostility is exactly what she needs: it will strengthen her image: "I will be looked at with respect: paintings that get bottles of ink thrown at them, that can inspire such outraged violence, such uproar and display, must have an odd revolutionary power. I will seem audacious, and brave. Some dimension of heroism has been added to me" (CE 354). Elaine knows that she will benefit from this event (the reader may suppose that Charna is bound to capitalize on it and give it proper media attention). Elaine thus mirrors Atwood's own capacity to review imagery about herself and to contemplate the resulting myths.

Image and voice construction and the ensuing dynamics of sales become the focus of one of Atwood's short stories, "Hairball." The main character, Kat, is an editorial director of a women's magazine. Thanks to her marketing expertise, she is well aware that the purpose of image building is to boost sales. Her technique consists of "working with the gap between reality and perception," bombarding the readers of the magazine with "images of what they ought to be," "mak[ing] them feel grotty for being the way they are" and then "hitt[ing] them with something new, something they've never seen before, something they aren't." Because, "nothing sells likes anxiety" (WT 49). In other words, it is all about constructing a voice that will echo the reader/consumer's own inner voice – a voice which, like Elaine's voice in *Cat's Eye*, is filled with self-doubt. Another one of Kat's skills is using the right language and voice to convince the directors of the magazine about her editorial ideas – a language saturated with images targeting their male egos. She deliberately uses a tone and terms they are likely to find attractive and that they will identify with: "'Fashion is like hunting,' Kat told [the board of Directors], hoping to appeal to their male hormones, if any. 'It's playful, it's intense, it's predatory. It's blood and guts. It's erotic.'" Thus she creates an image of the "erotic" "hunter," both "intense" and "playful," with "blood and guts," which she feels they will respond to – she ends up "go[ing] way too far," and the board refuses her daring ideas (52). But Kat's strategy, revolving around the concept of image and identification, is nonetheless a typical marketing technique, which she indifferently applies to the readers of the magazine, the board of directors, and also her lover. All are encouraged to buy something from her on the basis of an ideal – a possible equation with a fantasized image. "Hairball" thus illustrates Baudrillard's theory, according to which the process of consumption serves the purpose of image identification. According to Baudrillard, it is not the object itself that the consumer is after, but the status related to the object. Thus, the logic of social consumption revolves around the manipulation of social signifiers (Baudrillard 79). Advertising messages address the insecure inner voice in each one of us – the one that is defeated, laden with dissatisfaction and self-criticism. Highlighting the dynamics of the commercial voice addressing the consumer's dissatisfied inner voice is a recurrent theme in Atwood's fiction – one that she deals with, with a great deal of humour.

Many of Atwood's protagonists enjoy the power of making up and controlling such social signifiers. Other examples include Rennie in *Bodily Harm*, making up trends and proving them to become real, and Zenia, in *The Robber Bride*, creating images her friends want to conform to. Even Charis, who has absolutely no marketing skills, realizes that her employer's shop would not survive if it did not anticipate rapidly changing fashions.

Atwood's novels are also replete with examples of heroines experiencing the inevitable tension between art and marketing, and sometimes the bitter disappointments of commercialization. Marian, in *The Edible Woman*, vaguely understands that the marketing company she works for, Seymour Surveys, equates Moose Beer with the Canadian identity: the commercial jingle suggests that drinking the beer is a wilderness experience. For the nameless narrator of *Surfacing*, the confusion between natural objects and manufactured ones, and the commercialization of Canadian identity, is a source of disappointment; when she spots the three stuffed Mooses, dressed in human clothes, in the gas station, she is annoyed because she clearly disapproves of the exploitation of symbols and the commercialization of the North (S 7).

The "pornography of representation" (to use Susanne Kappeler's expression) inflicts possible violence on Atwood's heroines. It prevents them from finding their own voice and it allows their insecure inner voice to take over. However, when the protagonists become aware of this repression, they engage in an identity and voice construction process. Both Anna in *Surfacing* and Marian in *The Edible Woman* run away from a male photographer and his attempt to achieve control via fixed representation. Their intuitive reactions point to the necessity of resisting the entrapment of representation. In the same way, the narrator of *Surfacing* and Rennie in *Bodily Harm* are both led to resist influence from the hierarchy and refuse imposed trends. Rennie, who specializes in superficial and catchy articles on lifestyle, finally questions her own involvement in perpetuating the "pornography of representation" and reviews her choice of locking herself into one type of writing. Image construction, and the ensuing creation of models and trends, inevitably raises the question of power politics. Atwood's preoccupation with power relations and polyphony of voices is visible in her ability to keep track of who is actually in control, both in her novel-writing strategies and her dealings with the public.

So it appears that Atwood does have one thing in common with many of her protagonists and that is her ability to review the power of representation and image construction. Furthermore, her understanding of context leads her to pay in-depth attention to the superficiality of our consumer society. Not only do her novels explore the structures of image-building, representation and resistance in a late twentieth century context, but both her critical and artistic work highlight the forces that reshape the landscape of the artist, particularly as they affect the voice of the writer, whether as the accomplice or the victim (or both) of those forces. As literary bestsellers, Atwood's novels are situated at the intersection between art and commerce. This intersection is often said to be the "bloody crossroad" or the "sanguine [...] piece of ground" where the literary voice is sacrificed for the sake of marketable voices (if the artist resists all forms of commercialization, it is the artist who is sacrificed "at the altar of art"). Both literary authors and editors resent the power of commercialism. Gerald Howard comments: "[...] literature is the very last thing publishing is about [...] publishing is about power and money and ego sharp practices" (Howard 62).

Atwood has set out to prove that, although the publishing scene sadly corresponds to Howard's description of it, literary authors have a right to refuse to "starve their bellies." She is convinced that, thanks to Hyde's teaching, they will not only learn to survive, but they will continue to play their crucial role within society. Atwood's reviewing of Hyde's work demonstrates her belief in the artist's social function and her total commitment to the defense of the "gift economy." Her relationship with the media clearly shows her capacity to use the media and yet maintain an ironic distance. As I have suggested, Atwood's minor art of self-promotion and her experience with constructing a public speaking voice are not only useful for the promotion of her work, but also for her work *per se*, as she manages to turn her experience and her practical knowledge of image construction into useful material for her writing. Thus, it is not difficult to imagine Atwood's response to an "[intellectual's] sneer [about writing] a *bestseller*" (ND 68): it is no more necessary for an artist to feel guilty about promoting his work than it is for him to inflict deliberate sufferings upon himself. In *Negotiating with the Dead*, Atwood reports the question of an aspiring young writer: "Is it necessary to suffer for a creative voice to emerge?" Her answer to that question has tended to be: "Don't worry about the suffering [...]. The suffering will occur whether you like it or not [...] many times, the suffering is a *result* of the writing, rather than its cause. Why? Because there are a lot of people out there who'll be damned if they let you get away with it, you jumped-up smarty pants. Publishing a book is often very much like being put on a trial, for some offence which is quite other than the one you know in your heart you've committed" (108).

Atwood underlines that those who praise the author unconditionally because of his success are as ignorant as those who criticize the author's success regardless of the author's writing. This unconditional praise which will be referred to as "iconization" is present in Atwood's epitext, fiction and poetry. We may now turn our attention to this concept in relation to the voice potentially fictionalized by the author and iconized by the reader[1].

---

[1] Critics themselves are not immune to the iconization of authors. In her introduction to critical work in a special issue of the *Journal of the Short Story* on Alice Munro, Héliane Ventura clearly states that the objective of the volume is *not* to embark on a "hagiographic enterprise dedicated to the praise of one of the greatest short story writers in contemporary literature" (Ventura 3). Ventura underlines instead how most critical contributions "concentrate on the various ways through which Munro turns life into story", displaying one's "need for self-dramatization or for 'calling attention' to oneself, which many people in her family seem to have 'in large and irresistible measure,' as she herself declares in the first part of her collection from 2006, *The View from Castle Rock*." (Ventura 3) While highlighting the story-telling reflection in Munro's work, Ventura states that the critical articles of the volume steer away from the iconic in order to focus on language – mainly "on the types of languages used in Munro's stories" (Ventura 3).

CHAPTER 12
Atwood's Treatment of the "Iconized Voice"

While highlighting the representations of both the poetic voice and the public persona, we have made the distinction between the poetic voice of Atwood's poetry and Atwood's public persona's voice. As we have seen, the staging of the poetic voice in Atwood's poetry is highly ambivalent: it includes representations of what Atwood calls the "voice" or representations of various creatures, including the sibyl, who stand for the writer's inspiring voice. The voice-persona is given physical and psychological characteristics: she is staged either as a disagreeable and unattractive creature or as a quiet and comforting whisper. She is either an entity which is part of the persona and yet separate, or an entity totally different from the "[t]he thing that calls itself / I" (CG 50) that is the one that does the living, and who speaks from the outside rather than from the inside. Furthermore, the poet is to be considered either as a singular figure or the poets are represented as a group or collective figure. The collective group of poets is portrayed as a caravan "looking for water" (TD 35), or "speak[ing] what they must" (TD 37).

Questions of representation affect not only the "voice", but also fictional characters and the self-fictionalized author. Atwood frequently self-fictionalizes herself as an "iconized author" since she has an extensive experience of this status. Therefore Atwood speaks not with *one* public persona voice but with many, depending on the occasion and the message she wishes to convey and depending on the media she is broadcasted through. Before we examine Atwood's use of these many public persona voices – all of which are in the first person pronoun – we may say a few words about the "autobiographical pact" theory put forward by Philippe Lejeune. Lejeune suggests the following definition of the pact: "[a] retrospective prose narrative written by a real person concerning his own existence, where the focus is his individual life, in particular the story of his personality"[1] (Lejeune 1989, 4). Through the input of many critics on the form of autobiography, the notion has evolved into a broader conception

---

[1] This definition includes four "elements": form of language (narrative, prose), subject treated (individual life), situation of the author (author and narrator are identical), and position of the narrator (narrator and principal character are identical). (Lejeune 1989, 4)

which suggests that autobiography is not restricted to self-reporting but can be widened to include many forms of artistic writing. Lejeune himself commented on his early definition in saying that the pact was as much a mode of reading as a mode of writing[2].

Sherrill Grace throws light on this matter by making five basic assumptions concerning the autobiographical pact which can be summarized as follows: first, she sees "a continuum, not absolute distinctions, between testimony at one end of the truth and reality scale and first-person novels at the other" (in Moss and Kozakewich 123):

> Surely the theory of auto/biography has taught us to understand that all life stories are artistic recreations, possibly very deceptive, inevitably unreliable, and hugely manipulative, even when they are classified as memoir, testimony, or diary. The trick comes in knowing how to read these texts and in learning how to tell the difference between types of fictionality and degrees of referentiality. And when the writer is as skilled an artist as Atwood, as superb a ventriloquist, then the knowing and learning are a challenge. (in Moss and Kozakewich 122).

Grace's second assumption is that we readers are "trained (conditioned, if you prefer) to accept, believe, or take for granted that when we read (or hear) a first-person voice we are getting the straight goods" (122). Her third assumption in relation to the autobiographical pact concerns the world we live in, which she describes as "an auto/biographical age – from 'reality TV' to [...] the privileging of auto/biography in book stores" (in Moss and Kozakewich 123)[3] ; fourth, Grace is convinced that "biography and autobiography are inextricably related to each other and to other genres, including theory and scholarly discourse" (123). This is particularly apparent, as we have seen in *Negotiating with the Dead* where Atwood intertwines her own experience of writing with her experience of reading and criticism. Last, Grace claims that "relationality (self-representation through another) is fundamental to the construction of identity in all modes of

---

[2] According to Lejeune: "Le pacte autobiographique est un mode de lecture autant qu'un type d'écriture, c'est un effet contractuel historiquement variable" (Lejeune 1975, 45).
[3] Grace also speaks of "the revival of portraiture and self-portraits, [...] the re-presencing of the body and the return of the author, [...] the obsessive production of life-writing texts and the privileging of auto/biography in book stores" (in Moss and Kozakewich, 123)

auto/biography, that the process of articulating self is dialogic [...]" (in Moss and Kozakewich 123)[4].

I have underlined Atwood's pervasive use of first-person pronouns, from her earliest poems (of which "This is a photograph of me", previously quoted, is still one of the best-known and finest examples) to her fiction (from her first novel to the last). The "autobiographical pact" is equally relevant when it comes to examining Atwood's public persona voice. I would like to show that all five of Sherrill Grace's assumptions apply to the many public speaking occasions to which Atwood has been invited and these assumptions throw light not only on Atwood's handling of the pact – which, as Sherrill Grace suggests is "so effective [in Atwood's hands]" (131) – but also on her position concerning the "iconized author".

It is a well-known fact that Atwood is often invited to act as a spokesperson for a number groups[5]. When she is asked to talk about her experience as a writer, Atwood has a special talent for self-fictionalization. Again, I will refer to *Negotiating with the Dead* in which Atwood shares many of her experiences of writing from childhood onwards. In doing so, she offers a wide range of metaphors and images which reinforce the "autobiographical pact", promoting her own version of the pact. We may take for instance the beginning of *Negotiating with the Dead*. The book opens with the questions raised in the title of the first chapter: "Orientation: Who do you think you are? What is "a writer" and how did I become one?" As the title indicates, this chapter sets out to be

---

[4] The theoretical background for Grace's work is Gilmore, Rhiel and Suchoff who highlight that we live in a biographical age. Grace also refers to theorists such as John Paul Eakin, Susanna Egan, Leigh Gilmore, Sidonie Smith, and Julia Watson (to name a few) and their work on the construction of identity as a dialogic process. Finally, Grace mentions Paul de Man's concept of apostrophe as the impetus behind the specular structure of autobiography which, Grace claims, "is some version of Lejeune's pact" (in Moss and Kozakewich 123).

[5] There are many categories of people that Atwood can be a spokesperson for: for example artists, activists, women, Canadians. There are all sorts of cross-categories or sub-categories that can be evoked here: female writers, human rights activists, ecological activists, literary writers who happen to be successful or, on the contrary, unsuccessful writers embracing the new technologies of the XXIst century, writers refusing to embrace these new technologies, unknown writers trying to gain visibility, famous writers with tremendous visibility, insecure writers, aspiring writers or potential writers trying to figure out how to become writers etc. To a certain degree, Atwood can identify with the experiences of the people belonging to all of these various categories. Recently, the Big Think site ran an interview with Margaret Atwood in which she addressed many of the issues mentioned here. She talked "about Canadian humor, her creative process, dystopian versus apocalyptic literature, the reasons to preserve physical books, despite the rise of the e-reader, and the appeal of blogs and Twitter" (NYRblog March 29, 2010).

"autobiographical". However the reader soon realizes that it is only the gateway to a broader reflection on writers, one in which she performs an "autobiographics" of herself as a writer, to use Leigh Gilmore's expression[6]. Atwood's "I" in this first chapter of stands for a multiplicity of voices of writers. Paradoxically, here the first person singular is a pronoun that stands for a plural.

In Autobiographics: A Feminist Theory of Women's Self-Representation, Gilmore defines "autobiographics" as a hybrid text that willfully positions itself outside of the normal scope of autobiography in order to make a statement or to speak of an experience that would be too difficult for the life writer to portray using the techniques of traditional autobiography. She describes these texts as being "not content with the literary history of autobiography" and that instead they seek to mark their own "location in a text where self-invention, self-discovery, and self-representation emerge" (Gilmore 184). Furthermore, she claims that these texts move beyond "autobiography" in the authors' attempts to create for themselves, an identity that is more multifaceted and self-reflexive than can be found in a traditional autobiographical relating of facts. If the mark of autobiographics is, according to Gilmore, a self-reflexive process which "is concerned with interruptions and eruptions, with resistance and contradiction as strategies of self-representation" (Gilmore 184) implying agency in self-representation and if it is a form of writing "that emphasizes the biographical I" (Gilmore 184), its narratives are necessarily written in fragments. In the case of Negotiating with the Dead, Atwood mixes different fragments which include self-fictionalization and quotes from journals and autobiographies of other writers. As Atwood resorts to intertextuality, she weaves into her text the many voices of writers and commentators before her. In the resulting "autobiographics", Atwood states her own method of reading and writing, offering many metaphors for the reader to understand the role, position, vocation, tribulations, etc. of the writer. For example, Atwood suggests the writer is like a grave-digger: someone who does not just dig one grave (as most people can), but who digs many (as a true professional in the business of digging graves):

> As for writing, most people secretly believe they themselves have a book in them, which they would write if they could only find the time. And there's some truth to this notion. A lot of people do have a book in them – that is, they have had an experience that other people might want to read about. But this is not the same thing as "being a writer."

---

[6] See the very title of her book: *Autobiographics: a feminist theory of women's self-representation.*

> [...] everyone can dig a hole in a cemetery, but not everyone is a grave-digger. The latter takes a good deal more stamina and persistence. It is also, because of the nature of the activity, a deeply symbolic role. As a grave-digger, you are not just a person who excavates. You carry upon your shoulders the weight of other people's projections, of their fears and fantasies and anxieties and superstitions. You represent mortality, whether you like it or not. And so it is with any public role, including that of the Writer, capital W; but also as with any public role, the significance of that role – its emotional and symbolic content varies over time. (ND 26)

It is interesting to notice that the tone of voice in this "autobiographics" is not unlike the tone of voice of the poetic voice in several poems from Atwood's later poetry. Atwood's epitext – *Negotiating with the Dead* is the transcription of a series of conferences and therefore qualifies as epitext – has a poetical quality akin to her creative work. Indeed, humorous metaphors abound – the unflattering image of the grave-digger for example comes to mind when reading yet another unflattering portrayal of the writer in the following stanza from "Owl and Pussycat, Some Years Later" (TD 29-34):

> Is this small talent we have prized
> so much, and rubbed like silver
> spoons, until it shone
> at least as brightly as neon, really
> so much better than the ability
> to win the sausage-eating contest,
> or juggle six plates at once? (TD 30-31)

This example as well as many more first-person pronoun anecdotes in *Negotiating with the Dead* serve to illustrate all five of Sherrill Grace's assumptions concerning the "autobiographical pact": first, there is "a continuum" (Grace in Moss and Kozakewich 123), and not an absolute distinction, between the testimony in *Negotiating with the Dead* and the first-person creative work. *Negotiating with the Dead* itself qualifies as a hybrid genre, at the crossroads between an epitext resulting from Atwood's conferences, fragments of memoirs, and critical work: the different voices complete each other and flow into one another. The genre-challenging quality of Atwood's writing and capillary links between the different forms of writing serve to reinforce this idea of "a continuum" between the personal and analytical writing and the fictional writing. Second, Atwood is aware that we readers are trained to "take for granted [what] we read (or hear)" (Grace in Moss and Kozakewich 123); she is equally aware that – third assumption – we live in "an auto/biographical age", and she therefore plays on our expectations and beliefs by sharing her "life story" in *Negotiating with the Dead*: she addresses an audience who is eager to catch a behind-the-scenes glimpse of her life, and stages the personal anecdotes to suit the taste of a broad public. Fourth, the mixing of references in *Negotiating with the Dead* – from the personal to the scholarly – shows that autobiography is concerned with "interruptions and eruptions" (Gilmore, 184), displaying self-representation strategies connected to other genres, including essays, interviews and many different forms of writing. Last, the objective stated in *Negotiating with the Dead* – to help the young writer in the process of writing – is in keeping with the assumption that the process of articulating the self is dialogic and that "relationality (self-representation through another) is fundamental to the construction of identity" (Grace in Moss and Kozakewich, 123).

As for the above quoted metaphor of the writer as a grave-digger (which is akin to a wide range of metaphors from sausage-eating contestants to plate jugglers, in both her epitext and her poetry), it further illustrates how Atwood uses the "autobiographical pact" for the purpose stated in the opening paragraphs of *Negotiating with the Dead*, steering the attention away from her own life story to more profound questions concerning writers: she mocks the pedestal on which poets like to place themselves, claiming, in essence, that poets are no different from other human beings doing their jobs to the best of their abilities. The art of mocking the iconized writer illustrated by examples previously quoted taken from both Atwood's poetry and fiction is what York calls Atwood's "meta-iconography" (in York 229).

One cannot help but wonder why Atwood's meta-iconography plays such a large role in her handling of the "autobiographical pact". I would simply suggest that it is linked to the author's own experience and observation of the phenomenon of "iconization". Critical work on Atwood serves to support this suggestion. York outlines Atwood's literary iconization in two opposite manifestations: as a celebrated icon and as the personification of a witch. Hönninghausen caricatures the many voices and "styles and phases" attributed to Atwood: "Canadian nationalist, literary lobbyist, liberal parodist, Amnesty International activist" (York in Nischik, 97). Atwood supposedly "changed back and forth from poet to prose writer, from aggressive feminist harpy to soft-souled wife and mother, from progressive young woman to stone-faced sibyl" (York in

Nischik, 97). "She has attracted as much buckshot as veneration" (230) York points out. To illustrate this comment, York quotes Robert Fulford and his examination of "the darker side of literary iconization": " 'Do Canadians fear excellence?' [...] 'Consider the case of Atwood.' Atwood is now a 'case,' a literary psychosis in search of medication." (in York 230). How can one account for the negative reviews and responses to novels such as *Life Before Man*? Since most of the negative criticism stems from the Canadian readers themselves, it has been suggested that the reason lies with Canada's inferiority complex and unsatisfying exploration of the notion of nationhood. Trying to provide a simple explanation to this question, York resorts to an anecdote concerning Fulford and an American professor: "How would you like it if your sister won the Nobel Prize? The American professor who provoked Fulford's question by wondering aloud why so many Canadian readers seemed to despise Atwood replied in one word: 'shitty.'" (in York 230). Few contemporary authors of her literary caliber have been subjected to such iconization in the two aforementioned opposite manifestations.

It is thus hardly surprising that Atwood's work itself should examine the basic paradox of iconography. She does so in all sorts of humorous ways which we have previously underlined and many more examples are to be found in York's article (in York, 229-252). While Atwood playfully thumbs her nose at the iconic in her meta-iconography, as can be observed in certain poems and passages of *Negotiating with the Dead*, her tone becomes more serious when she deals with the subject of her creative work: this tone reflects the fact that Atwood obviously values the work of poets and considers it to be different from any other line of work. In "The Poets Hang on" (TD 35-37), although she claims that poets can be pretentious, she recognizes that they "know something" – something she endeavors to define:

> When asked about it, they say
> they speak what they must.
> Cripes, they're pretentious.
>
> They know something, though.
> They do know something.
> Something they're whispering,
> something we can't quite hear.
> Is it about sex?
> Is it about dust?

Is it about fear? (TD 36-37)

The poem "The Poets Hang On" ends with this series of unanswered questions which point to a "gift or unusual ability that sets an artist apart" (ND 26). Atwood thus highlights the fact that it is just as ridiculous to place artists above all other human beings as it is to believe that anyone can be a writer: the "apparent democracy"[7] of writing is misleading, and this is the parallel she suggests between different artistic modes:

> To be an opera singer you not only have to have a voice, you have to train for years; to be a composer you have to have an ear, to be a dancer you have to have a fit body, to act on the stage you have to be able to remember your lines, and so on. Being a visual artist now approaches writing, as regards its apparent easiness – when you hear remarks like "My four-year-old could do better," you know that envy and contempt are setting in, of the kind that stem from the belief that the artist in question is not really talented, only lucky or a slick operator, and probably a fraud as well. This is likely to happen when people can no longer see what gift or unusual ability sets an artist apart. (ND 26)

Here Atwood criticizes other people's perception of artists as envy and jealously leads them to question the talents of such artists. Instead, the writer, according to Atwood, should be seen as both a gifted individual and one who shouldn't place himself above anyone else. The representations of the writers that Atwood offers in her epitext are as much about dispelling false or conceited images about iconized authors as about sharing testimonies of writers such as herself. They are also about confronting her own ideas about writing as a profession with the ideas of other writers[8]. Atwood's message, as we have seen, is that writers are different

---

[7] This is what Atwood means by "apparent democracy": "its availability to almost everyone as a medium of expression. As a recurring newspaper advertisement puts it, "Why Not Be A Writer?...No previous experience or special education required." Or as Elmore Leonard has one of his street crooks say, ' ...You asking me...do I know how to write down words on a piece of paper? That's what you do, man, you put down one word after another as it comes in your head...You already learned in school how to write, didn't you? I hope so. You have the idea and you put down what you want to say. Then you get somebody to add in the commas and shit where they belong...There people do that for you'" (ND 25).
[8] For example Atwood comments: "I didn't encounter any writing about writers and their writing lives until I'd made it to university and had run headlong into Cyril Connolly's *Enemies of Promise*, originally published in 1938 but reissued in time for me to be frightened by it. It lists the very many bad things that can happen to a writer to keep him –

and yet not superior to other people – and this is largely reflected in the representation of her own public persona in her epitext and in her poetry.

Atwood's handling of the "autobiographical pact" goes from the creation of a meta-iconography to a humorous treatment of the trivial. For example, many jokes and comments have been made, both in her poetry and in her epitext, about Atwood's curly hair. "Well, the hair / was always difficult" (MBH 123) claims the persona in "Shapechangers in Winter". On her blog and Twitter page similar comments abound from many readers with varying degrees of humour. Atwood's humorous attitude to her curly hair serves the purpose of reinforcing the pact and playing into the readers'/audience's desire to interact with the "real" Atwood. But it is also a strategy to deal with the subject of aging, as Jamieson underlines in her analysis of the poem "Shapechangers in Winter" (Jamieson in Moss and Kozakewich 269-278).

Another example of Atwood's handling of the pact is perhaps to be found in her poem "Voice", previously quoted, and which I would like to come back to in order to show how Atwood both mocks and cherishes the iconized author. Throughout the volume, *The Tent*, Atwood not only chooses to stage her poetic voice as an aging voice, but also the speaker's reaction to this. And the speaker is both the public persona who is still receiving a fair amount of attention and the private persona observing the phenomenon of decline. The two personae (public and private) are grouped together in one entity designated as "us" ("Invitations to perform cascaded over us. All the best places wanted us", TT 22). But the plural of "us" also indicates that the two entities are separate, one causing the other to fear the end of an era. The decline of the "voice" is predictable. Like an aging actress who is deprived of her youthful beauty, the aging persona is deprived of her "voice". It is common knowledge, the speaker of the poem claims that, among the entourage of a writer, a "voice" can only occupy center stage for so long. Through the speaker's statement, Atwood emphasizes the physicality of the voice which, like a "dead shrub", begins to shrivel[9]. It becomes apparent why Atwood also underlines the fear experienced by the speaker as she observes the

---

him is assumed – from producing his best work. These include not only the practice of journalism – a bloodsucker for sure – but also popular success, getting too involved with political agendas, not having any money, and being a homosexual. About the most effective thing a writer could do to support himself, said Cyril Connolly – both he and I were living then in the age before the proliferation of grants – was to marry a rich woman. There wasn't much hope of this for me, but all other avenues, according to Connolly, were fraught with peril." (ND 66)

[9] As the persona indicates: "all at once, [...] people said – though not to me – my voice would thrive only for a certain term. Then, as voices do, it would begin to shrivel. Finally it would drop off, and I would be left alone, denuded – a dead shrub, a footnote." (TT 22).

"shrivelling". Her only advantage is that she is one step ahead of her entourage ("Only I have noticed it so far"). But she can clearly see it happening and is gradually overtaken by fear: "There's the barest pucker in my voice, the barest wrinkle" (TT 22). And fear is described as a spreading evil, "a needleful of ether, constricting what in someone else would be my heart" (TT 22). Atwood personifies the "voice" (all the while pointing to the artifice of this personification – "constricting what in someone else would be my heart", TT 22): she does so in order to underline the power of this rampant fear. However, it is the humour and not the fear which predominates as the last paragraph of the poem reveals:

> Soon it will be time for us to go out. We'll attend a luminous occasion, the two of us, chained together as always. I'll put on its favourite dress, its favourite necklace. I'll wind fur around it, to protect it from the drafts. Then we'll descend to the foyer, glittering like ice, my voice attached like an invisible vampire to my throat. (TT 23)

In this last paragraph the representation of the voice as a persona is intertwined with the representation of the speaker herself. The two are pictured as one celebrity attending a "luminous occasion". They are "chained together as always". The voice-persona acts as a dictator, depriving the speaker of an ordinary life, enveloping her with a glamorous dress and necklace, but, ultimately, leading her to a decline that no one escapes from. The metaphor of the vampire attached to the speaker's throat is particularly eloquent in revealing how much life and blood the speaker is allowing her "voice" to suck out of her. The humour of the poem "Voice" is very similar to Atwood's own humour in personal exchanges. For example, in a private conversation with Reena Khandpur and myself, Margaret Atwood commented[10] on readers who want to see celebrities like herself on TV or in glossy magazines and follow them as they get older: "They want to watch you decay". Atwood is prompt to mock the public's eagerness to leer on the less glamorous elements of the lives of "celebrities" and perhaps this serves as a reminder that the audience's attention is not as valuable as those who dream of fame think it is.

While the act of de-iconizing an icon has become a virtual trademark of Atwood's later work, so too has the act of humanizing the icon. It is particularly

---

[10] This conversation took place as we were heading for breakfast before the Ottawa interviews. A lady came up to Margaret and commented on the author's hair which was no longer dyed black: "I preferred you with black hair", said the lady. Atwood smiled politely and we went off to our breakfast table where she proceeded to mimic some of the ludicrous comments she gets from total strangers and smiled again as she shrugged them off.

apparent in Atwood's last volumes of poetry *The Tent* and *The Door*. And poems such as "A Voice" (TT 20-23) and "Owl and Pussycat, Some Years Later" (TD 29-34) remind the reader of Atwood's "Shapechangers in Winter" (MBH 120-125). At one point "the past / lets go of and becomes the future" (124). And "the trick is [then] just to hold on / through all appearances; and so we do" (MBH 125). Atwood resorts to humour to lead the way, for all of us reflecting on aging, whether iconic figures or not.

CHAPTER 13

Atwood on the Internet: Epitextual Strategies and Categories of Voices

Critics, journalists, biographers, and Atwood's many collaborators (agents and publishers) have commented on Atwood's "public persona voice" on the Internet. In the age of digital technology where so many commentaries concerning public personae are readily available, these voices are part of an author's epitext; the term epitext is to be taken in its broad sense here, that is everything the author says or writes outside the creative work itself. Here I must refer to Genette who defines three notions in his theoretical book *Paratexts: Thresholds of Interpretation*: the paratext, the peritext and the epitext. In defining those terms, Genette is interested in the relationship between books and readers – and, at times, in how other discourses by authors (and by publishers involved in presenting the bounded volumes) stand between books and readers. The difficulty in understanding the concept of the paratextual is that it has no fixed location, located, as it were, in the cartographically blurry critical space that Genette calls "threshold". The paratextual elements are arranged so as to introduce the work and contextualize it. The possible forms of epitexts can be extremely diverse and scattered over all the existing types of media. To convey the core elements of the relationship between the different elements of the paratext, Genette formulates a simple algorithm: "Paratext = peritext + epitext". The peritext includes elements "inside" the confines of a bound volume – in other words, everything between and on the covers. The epitext, then, denotes elements "outside" the bound volume – public or private elements such as interviews, reviews, correspondence, diaries etc. The author's epitext includes new forms of language to support different tones and voices. Atwood provides us with a fascinating example as she interacts dynamically with her large audience.

I will first describe the different Internet voices, focusing on the main categories of voices (Margaret Atwood's office voice, social media voice from her blog voice and her Twitter voice) and other media voices (such as the one Atwood uses on the radio, on TV or with the press), and highlight their similarities and specificities. I will also focus on Atwood's experimentation with Internet technology. I will take the example of two book tours concerning the last two volumes of her trilogy – *The Year of the Flood* and *Maddaddam* – as well as

Atwood's experimentation with Wattpad and Fanadoo to illustrate how Atwood's use of the Internet serves several purposes: from reinforcing the "autobiographical pact" to conveying key messages all the while experimenting with different forms of language, Atwood capitalizes on social media and other Internet functionalities.

MARGARET ATWOOD'S OFFICE VOICE, SOCIAL MEDIA VOICE AND TWITTER VOICE

Trying to describe Margaret Atwood's voice on the Internet is a complex task because it is impossible to cover all the material concerning the author on the Internet (nearly 5 million links appear when you google Margaret Atwood). However the Margaret Atwood official website is a good place to start; it was revamped in 2013 and it is connected to many different Atwood voices on many other sites or platforms. The voices can be put into four categories I wish to define: Margaret Atwood's office voice, her Internet article voice, her social media voice and her Twitter voice.

To start with the "office voice", O. W. Toad is an anagram of the letters in Atwood's last name and it is also the office's company name. Therefore I will call Atwood's "office voice" the O.W. Toad voice. In the pre-2013 version of Atwood's site, the information given on the home page was less impersonal than in the new version of her site. In both versions, the O.W. Toad voice describes the way the office is run, indicating the role of Atwood's assistant, Sarah Webster, and mentioning other full-time or part-time employees. In the pre-2013 version, Atwood's home-page address used to be signed with Margaret Atwood's own hand signature and it was accompanied by a very attractive and recent picture of the author smiling warmly. Removing the picture and signature, in the new version of the site, may be Atwood's way of removing the pedestal that her fans persistently place her on. It may also simply point to a desire for change, a web design that looks more focused on the books themselves rather than the author. While the new version shows visuals of her books, in both versions of Atwood's site, the O.W. Toad voice makes a number of statements (concerning Atwood's work and schedule) and provides answers to frequently asked questions[1]. The

---

[1] Examples of FAQs on Atwood's site: Can you provide me with a blurb for my book?
Can you read my manuscript and help me get published?
Can you tell me what a particular poem / novel ending / symbol means?
Can you come and read at our university / reading series / charity fundraiser?
Can you donate something for my charitable cause?
Can I have permission to reprint an Atwood work?

tone of the voice is professional, business-like, practical, precise, polite and concise. In other words, it indicates clearly what type of information the office can or cannot provide. Indeed, if the O.W. Toad voice welcomes the "visitor" on Atwood's website, it is also quite an expert at turning the "visitor" down politely. The contact page includes a message which clarifies things to anyone who is about to send Margaret Atwood a request on any of the subjects which are commonly addressed to Atwood's office (this message used to be on the home page). Atwood's office has clearly anticipated who will be visiting the website (readers, publishers, and fellow writers) and for what purpose (written blurbs or quotations, advice to writers, participation in events and donation to charities and causes)[2], and the O.W. Toad voice is given a role to play in informing visitors about what can and cannot be expected from Margaret Atwood.

It is the same O.W. Toad voice which communicates publicly on every issue related to Margaret Atwood's work, commitments and book tours. The O.W. Toad voice speaks for Atwood as a writer, but also as an *engaged* writer and she never misses an opportunity to highlight the organizations with which she is involved or which she supports, whether in connection with the environment[3], literature[4] or business[5]. Atwood's official website lists out all the links related to

---

What is your favourite book? Colour? Food?

[2] For example, on the home page, it greets the reader with the following warm welcome: "Welcome readers! I am very pleased that you are interested in my writing and I hope this site helps you find what you are looking for." The website also includes a full list of guidelines about what the office, can and cannot do: "1. Due to the sheer volume of requests I receive, for any and all requests, the office and I require a minimum of one week's advance notice. Any requests that we receive on short notice will be declined.
2. For many, many years, I have not written blurbs or quotations for other books (See http://www.margaretatwood.ca/book_blurbs.php). The volume was simply too high.
3. I cannot write an introduction to your book.
4. Advice to writers can be found on this website, in my book *Negotiating with the Dead: A Writer on Writing*, in my various books of essays, and on my blog from time to time, through www.yearoftheflood.com.
5. For legal reasons, I cannot read unpublished manuscripts; please do not send your manuscript.
6. I already give to a large number of charities and causes; please do not add to the requests. We're full up.
7. My office can no longer send 'sorry, can't do it' or 'Thank you for the book' replies to solicitations as above, books sent, or other such items. Please think about the paper, postage, and fuel wasted with each request. Thank you for respecting our planet!"
[3] BirdLife, Forest Stewardship Council, Markets Initiative, Nature Conservancy, Pelee Island Bird Observatory, World Wildlife Fund.
[4] Griffin Poetry Prize, Harbourfront Centre International Readings, League of Canadian Poets, PEN Canada, Writers' Union of Canada, Literature for Life.
[5] LongPen evolved into the iDoLVine platform. See Natalie Samson's article entitled "LongPen goes digital as iDoLVine" (Quill & Quire blog May 17, 2011).

these activities. Furthermore, the O.W. Toad voice provides information on where to find the author on blogs and social media websites and points to the other Atwood voices on the Internet. Several voices labeled "Atwood" are not managed by Atwood herself: for example, Margaret Atwood's official Facebook page is not monitored by Atwood herself, but by her publishers (yet another voice under the Atwood umbrella) which highlights Atwood's work for obvious promotional purposes.

Margaret Atwood has a blog (http://marg09.wordpress.com/) and she is present on many social media, including Twitter. Office voice, blog voice, Twitter voice: what distinguishes these three cyberspace voices? The differences have as much to do with the type of social media itself as with Atwood's way of using these media because Atwood simply adjusts to the specificities of each type of media. Thus Atwood's blog voice is not an office voice. Unlike the O.W. Toad voice which speaks in anticipation of requests, the blog voice spontaneously posts articles and comments. However, it seems that Atwood has neglected her blog in favour of other modes of online presence. The comments on her blog date back to 2012, for example: "My Tribute to Jay MacPherson, Delivered at Victoria College, June 11, 2012", "Looking Back on Earth Day 2010", and "Dead Author T-shirts". The blog voice is very journalistic but it is also the voice that gradually withdraws into silence, the voice that encourages interaction between readers and fans by providing a space for them to meet and communicate, but which rarely joins in the conversation. Indeed, Atwood does not respond to comments left on her blog and many of the readers' comments are not worded in anticipation of a reply: they mostly express appreciation for Atwood's blog postings (some simply thank Atwood for her posts). Margaret's blog voice is present not just on her own blog (although discreetly) but on other blogs, namely in blog articles where she makes meta-communicational comments about social media.

While the blog voice is casual and humorous or journalistic, it is not as chatty and interactive as the Twitter voice. The Twitter voice seems to be one that Atwood enjoys most in cyberspace (it may also be the reason why she neglected the blog voice): the Twitter voice is the one that frequently makes jokes, brings all the fresh news, and never fails to make an appearance in the form of a post, several times a week. Frequently, this voice will get involved in interacting with readers, fellow artists, fellow activists and friends. Indeed, Atwood not only understands the power of Twitter but she also seems to enjoy using the tool and does so at regular intervals: her "followers" can read a couple of lines by her every week. From the comments in response to her tweets, I gather that most followers, like her fans, enjoy being kept informed about everything concerning her schedule, and they usually find her tweets instructive (there are many tweets where Atwood shares the material she reads[6] or the places and things she discovers). Atwood has perfected a tweeting style which allows her to pack in a great deal of humour into the 140 character limit: for example, on March 2, 2013, as she comes back to Toronto after much traveling: "Now, jet-lagged, I will bump into furniture for a while and catch up tomorrow... Nitee Nite".

Tweeting is such a regular habit and Atwood uses the platform so effectively, that she now has about half a million fans. As a result, Atwood is not just on Twitter now: she is in Tweetwood. Tweetwood is the land of Twitter celebrities[7] where users have access to celebrity tweets and conversation, and where trends are mapped out in relation to these tweets. In Atwood's case, the main trends highlighted on Tweetwood at the beginning of 2013 are her latest writing on Wattpad (Maddaddam) and the festivals and events she has attended and her latest endorsements – which we will come back to, as we highlight how Atwood's epitext and "real life" commitments affect the "autobiographical pact".

If many writers and amateurs have embraced the idea of poetry on Twitter, Atwood has not done so herself. What Atwood's Twitter voice achieves is mainly the communication of quick and concise information which have a potential to go viral. Indeed Atwood herself has not gone into exploring the specificities of a 140-character poetic voice and she repetitively highlights the value of Twitter for the promotion of ideas or products. It is difficult to determine a cross-fertilization between her tweets and poetry[8] because of the sheer volume of Atwood's non-poetic tweets. That is not to say that none of her tweets are poetic but her followers are given the impression that Atwood does not set out to be poetic and prefers the spontaneous and quick communication on Twitter to the elaborate,

---

[6] For example : on Feb 26 2013: "50 unseen Rudyard Kipling poems discovered http://gu.com/p/3e38y/tw via @guardian" and on March 1 2013: "On plane, read What Matters in Jane Austen? by John Mullan. 'Twas vastly entertaining, I declare! (Fans self. Picks strawberry. Blushes.)"

[7] Tweetwood is the largest celebrity portal based on Twitter, with more than 3000 Twitter celebrities categorized into different sub portals (by nationality, artistic category, etc.). Along with all the standard functionality users see on Twitter, Tweetwood has a number of features allowing users to track and share twitter conversations between celebrities. Twitter trends gives users a quick glimpse of what is trending among celebrities. Trends on Tweetwood are different from Twitter trends as they are based on celebrity tweets which are said to be a better measurement of popularity.

[8] Cross-fertilization does occur. For example, the bottle image Atwood uses in her poetry resurfaces in one of her Twitter comments on Feb 28, 2013: speaking about an appearance, she says: "... it wasn't me. But I have bottled my voice for insomniacs. That'll be $50 a drop." Indeed, this Twitter comment implies that celebrity's voice is in the bottle. A price tag is added, to the metaphor which runs from her poem "A Sibyl" to "Bottle".

finely constructed approach of groups such as the Twitter Poetry group [9]. Atwood's promotion of poetry on the Internet has found other outlets in which the 140-character restriction does not apply.

REINFORCING THE AUTOBIOGRAPHICAL PACT

One of the most powerful things about Atwood's use of the Internet and different forms of social media such as Twitter is that it allows the reinforcement of the "autobiographical pact". This is achieved through various strategies which I would now like to suggest and illustrate. For easier future reference to these strategies, I will assign them a reference letter from A to D:

A. The first strategy consists in achieving "real virtual presence" on a network of social media. It is indeed the "real" Margaret Atwood who achieves this "virtual presence" which her followers find so attractive.
B. Secondly, Atwood excels in meta-communication which leads to a "realness" effect as she includes anecdotes about herself communicating in the Web 2.0 era and as she enters the debate concerning new strategies for publishing and promotion.
C. Thirdly, Awood's experimentation with new forms of media, from Twitter to Wattpad and Fanado, fuels the media with stories about Atwood and her curiosity or endorsement of new technologies. Atwood remains present in her readers' minds as a "real" person trying out new things and embracing modernity.
D. The fourth and last strategy occurs when the themes to be found in Atwood's poetic and fictional work are illustrated and reinforced, through personal engagement and activism of the author. The reader who is familiar both with the author's creative work and her personal commitments to various causes will appreciate the coherence between the author's "real" life and imaginative life.

---

[9] See Charlotte Cripps's article entitled "Twihaiku? Micropoetry? The rise of Twitter poetry" (*The Independent* 16 July, 2013). Also see Kaitlin Hawkins comments about "writers, translators, poets, and authors [who are increasingly] getting creative with their Tweets [...]. Micro poetry, flash fiction, and mini-stories often appear in the Twitterverse from the feeds of well-known writers, including Margaret Atwood (@MargaretAtwood), Sherman Alexie (@Sherman_Alexie), and Salman Rushdie (@SalmanRushdie). One user, @TalesonTweet, is collecting such tiny creative pieces from authors around the globe in an effort to promote creativity and literature across Twitter." in her article "Tales on Tweet." (worldliteraturetoday.org September 6, 2012).

Let us illustrate the above four points (summarized by the following key expressions: "real virtual presence", "meta-communication", "experimentation with new forms of media", "engagement and activism"), through various examples which often show how the different strategies are combined, resulting in an extremely effective reinforcement of the "autobiographical pact".

Atwood's "real virtual presence" on Twitter is what her followers find so attractive. It would be easy enough for her to sub-contract her tweets to her secretary but she prefers to write them herself. Her clever wording (both precise and humourous, as I've pointed out) give her tweets an "authentic" feel to them. Furthermore, Atwood's capacity for meta-communication needs to be underlined here. From her very first volumes of poetry onwards, Atwood has been known to reflect on the act of communication, exposing practices which lead to abuse, and underlining the importance of resistance. Feminist readings of *Power Politics* or *True Stories* for example highlight how Atwood exposes the language of the oppressive lover or ruler, and the one of the oppressed. In relation to new medias, Atwood's meta-communication is equally powerful, although perhaps less serious in tone. Her playful speech at the O'Reilly Tools of Change for Publishing (TOC) conference in 2012[10] about the writer's share of the "publishing pie" getting increasingly smaller is an example of her recent reflection on how new communication and publishing tools impact on the writer's financial situation and therefore his/her very capacity to survive and write. Another example that I would like to expand on here is Atwood's commentaries of her use of Twitter as it will give me an opportunity to illustrate all four of the above mentioned strategies – from A to D.

On different occasions which are reported on various media, Atwood has explained how she plunged into the world of Twitter; the most complete account of this event is to be found on the New York Book Review blog (NYRblog) on March 29, 2010. In this article, Atwood turns the whole Twitter discovery process into the story of a mature writer embarking on a Web 2.0 adventure, thus simultaneously illustrating strategies A, B and C: she highlights her "real virtual presence" on Twitter (strategy A), and portrays herself as someone who explores

---

[10] To summarize Atwood's talk at the 2012 TOC conference, "Publishing" originally meant simply to make public. That meaning, and the processes and technologies by which "publishing" has taken place, has changed radically over the years, and is in the process of changing yet again. The pie – the author and work, and the packaging and sale of the latter – has been divided up in various ways through the years, with bigger and smaller pieces for members of the book chain. We are now in the midst of the largest publishing changes and challenges since Gutenberg. How will they affect the author? What tools are newly available to him/her? Atwood's talk was illustrated with her own drawings.

and embraces new communication tools (strategy C) and, finally (strategy B), she unfolds a full meta-communication commentary by telling us about how she became a regular Tweeter. Indeed, she explains how she came to understand the logic and usefulness of Twitter. From opening an account, to building a base of "followers", Atwood portrays herself "diligently" asking for advice every step along the way[11]. Her tone is humorous, self-mocking. For example, Atwood explains that, as she attempted to set up a Twitter account, she discovered that there were already two Margaret Atwoods on Twitter and so she reacted immediately: "I gave commands; then all other Margaret Atwoods stopped together. I like to think they were sent to a nunnery, but in any case they disappeared. The Twitter police had got them. I felt a bit guilty." (NYRblog March 29, 2010). Atwood discovered the effectiveness of Twitter and "one follower led to another [and] the numbers snowballed". Since her comment on the New York Book Review blog, Atwood has not only gained hundreds of thousands of followers but she has managed to make Twitter a key promotional tool. Further comments on the process of tweeting include remarks on:

- Twitter's promotional effectiveness (she explains how useful Twitter was in attracting an audience at some badly-planned "Year of the Flood" event),
- Twitter vocabulary which Atwood revels in learning – mainly acronyms such as "LMAO ('Laughing My Ass Off,' as one Twitterpal informed me)",
- Twitter's addictiveness (she voluntarily admits to being "sucked into the Twittersphere like Alice down the rabbit hole").

Atwood's description of the Twittersphere is in itself a creative treatment of the Twitter reality. Atwood combines strategies A, B and C[12], strengthening the autobiographical pact, but she also adds playful metaphors, giving the whole story an elaborate fictional quality. For example, Atwood describes the

---

[11] In Atwood's own terms: "I was told I needed 'followers.' These were people who would sign on to receive my messages, or "tweets," whatever those might turn out to be. I hummed a few bars from 'Mockingbird Hill' – Tra-la-la, twittly-deedee – and sacrificed some of my hair at the crossroads, invoking Hermes the Communicator. He duly appeared in the form of media guru McLean Greaves, who loosed his carrier pigeons to four of his hundreds of Twitterbuddies; and with their aid, I soon had a few thousand people I didn't know sending me messages like 'OMG! Is it really you?' 'I love it when old ladies blog,' one early follower remarked." (NYRblog March 29, 2010)

[12] As previously mentioned, these strategies are: A. "real virtual presence", B. meta-communication, C. embracing of new technologies.

characteristics of the Twittersphere contributors, comparing her Twitter followers to fairies as if she were speaking about a magic land: the followers provide advice, she explains, on technical elements she is not familiar with and they help her promote her work:

> The Twittersphere is an odd and uncanny place. It's something like having fairies at the bottom of your garden. How do you know anyone is who he/she says he is, especially when they put up pictures of themselves that might be their feet, or a cat, or a Mardi Gras mask, or a tin of Spam? (NYRblog March 29, 2010)

The Twitter contributors who are like "fairies" are surprisingly efficient and they amuse and intrigue Atwood with their "Mardi Gras mask[s]". The description moves away from fairy-tale and carnival metaphors and provides concrete examples to illustrate the support Atwood receives when she is looking for specific information – such as "artificially-grown pig flesh, unusual slugs, and the like" (NYRblog March 29, 2010). Further details are given as Atwood marvels at the ability of her followers to "deduce" her interests and to produce promotional material – such as a badge which reads "call me a visionary, because I do a pretty convincing science dystopia" (NYRblog March 29, 2010). Twitter's concrete results are listed[13]: Twitter reinforces the support she receives when she goes on book tours as the example of special badges made by followers indicates.

Beyond the energizing book-tour support reported by the author herself, Atwood says she enjoys the interaction with Twitter followers, especially when she needs to do research for her writing. It is the swiftness of their responses which she finds most striking: "They're sharp: make a typo and they're on it like a shot, and they tease without mercy. However, if you set them a verbal challenge, a frisson sweeps through them." Atwood gives examples of verbal challenges and typo corrections. For example: "[My Twitter followers] did very well with definitions for "dold socks"—one of my typos—and "Thnax," another one." What gives Atwood a particular thrill is when she finds that her followers surpass themselves in creativity by coming up with self-mocking and politically

---

[13] Atwood lists out what she has managed to do thanks to the help of her followers: "But despite their sometimes strange appearances, I'm well pleased with my followers – I have a number of techno-geeks and bio-geeks, as well as many book fans. They're a playful but also a helpful group. If you ask them for advice, it's immediately forthcoming: thanks to them, I learned how to make a Twitpic photo appear as if by magic, and how to shorten a URL using bit.ly or tinyurl. They've sent me many interesting items [...] (They deduce my interests.) Some of them have appeared at tour events bearing small packages of organic shade-grown fair-trade coffee." (NYRblog March 29, 2010)

correct responses to her own comments: "[T]hey really shone when, during the Olympics, I said that 'Own the podium' was too brash to be Canadian, and suggested 'A podium might be nice'." (NYRblog March 29, 2010) And Atwood then lists out the variations of this phrase which poured onto a feed tagged #cpodium: "'A podium! For me?' 'Rent the podium, see if we like it.' 'Mind if I squeeze by you to get onto that podium?' (NYRblog March 29, 2010). "I was so proud of [my followers]", Atwood concludes, "It was like having 33,000 precocious grandchildren!" (NYRblog March 29, 2010)

The number of "precocious grandchildren" has multiplied by almost twenty since Atwood made the above comment. Many followers enjoy the verbal challenges on Atwood's Twitter page. Others like to be active in Atwood's causes: "They raise funds for charity via things like Twestival, they solicit donations for catastrophe victims, they send word of upcoming events" (NYRblog March 29, 2010). The Twitter experience is not always a pleasant one for Atwood. Some visitors express their disagreement, dislike or rejection. In Atwood's own terms: "Once in a while, they're naughty: I did get word of a fellow who'd made a key safe by hollowing out one of my books. (Big yuks from his pals, one of whom ratted him out to me and even sent a pic.)" But Atwood knows how to defend herself: "[A]fter I threatened to put the Purple Cross-eyed Zozzle Curse on him, he assured me that no disrespect was intended. (He was forgiven.)" (NYRblog March 29, 2010). Another example of meta-communication about Twitter is when Atwood compares Twitter to the activity of diary writing and letter writing or even to that of African drumming ("Even African tribal drums, for instance, could send very complex messages over great distances")[14]. Atwood underlines that these forms of communication (from diary writing to African drumming) are no different in nature from the things we have always been doing: "communicat[ing] with one another, send[ing] messages to one another, and perform[ing] our lives. We've been doing that for a long time." (Atwood on Big Think Jan 8, 2014) Atwood's meta-communicational comments

---

[14] See the following paragraph: "People used to perform their lives [...] to themselves in their diaries, and also through letters to other people. So for me, anything that happens in social media is an extension of stuff we were already doing in some other way. So, it's all human communication. And the form that most closely resembles the "tweet" is the telegram of old, which also was limited because you paid by the letter. And so short communications very rapidly sent.
So all of these things, the postal service, et cetera, they're all improvements, if you like, or modernizations of things that already existed earlier in some other form. Even African tribal drums, for instance, could send very complex messages over great distances. They were very rapid, they were very well-worked out and communications could just go like wildfire using that medium of communications." (in Miller Big Think Jan 2, 2014)

about Twitter provide the author with an opportunity to contrast the evolution of society to the continuity of the human stuff we are made of. Indeed, our need to communicate quickly and efficiently is not new, and neither is it specific to our Western culture. However technology offers new possibilities of achieving quick communication to an ever widening group. It also allows us to "perform our lives" in instantaneous multimedia ways. But neither the degree of efficiency in communications nor the way in which we "perform our lives" changes the nature of fundamental communicational needs. Audience and mirrors are recurrent tropes in Atwood's poetry. Lines such as "You ask [...] / for the one forbidden thing: / love without mirrors and not for / my reasons but your own." (PP 55), read as yet another comment on our need for mirrors (like the "you" in the poem "They were all inaccurate", PP 55) which we often mistake for love. As the age of the Internet is providing an excess of mirrors and performance opportunities, Atwood's creative message is only reinforced, leading the reader to reflect on the narcissistic functioning of both individuals and society as a whole.

CRITICAL RESPONSE TO ATWOOD'S PRESENCE ON THE INTERNET AND DEDICATION TO ART

There are a number of on-going debates about Atwood's presence and her views on Twitter. These debates will give me an opportunity to show how Atwood's "autobiographics" on the Internet voice is thematically related to interrogation in her creative work and to comments in *Negotiating with the Dead* (the D strategy, in relation to the autobiographical pact). One of the themes to be found in Atwood's poetic and fictional work, has to do with the writer's dedication to his/her art. The reader who is familiar both with the author's creative work and with her personal commitment to writing routines will appreciate the coherence and similarities in the messages conveyed by the author's "real" life and her imaginative life. Atwood's presence on the Internet has not put into question her theory about a writer's dedication to his/her art, nor has it threatened her own creative life by bringing in too many distractions. On the contrary it has come to reinforce the autobiographical pact because her central message concerning artistic creation (expressed in *Negotiating with the Dead* but also in her fiction and poetry) has been put to the test and seen to hold up, thus leading the readers of her creative work to think that Atwood *speaks from experience*.

We may start with the critical debate which set in when Atwood shared her view that "Twitter, internet boost[ed] literacy"[15]. At the Toronto nextMEDIA conference (for media professionals) in December 2011, she claimed: "I would say that reading, as such, has increased. And reading and writing skills have probably increased because what all this texting and so forth replaced was the telephone conversation." She also emphasized that people had to actually be able to read and write to use the Internet and concluded: "So it's a great literacy driver if kids are given the tools and the incentive to learn the skills that allow them to access it." (ibidem). Critics respond to Atwood's position by saying Twitter has a diluting effect on the written word, to which Atwood argues: "It doesn't depend on the technology, it depends on the users…"[16], which leads to more debates and criticism concerning the decrease of literary quality that comes with rash publication[17]. Atwood, however, does not get drawn into these debates. As we have pointed out in relation to her "blog voice", she often makes a point on a given media (in an article, or on the radio for example) and then allows the interaction to carry on without her.

Negotiating with the Dead is probably Atwood's best defense to any criticism that may arise in connection with her comments in the media. Although *Negotiating with the Dead* was written before Atwood took to social media, her mode of presence on Twitter is an illustration of her advice to young writers in that it shows that the discipline mapped out in *Negotiating with the Dead* always prevails when it comes to her creative work. The Internet is not a place where Atwood embarks on a collaborative writing adventure even if she enjoys the help from followers on particular questions. The skills involved in sending out a call for help on specific questions and then sifting through the responses without getting sucked into wasting hours of writing time on these matters, may not be something that a budding writer fully masters – hence the relevance of *Negotiating with the Dead* in the social media era. Indeed, the concept of protecting the gift sphere has not been outdated by Twitter. Not only does it still apply in the age of Internet communication but perhaps it is all the more important given the strength of character that it takes to isolate oneself from the

---

[15] See Margo Kelly's article: "Margaret Atwood says Twitter, internet boost literacy" (CBC Jan 8, 2014).

[16] See comments on the Biblioklept blog (Biblioklept.org) from Jan 10, 2014 onwards.

[17] One criticism to Atwood's comment read: "[Atwood] says one of the positives of Twitter is the ability to get your questions answered quickly. From a literary or creative perspective, she misses the idea that convenience and speed are not necessarily positive qualities. What about the inspiration that comes from searching for an answer in a conversation with a stranger on the bus, or the encounters on a walk to a library?" (Turner Biblioklept Jan 11, 2012)

temptations of spending time on social media. For Atwood, interacting with hundreds of thousands of followers could have turned into a full-time job but it has not. Atwood's use of Twitter illustrates how she embodies the balance between relationship to and separation from others – a subject extensively developed in *Negotiating with the Dead*.

While this is one important example of Atwood's recommendations, her comments published on the Internet highlight the very themes of her work. I would now like to turn to the "Year of the Flood" tour for another example of concordance between her Internet epitext and themes to be found in her creative writing.

MARGARET ATWOOD'S VOICE DURING THE "YEAR OF THE FLOOD" TOUR

The "Year of the Flood" tour is a unique tour which I will describe in full before showing that it is another striking example of strategy D, where Atwood's many epitextual voices are all in keeping with the themes to be found in Atwood's poetic and fictional work. Indeed, the "Year of the Flood" tour provides an illustration of how Atwood's personal commitment and activism present a harmonious fit which strengthens the autobiographical pact.

As extensively reported by the media, on the eve of her 70th birthday, Canadian writer Margaret Atwood set out on a highly innovative international book tour[18], criss-crossing both the British Isles and North America for the launch of her new dystopian novel, *The Year of the Flood*. What led Margaret Atwood (who seemed so averse to doing author tours that she invented the "LongPen"[19]), to embark on such an adventure? This 16-week, six-country tour involved staged readings as well as musical performances. Starting her tour on October 4 2009 in Denver, she appeared in 10 U.S. cities and many more British Isles locations. In a press release issued by her office (the O.W. Toad voice), Atwood claims she chose not to mount a traditional tour:

> I wanted to do some non-publishing things of mine, such as raise awareness of rare-bird vulnerability and heighten Virtuous Coffee

---

[18] Many journalists reported on the novelty of Atwood's book tour – for example, James Bradshaw in "Atwood Promotes New Book via Live Theatre" (*The Globe and Mail* August 17, 2009) and Bruce DeMara in "Margaret Atwood Offers More Bang for the Book" (*The Toronto Star* August 18, 2009).

[19] "LongPen" is an electronic book-signing device authors can use to sign physical books in remote locations while on a virtual book tour. See Oliver Burkeman's online article in *The Guardian* in March 2006 (entitled "Atwood sign of the times draws blank").

> Consumption (Arabica, shade-grown, doesn't kill birds) and blog the seven-country dramatic-and-musical book tour we were about to do. Anyway, the publishers were at that time hiding under rocks, as it was still the Great Financial Meltdown, not to mention the Horrid Tsunami of Electronic Book Transmission. "That sounds wonderful, Margaret," they said, with the queasy encouragement shown by those on the shore waving goodbye to someone who's about to shoot Niagara Falls in a barrel. (NYRblog March 29, 2010)

The criticism voiced by professionals and humorously reported by the author herself only underlines the audacity of Atwood's new book tour concept. For this "non-publishing" tour Atwood conceived and executed something totally unexpected: a theatrical version of her novel: several cities were treated to a full hour-long performance, with Atwood as narrator, and local actors acting out scenes, and local choir singing a selection of the 14 hymns of the novel (one hymn for each chapter, with music composed by Orville Stoeber). To say a few words about the novel, *The Year of the Flood* is the second volume of Atwood's dystopial trilogy (which starts with *Oryx and Crake* and is then followed by *The Year of the Flood* and *MaddAddam*). *The Year of the Flood* follows a cult of spiritual gardeners who survive an ecological apocalypse described as the "waterless flood". The book is partially constructed around the hymns scattered throughout the book and sung by its heroes and heroines. Many of the hymns are sung in praise to a specific new millennial patron saint whose knowledge, experience and wisdom they believe holds a key to spiritual and environmental rebirth— philosopher Henry David Thoreau, environmentalist Rachel Carson, naturalist Euell Gibbons, and handicapped Canadian athlete Terry Fox among them. Thus the novel contains a patchwork of voices many of which serve to illustrate the dangers of totalitarian regimes, in the same vein as other great dystopian novels by Atwood, namely *The Handmaid's Tale* and *Oryx and Crake*. Sady Doyle, in his article entitled "Dystopia, for the 'Lulz'" published on the *In these Times* website, commented on Atwood's dystopian trilogy as well as on the book tour and the author's promotional and non-promotional public appearances simply to underline how this well-established author no longer had anything to prove and therefore could "do what she like[d]":

> Of all the Great Living North American Writers, Margaret Atwood may be having the most fun. Having firmly established her cred as a serious writer with works like *The Edible Woman* and *The Handmaid's Tale*, she's now earned the right to a certain level of goofiness: Spending her

days on Twitter, attending Comic-Con, and devoting the past 10 years to a post-apocalyptic saga filled with bad puns and mutant pig-beasts. It's hard not to envy her: She's done her work and assured her legacy—now gets to do what she likes. (Doyle, in.these.times.com August 22, 2013)

This comment puts Atwood's recently-published trilogy in a different category from her previous work: Doyle places the author's best "serious" work behind her and considers her present work to be the expression of a well-earned freedom: the right to "[go for] a certain level of goofiness". This criticism of Atwood's trilogy is further expanded in the article with the analysis of several of Atwood's recent characters – for example: "[Zeb] never seems as rich or as complicated as Atwood's characters at their finest" (Doyle, in.these.times.com August 22, 2013). Although Doyle's review is critical of Atwood's trilogy, it is also a tribute to the author's ambition to write a story about "the end of humanity" and it echoes many critical commentaries which praise Atwood for her ability to weave into her fiction ecological themes which are of the greatest importance today[20]. It may also be worth pointing out that Atwood is experimenting with a new type of voice in the trilogy: this voice seems to think in terms of future cinematographic adaptations, turning many situations of the novels into scenes the reader can visualize vividly. As Atwood appears to be highly aware of the theatrical potential of the *Year of the Flood*, she has extracted scenes that work well visually in order to script a performance for her book tour. This script is like a storyboard of her novel: it is composed of 26 sequences taken from the novel, alternating between a narrator's voice summarizing events, the choir voices singing hymns which are neo-pagan rituals and which emphasize Atwood's

---

[20] These comments leave aside what Michele Roberts describes as "the fullness of [Atwood's] text, re-made by the shared activity of writer and reader." Robert comments on how Atwood demonstrates "foreground[s] questions of storytelling, writing and creativity [in p]rominently displaying the way she has constructed her novel, she forces the reader to understand that this is part of its subject. We are not allowed to be passive consumers of her tale but have to pay attention to how stories arrive, change and last." (*The Independent* August 16, 2013). Robert Lennon also focuses on the speculative genre and metafictional value of Atwood's text: "It should surprise no one that the author of such grand metafictions as *The Blind Assassin* would turn [the *MaddAddam*] trilogy into a manifesto about the power of language. But it does come as a surprise, a strangely satisfying one. Atwood's reinvention of herself as a bestselling speculative-fiction writer is the ultimate frame story here: the *MaddAddam* trilogy is, at its heart, a love letter to literature, the endlessly rewarding, protean pursuit that has sustained her, and that is lucky to have her as one of its foremost practitioners." (*The Globe and Mail* August 30, 2013). Finally, Peter Kemp argues that Atwood's *MaddAddam* "is both an adventure story and a philosophical meditation on humanity's predilection for carnage and creation." (*The Economist* September 21, 2013).

message in her novel[21] and the voices of characters experiencing given situations. These scenes that Atwood has chosen have different locations which are highly representative of the novel's wide range of sites, and the situations are extremely colourful (such as the scene where Toby, with her binoculars, spots a couple of people in the distance: three men in camouflage outfit leading a huge bird on a leash. This bird has blue-green iridescent plumes and the head of a woman; the bird woman is in fact Toby's friend Ren, dressed up in glitz and fleeing Scales and Tails where she had been locked up and waiting to be rescued). Such colourful scenes often include surprise effects which work equally well from a cinematographic point of view, offering suspense and special effects through movements, costumes and backdrops. This example illustrates how Atwood has developed the skills of creating a narrative voice as a clever "picture maker" according to Butler's definition. Indeed Butler highlights the importance of the narrative voice thinking in terms of the "basic building blocks of a film" in order to craft a story which is likely to work well cinematographically:

> The shot is the basic building block of a film [...]. And, of course, shots are connected into scenes and scenes are developed into sequences [...]. These concepts describe not only the inevitable flow of the film but also the narrative voice as picture maker. These pictures have a life in time. They begin, they develop, and they end in equivalents of the filmic concepts. As in film, it is the manipulation of these 'shots' accumulating into 'scenes' and 'sequences' that creates meaning and produces the rhythm of the voice of the narrator. (Butler 65-66)

In the *Year of the Flood* script Atwood displays her ability to extract scenes from her novel and turn them into an accumulation of shots, recreating the rhythm of the novel. In the "Wake of the Flood" which reports on the many unique performances of *Year of the Flood*, it becomes apparent how each of the interpretations of *Year of the Flood* script highlights the potential of Atwood's script in terms of theatrical adaptation.

Over the years, Atwood's collaboration with artists in different fields may have increased the author's interest in the synergies to be found in such collaborations. She has indeed seen the adaptation of several of her novels or short stories for theater or dance performances; she claims that she cannot take

---

[21] These hymns add popularity to the performance and they also highlight the mystical, Blakean overtones of Atwood's text. They were composed by Orville Stoeber, in a devotional style – influenced by a mixture of gospel, country ballads, jazz and folk.

credit for the artistic achievements of those who adapt her work, but she does delight in the opportunities of being invited to rehearsals and to comment on the on-going fine-tuning of the performance. It is hard to tell how this experience (on *The Handmaid's Tale* for example, adapted three times, as a film, a musical, and a dance performance, or on various volumes of short stories[22]) has influenced her work, but since Atwood is naturally inclined to draw an artistic benefit from her diverse experiences, it is hardly surprising that the narrative voice of her later novels should have developed this cinematographic quality which her *Year of the Flood* book tour illustrates.

Atwood herself commented on the book tour by explaining that the non-traditional format of the tour served not only an ecological but also an artistic purpose: "It's a chance to break free from the traditional structure of a book tour" Atwood said in a statement to *The Toronto Star*[23], and she added: "It's also a great chance to work with other creative minds and see their interpretation of the story come to light."[24] The artistic goal, in the post-publication stage, became a collaborative one, as the author's wish was to encourage locally-produced performances and to make her book tour a participative and grass roots project: she joined volunteers in a loose-knit, production aiming at raising the public's awareness of, to quote Atwood on the tour, "the fragile natural world and our vital connection to it". With Atwood herself taking on the role (and voice) of the narrator, and with the input of a local cast, the theatrical version of *The Year of the Flood* was performed, in every city of the tour. Although Atwood did not repeat the experience for the promotion of the third novel in the trilogy, she took the opportunity of the *MaddAddam* book launch to reaffirm her ecological beliefs and values, and, as Atwood's trilogy is being translated into other languages, the experience of the unusual *The Year of the Flood* book tour expands to other countries: Japan and now France, with the "Festival Atlantides"[25] in Nantes.

---

[22] On the subject of the adaptation of Atwood's short stories, see Shannon Hengen's article "Sensory Appeal in *The Atwood Stories* on TV." (in Evain, Khandpur 35-42) and, more recently Jen Zoratti's article, "Choreographer's adaptation of Margaret Atwood's dystopian novel strikes current chord" (*Winnipeg Free Press* January 8, 2014) or Alison Flood's article, "Margaret Atwood Takes to Stage with Emmerdale and Only Fools Stars" (*The Guardian* August 19, 2009) and Stephen's Hunt review, "Artistic Worlds Collide for Choreographers at Alberta Dance Festival." (*Calgary Herald* August 31, 2013).

[23] This comment and many other comments by Atwood on her book tour were echoed by the press. See the press articles in bibliography.

[24] See press release on the *The Year of the Flood* site.

[25] It has been my privilege to translate the *Year of the Flood* performance into French.

COHERENCE BETWEEN THE CREATIVE AND PROMOTIONAL VOICES

The unique book tour for the launch of *The Year of the Flood* gives us an opportunity to hear the following voices performed on stage: Atwood's fiction voice (extracts of the novel itself), her poetic voice (as many poems equally highlight ecological preoccupations), her public persona voice, her activist voice and her different Internet voices previously mentioned. To this list, one should add Atwood's filmic voice on a documentary as Atwood's odyssey was captured in Ron Mann's film: "In the Wake of the Flood". Pushing the boundaries of what qualifies as a documentary, "In the Wake of the Flood" mixes footage of the tour, archival materials and evocative behind-the-scene material in featuring Atwood "on the road and at home as an aging but buoyant literary rock star spreading a message of warning and hope as she staged and participated in the novel production"[26].

The movie "In the Wake of the Flood" reveals the warm super-star welcome Atwood received in each community she visited. The documentary chronicles Atwood's journey from Edinburgh, London to New York City, Toronto and Vancouver. It evokes Atwood's adventurous childhood in the backwoods of northern Quebec, and features conversations with activists and fellow travelers. The movie also highlights Atwood's conception of the tour: to move beyond the presentation of her book and related ecological issues and to inspire her audience into awareness and civic action. Both the movie and the press underlined that, in keeping true to the novel's environmentally-conscious theme, Atwood left "a light carbon footprint behind her" (taking the train instead of traveling by air, whenever possible). The movie culminates in Sudbury, Ontario where the author is celebrated on her birthday. The movie press release thus concludes: "'In the Wake of the Flood' combines these artistic and narrative threads in its evocation of Atwood's achievement and worldview, following her as she shares her life and ecofable with her audience and us. 'In the final 100 days of my 69th year, I decided to change the way I'd been doing things.'"[27] While there is much to say about how the form of "autobiographics" contributes to the reinvention of the book tour, I now wish to comment on Atwood's handling of strategy D. This strategy, as previously mentioned, consists of reinforcing the links between poetic and fictional work through personal engagement.

---

[26] See press release on the *The Year of the Flood* site.
[27] See document uploaded by Atwood's assistant on docstoc: http://www.docstoc.com/docs/74700803/1-In-the-Wake-of-the-Flood and Brian Johnson's online article "In The Wake of the Flood. Margaret Atwood: The Year Of The Flood." (yearoftheflood.com March 9, 2013).

We may ask ourselves to what extent Atwood's "Flood tour voice" is coherent with the Atwoodian creative voice. Perhaps Atwood's voice, on this unusual book tour, does carry a message which is similar to the one in her poetry and one could go as far as to say that the "Flood tour voice" is a possible embodiment of poems by Atwood. Indeed, the form chosen by the "Flood tour voice" is more accessible than the poetic form and it is in direct contact with an audience greater than Atwood's poetry readership. However, this "Flood tour voice" is driven, I would suggest, by the same authentic belief as that expressed in many of Atwood's poems – a belief that commands a respect of the planet we live on. For example, "A Moment" from *Morning in the Burned House* conveys that very message by highlighting the importance of considering the land we live on not as a place we own but as a place we visit (or borrow from our descendants, as an old Indian saying puts it):

> The moment when, after many years
> of hard work and a long voyage
> you stand in the centre of your room,
> house, half-acre, square mile, island, country,
> knowing at last how you got there,
> and say, *I own this,*
>
> is the same moment when the trees unloose
> their soft arms from around you,
> the birds take back their language,
> the cliffs fissure and collapse,
> the air moves back from you like a wave
> and you can't breathe.
>
> No, they whisper. *You own nothing.*
> *You were a visitor, time after time*
> *climbing the hill, planting the flag, proclaiming.*
> *We never belonged to you.*
> *You never found us.*
> *It was always the other way round.* (MBH 109)

This poem is about striving – trying, struggling, pouring one's efforts into the universe – and, as a result, one is part of the universe. As soon as one stands back and says "now the job is done, I've completed it and I own *this*", everything is lost: one becomes divorced from the world. In other words: one is part of the world while struggling; one starts to die, one divorces oneself from the world, when one wants to sit back and *own* one's accomplishments.

The message of this poem which was published several years before *The Year of the Flood* is precisely the point Atwood is making when using her "Flood tour voice". In both cases Atwood addresses us – the "you" of the poem, the "you" of the book tour – to say that life is a process of constant discovery and issuing out the warning that, once "you" decide you no longer need to explore, and pour your efforts into the universe, then you have lost everything because you are no longer part of the universe. The "Flood tour voice" which mixes the many voices of the novel with the engaged author's voice defending ecological efforts entreats us to put more energy into "saving the planet". This same "Flood tour voice" views the world as a place borrowed from the generations after us as opposed to inherited from the ones before us, and this worldview has a direct consequence on how we treat nature and the world we live in – much like the voice of the poem "A Moment".

While this example serves to illustrate strategy D, it equally shows the power of poetry and its relation to an author's commitment to various causes. In a conference about Jorge Luis Borges, Alberto Manguel, echoing Malraux, said about writers such as Louis-Ferdinand Céline: "l'homme aurait dû lire l'écrivain"[28]. It is as if Atwood the activist had heeded Malraux's and Manguel's advice and taken inspiration from her own poetry in order to decide on how to lead her own life. This goes to show that the two-headed image in Atwood's poetry does not necessarily imply a totally schizophrenic nature and it is this coherence between the "person" and the "writer" which, we, the readers long to see, in our perhaps slightly childish need to hear the voice of role-models.

MARGARET ATWOOD ON WATTPAD AND FANADO

To complete this tour of Atwood's voices on the Internet, I would like to mention Atwood's experience on Wattpad and Fanado. These experiences show how Atwood's voice has the capacity not only to adapt to a changing environment but to speak in favour of those changes which she believes will help writers. I shall begin by describing Wattpad and Fanado and Atwood's involvement with these systems. Atwood's writing on Wattpad as well as her endorsement of Wattpad

---

[28] This conference took place in the language department of the Nantes University in May 2013, Alberto Manguel quotes André Malraux concerning Louis-Ferdinand Céline : "... si c'est sans doute un pauvre type, c'est certainement un grand écrivain." Voir *Céline : Lettres à la NRF : 1931-1961* (Céline, Fouché and Sollers 84).

and Fanado give her an opportunity to speak in a range of different voices. Having identified these different voices, it will be necessary to highlight the links and cross-fertilization between the messages of the different voices – mainly in relation to Atwood's treatment of the iconic. Again, I will show that the nature of these links is mainly thematic and not aesthetic, nor linguistic. Finally, concluding on Atwood's comments, the link between social media and our need to "perform ourselves" will be further illustrated.

Whether Wattpad and Fanado are likely to become as popular as Youtube, Twitter or Facebook, the future will tell. The uncertainty behind these two recent ventures has not prevented Atwood from embracing these systems and giving them her full support. Wattpad is often said to be a YouTube-like platform for stories and texts. It describes itself as "the best place to discover and share stories" or a "new form of entertainment connecting readers and writers through storytelling". Thousands of new stories are added every day by an active community of readers and writers. The platform has a built-in feedback mechanism which allows Wattpad writers to receive encouragements from the community. The Wattpad users' texts are available to all for free on all devices including mobile.

To say a few words about the Wattpad community and its texts, according to recent statistics, about nine in ten users are readers rather than writers. The community is young and growing throughout the world[29]. The most popular genres on Wattpad.com and the Wattpad mobile app include Romance, Paranormal, and Fan Fiction. The site is also home to poetry, humorous texts, science fiction, thrillers, and others. Atwood's profile page on Wattpad introduces the author and her opinion concerning Wattpad: "I've been a writer since 1956. I've seen writing and publishing change a lot over the years. I look forward to exploring the ways Wattpad connects people to reading and writing, and may help give them confidence through feedback from readers." This simple statement in lieu of a biography not only reveals Atwood's curiosity about the new tool but it expresses her desire to see the site's effectiveness in giving budding authors "confidence through feedback from readers". In 2013, the statement was expanded to include the links to all of her websites and webpages[30].

Since Atwood became a Wattpad member in June 2012, she has become the main vocal ambassador for the site. She is co-writing *The Happy Zombie Sunrise*

---

[29] Around four in ten users are U.S. based; traffic also comes from the U.K., Canada, the Philippines, Australia, and more. Approximately 75 percent of users access the site through their mobile device.
[30] These links are also to be found on her main web site: http://margaretatwood.ca.

Home with author Naomi Alderman on the site, as well as judging Wattpad's poetry contest, charmingly named after her – the "Attys". Atwood has repeatedly given her public support to this form of democratization of written content and stated her motivation for doing so: for example, she wrote of Wattpad in the *Guardian*, "No one need know how old you are, what your social background is, or where you live. Your readers can be anywhere." (Atwood, *The Guardian* July 6, 2012) In short, she claims that for or all young writers, no matter where they are located, Wattpad is a safe space to share one's writing.

Atwood also believes Wattpad allows writing experimentation. Many members of Wattpad's community upload work in progress: unfinished books or chapters, fragments of poetry – anything they wish to receive feedback on. In a piece she wrote for the *Guardian*, Atwood talked about how Wattpad could help young writers develop their own voices, by putting them in touch with readers: "[...] if you're worried about adverse reactions from your teachers, your grandmother, or others who might not like you writing about slavering zombies or your relatives, you can use a pseudonym", Atwood advises in *The Guardian* (July 6, 2012). Not only that, she adds "you'll have readers who leave encouraging comments on your message board, thus boosting your morale." (Atwood, *The Guardian* July 6, 2012)

Writers of her generation, Atwood says, did not have these tools at their disposal: they had to scribble in notebooks or private journals. Sometimes they got a chance to publish in high-school yearbooks unless they preferred to keep most heartfelt writing in their "sock drawers" for fear of ridicule. Atwood also tells about her own experience, as she grew older, in helping to create literary magazines and presses. Most of these ventures in the 60s and 70s in Canada received institutional financial support but were chronically underfunded. The feedback that Wattpad writers receive recreates the readership of small literary magazines and presses without burdening young writers with the financial responsibility of the media they publish on. In its editorial form, Wattpad can also be compared, Atwood claims, to the serialization of novels back in the XIXth century which stimulated authors like Charles Dickens.

Is there a contradiction between Atwood's message at a TOC conference in 2012 about the writer's share of the "publishing pie" diminishing and her support of a free publishing platform? Atwood's position can be clarified as follows: if one considers the various stages involved in becoming a writer, the Wattpad platform is helpful mainly as writers are starting off and in need of encouragement and attention. For slightly more mature authors, Wattpad may ensure further promotion by engaging with readers. What then happens to the young writer as he/she decides to embark on a writing career does not fit into the restricted commentaries concerning Wattpad and, as we have seen, Atwood's large epitext on that subject reveals her understanding of the complexities of the changing environment in publishing. Coming back to the sole subject of Wattpad, a close examination of Atwood's meta-communication about the platform, allows the reader to establish a link between these comments and *Negotiating with the Dead*. In the same way as *Negotiating with the Dead* aims at giving the budding author advice on protecting the "gift sphere", Atwood maps out the functionalities of the Wattpad tool: networks and communities like Wattpad, she claims, are not necessarily a replacement for the traditional publishing industry, but more like an incubator system, a space where authors can experiment and receive feedback. Mainstream publishers themselves, she points out, are taking an interest in the Wattpad community and offering the most popular writers attractive book deals:

> Publishers bring a lot to the joint venture that is producing a book. Not everyone wants to read those kinds of books, and not everyone wants to write them – but they remain a huge aspiration for many. For those who want to hone their writing skills, schools and tools are increasingly available. In my view, Wattpad is not a replacement for publishers, but a gateway leading to them. (Atwood, *The Guardian* July 6, 2012)

Atwood herself experiments with Wattpad as if she were an inexperienced writer. Never before had she co-written a novel. Her tackling of the zombie theme (particularly popular with teenagers) is new as well. Wattpad conveys a playful dimension to Atwood's new enterprise of collaborating with Naomi Alderman (the platform offers a combination of new features for Atwood from the episode format to the two authors taking it in turns to write and the audience's participation through the posting of comments). One could go as far as to say that Wattpad provides Atwood with a place to "play" with writing. The importance of play is something that Atwood underlines in her Toronto interviews with Reena Khandpur and myself – "we are a playing and experimenting creature" – and which she chooses to emphasize again in the final line of the interview, "[…] we are the animal that plays. […] Avoid boredom." (Evain, Khandpur 109)

Atwood's interest in the book industry's latest developments can also be seen in her commitment to help create an interactive artists' platform. As a follow-up to her "LongPen" invention, Atwood is also involved in a crowd-funded effort to create a service called Fanado that authors can use to connect with their readers[31]. Atwood resorts to an innovative business practice in order to raise funds for Fanado: in a campaign run by the crowd-funding service Indiegogo, Atwood offers donators the chance to become a character in her new novel. This initiative illustrates Atwood's desire to experiment with the new trends in the book industry, to entertain her audience, and to explore her own creative powers in different media.

In voicing her support to Wattpad and Fanado, Atwood speaks in her business voice, her inventor's voice and her advertising voice. All of these voices combine in one major endorsement statement, which, at times, is worded in a lyrical style. For example, Atwood concludes her article in the *Guardian* by declaring that "Wattpad opens the doors and enlarges the view in places where the doors are closed and the view is restricted. And somewhere out there in Wattpadland, a new generation is testing its wings." (*The Guardian*, July 6, 2012) This view which supports freedom of speech, followed by a comment concerning the young author's need to connect with his/her audience displays a certain poetic touch, and it also acts as a reminder of Wattpad's main audience all the while establishing a connection with Atwood's message in *Negotiating with the Dead*. Not only does Atwood's endorsement of Wattpad provide an encouragement to the young author but she also shows her willingness to carry on experimenting with writing – very much as she encourages young writers to – trying out new forms, collaborations and media. This experimentation may be a way to set herself new objectives, to stimulate her own capacities to explore the world and to renew her creative powers. And, as the above example demonstrates, Atwood sometimes plays with language even when she is speaking in her advertising voice. This comment brings us back to the capillary links between the different genres (poetry and fiction) and to the cross-fertilization between Atwood's different voices, even between the public persona voice and the poetic voice.

Atwood's desire to pioneer new writer feedback loops and publishing systems, provides many examples of Atwood's ability to navigate between "serious" artistic work and the publishing world. It is also illustrated by Atwood's treatment of the iconic, when contributing to the Wattpad platform: in response to criticism for giving her support to this new publishing system which, according to traditional publishers, is not worthy of an established author's attention,

---

[31] The idea behind Fanado is to give authors tools that they can use to interact with fans remotely, including the ability to share live video and audio of readings or get-togethers with a community, and to sign and distribute both electronic books and printed books, as well as CDs and other offerings related to a work. In some ways, Fanado is the logical extension of Atwood's earlier project "LongPen".

Atwood's comment echoes the meta-iconic discourses previously analysed in her poetry and fiction. Indeed, she is mischievous and is quick to mock those who mock her:

> Once again people are giving me strange looks. Why Wattpad? And, indeed, what pad? Wattpad, as in wattage, the kind that makes the lights turn on. "But Margaret," you can hear them whispering. "You're a literary icon at the height of your powers; it says so on your book covers. Why are you sneaking out with an online story-sharing site heavy on romance, vampires and werewolves? You should be endorsing Literature, capital L. Get back up on that pedestal! Strike a serious pose! Turn to stone!" (Atwood, *The Guardian* July 6, 2012)

Refusing to "get back on that pedestal" in order to behave like an icon is typical of Atwood's public persona, as is her desire to "have fun" and to be "goofy", as Doyle would put it, experimenting with "an online story-sharing site heavy on romance, vampires and werewolves" (Doyle, in.these.times.com August 22, 2013). Her own irreverence is also, as I have tried to underline throughout, a subject that she enjoys turning into material. Whether in poetry, prose, or in her epitext, including the various forms of social media previously mentioned, there is indeed a one and only signature behind this playful treatment of iconic figures. However, although the iconoclast comments of her work and epitext are thematically related, they are not to be placed on the same level. Atwood herself explains the different forms of language, placing the "social media language" in the category of a communication code as opposed to an artistic form of expression like fiction and poetry.

This brings me to the final point I would like to make in relation to one of Atwood's meta-communicational comments. When asked about the importance of appearance on the Internet ("it's about *being seen* sending a message, right?"[32]), Margaret Atwood takes a historical perspective and draws a parallel with the function of clothing in the XIXth century. She compares today's social lives with the social lives of the 19th century where "people coded themselves or were coded by the authorities according to their clothing". Because people differentiated themselves through what they wore, clothing became "a visual performance for the benefit of anybody looking at them". Clothing, Atwood claims, has become "much more horizontal" that is you "can't tell by looking at

---

[32] Margaret Atwood is interviewed for "BigThink" by Max Miller (2011).

somebody what level of society they come from [...] the jeans outfit is pretty ubiquitous". Therefore other guises come into play:

> So maybe we feel the need to perform ourselves in some other way. And if you think that what goes up on people's blogs is really the full content of their lives, of course, you're quite wrong. It's what they're doing in the spotlight. It's their turn. And this spotlight they can shine it on themselves and they can go in there and sort of dance about and create a persona for themselves. Of course it's not the whole story.

Our need to "perform ourselves in some other way", points to various languages: today's social media, like XXIst century dress codes, is a form of language used to put oneself in the spotlight. Atwood's comment about our need for differentiation, our narcissistic desire to be seen in the edited version we like to give of ourselves, raises the question not only of languages, voices, guises and representations but also of the "true story" – one of Atwood's leitmotivs previously quoted: where does the "whole story" actually lie? Atwood's epitextual or public persona voice brings us back to her creative work: her poetry, mainly the poem in *True Stories*[33] and her fiction, mainly the narrator's comment in *The Blind Assassin* concerning our need to "memorialize ourselves" (BA 95)[34].

To conclude on Atwood's voice on the Internet, it presents a distinctive addition to what Leigh Gilmore calls the author's "autobiographics", "the discursive signature of the [author as subject]" (Gilmore 14) and an effective "agency [of] self-representation" (14). All four of Atwood's strategies (A. "real virtual presence", B. meta-communication, C. embracing of new technologies and D. coherence of message conveyed through different modes of language) serve to reinforce the autobiographical pact. The question is now perhaps why Atwood chooses this form of "autobiographics" composed both of her incredible creative work of fiction and poetry and of a rich epitext. Sherrill Grace who comments that Atwood has "always written this way", ventures to explain why: "Perhaps

---

[33] "Don't ask for the true story; [...] / The true story is vicious / and multiple and untrue" (TS 3).
[34] "Why is it we want so badly to memorialize ourselves? Even while we're still alive. We wish to assert our existence, like dogs peeing on fire hydrants. We put on display our framed photographs, our parchment diplomas, our silver-plated cups; we monogram our linen, we carve our names on trees, we scrawl them on washroom walls. It's all the same impulse. What do we hope from it? Applause, envy, respect? Or simply attention, of any kind we can get?
At the very least we want a witness. We can't stand the idea of our own voices falling silent finally, like a radio running down." (BA 95)

because she is not a high modernist determined to erase the personal in favour of some illusion of godlike Joycean neutrality." And, most importantly to me, "[p]erhaps because the "I" voice feels right to her, and [...] because she has always understood the capacity of the autobiographical pact to call up "you," whether living or dead." (in Moss and Kozakewich 129).

And it is with Atwood's capacity to speak the "I" and to call up the "you" – whether she is addressing the environmental activist, the human rights defender, or the reader – that I would like to end, as I contemplate the complementarity between the different voices, the ability to play with form and medium, the coherence of the "autobiographics", the fictional, mythical, iconographical and virtual constructions and, most importantly, the generosity of multi-facetted Atwood in playing with these voices.

Conclusion

Atwoodian critics unite in saying that Margaret Atwood offers an intriguing and compelling body of writing as well as a rich epitext. The exploration of her voice and its representations, at the heart of this present volume, has led us on a journey to question the very nature of "a voice" and its different meanings according to critics and poets. While Atwood's literary work (more than forty books – a dozen novels, numerous collections of poetry, children's books, and countless essays) is attributed a unique voice-print, Atwood's epitextual voice comprises a wide range of voices which can be heard through many different medias and occasions: public appearances, countless radio and television programs, many webpages, published articles and even documentaries such as the fly-on-the-wall cinema *vérité* "In the Wake of the Flood" – not to mention her transcribed voice in press articles or on blogs and web sites. Atwood is, needless to say, one of the most acclaimed authorial voices of our times: her fans are eager to follow her whenever she makes a public appearance – on her book tours, through the media as well as on Twitter. Her popularity as an iconic figure is surpassed only by her literary talent as both a poet and fiction writer.

Atwood's writing has been described as being amongst "the best of contemporary writing" (Davey 162), combining "a visible sense of play – pun parody, self-parody, satire – with visible moral intent" (Davey 162), offering "gardens of textual delights" (Davey 162). She is "a writer of many facets" (Davidson 9), inspiring critics to write volumes such as *Various Atwoods* (York) which escalade into "*Multiplicitous Atwoods*[1]" (in York 2). Atwood's mistrust of "the received language" is often highlighted. It leads her to push the boundaries of modern writing, creating "intergeneric texts" (York 2) which are "laconic, vivid, concrete in their imagery, disturbing in their juxtaposition" (Davey 162), reversing stereotypes and Lakoff's idiomatic metaphors (Evain 2009 182-193), and subverting the subtexts that she embeds or implies in her own work.

Many levels of reading have been suggested of Atwood's work and the following labels are often used: poems "about Canada" or "post-colonial"; "female-empowered"; "descent"; and "metafictional" poems. Atwood's treatment of these themes is widely appreciated as it offers relevant material for all the different schools of criticism. Some readers and critics have expressed reservations about certain areas or elements of Atwood's huge body of work but

---

[1] York's italics.

these reservations have been diluted out over time in a sea of critical work. The sheer volume of research already on record demonstrates how Atwood's writing is worthy of our attention. Davey was once slightly critical in his appreciation of Atwood's work in saying that it was "[unnecessarily] gender specific" (Davey 164). He supported this argument by contrasting Atwood's approach to the less dichotomized approach of other Canadian advocates of affirmative writing such as Leonard Cohen, Jay Macpherson, John Newlove, Anne Hébert, Douglas LePan and Gabrielle Roy. Davey further claimed that he also had "reservations about the didactic tone that characterizes much of Atwood's writing, its overt sense of deliberate patterning and organization that often seems inimical to her endorsement of irrational energies." (Davey 165). As previously explained, Davey, in *Margaret Atwood: a Feminist Poetics*, undertakes to elucidate Atwood's writing according to the masculine and feminine dichotomy that informs both language and structure of the author's work. He defines masculinity and femininity in stereotypic ways: femininity, as we have seen, means "close to nature"; masculinity means power and control. He then fits Atwood's work into these established categories: the poetic work being essentially written, he claims, in a female language (as opposed to the critical work). Much of the driving force behind most of the Atwoodian monographs, as York points out, "has been, not surprisingly, the [...] burgeoning field of feminist theory" (York 3).

However, Atwood herself cringes when her work is labelled as "feminist". Although she emphasizes the importance of female language, she does not restrict herself to it in her writing both of poetry and prose. Her writing may encourage the reader to explore the dichotomy between the symbolic female and male spheres, it may also attribute particular value to the female sphere, but Atwood herself does not set out to defend borders. The comment she makes about borders, in a recent discussion about genres, would equally apply here: "[...] borders are increasingly undefended, and things slip back and forth between them with insouciance." (IOW 7). Indeed, Atwood's genre-challenging writing moves freely between, what Davey calls, the "feminine" language of irrationality, hallucination and disorientation and the more "masculine" structured, rational or systematic language, present even in her poetry. It is the freedom to resort to both of these forms and to infuse her writing with paradoxes, humour and irony which, I would suggest, best describes Atwood's writing. Davey himself dismisses his own reservations concerning Atwood's writing and states that a didactic interpretation of her work is in direct contradiction with one of Atwood's short stories "The

Festival of Missed Crass"[2]. As Davey underlines, this short story stages "Wordhoarders" whose job it is to "preserve whatever meaning [they] can", to "prevent first-order language from becoming second-order language" (Davey 169). Davey considers the Wordhoarder of Atwood's story to be "a kind of Atwood self-portrait" where the author is described as "a poet who in the tradition of Arnold and Pound sees herself as a custodian of language and culture, a protector and renewer of meanings." (Davey 169). Atwood's "Wordorder is Worldorder" illuminates what Davey describes as "the extraordinary focus of Atwood's novels on language, on the role of language in cultural health, and on protagonists who use language with either precision or imprecision." (Davey 169)

Atwood's passion for literary heritage is demonstrated in her abundant critical work and mainly in the controversial *Survival* which highlights the main themes of Canadian literature. The conscious scrutiny and world-recreation that Atwood undertakes in her own literary genre-challenging writing, is not incompatible with her also being a "custodian of language and culture". Atwood's precise use of language (whether female or masculine) serves to highlight "the role of language in cultural health". And she thus becomes, like the canonic writers to which she pays tribute in her critical writing or in her subtexts, both a "protector and renewer of meanings".

Coming back to the many critical labels ("about Canada" or "post-colonial", "female-empowered", "descent" and "metafictional" writing), Atwood's work, and mainly her poetry, can indeed be read on different staves simultaneously – the personal, social, cultural and universal. For example, her writing presents a portrayal of both external political and cultural repression *and* the internalized effects of various kinds of repression on the individual psyche. It is the plurality of levels of readings and perspectives which is most strikingly effective in Atwood's writing. Atwood's strategy concerning the use of personae in poetry is also particularly original. As we have seen, the author stages a wide range of personae which include many different figures from Greek mythology to popular culture. Atwood equally resorts to fairy tale characters, gothic figures and female figures who are traditionally voiceless (such as "Miss July"). These voices of the many personae come to challenge dominant cultural representations and expose the threats of these representations to society and to the individual.

While many critics highlight an interplay of voices in Atwood's writing, I have argued here that, beyond the vocal plurality, the reader distinctly hears the

---

[2] "The Festival of Missed Crass", later renamed "Forbidden Christmas" is a children's short story which was made into a musical for Toronto's Young People's Theater. See Atwood papers in the Thomas Fisher Rare Book Library. Box 115.

voice of a persona-soloist who sings out her particular truth. This Persona (with a capital P) is highly singular as she bears the mark of a rich experience which is capable of cultivating two modes of functioning related to integration and independence. She has shown her ability to reconcile the different parts of her extended identity and to celebrate them all. This voice is also a voice of lucidity which highlights and works through paradox. She demonstrates a great understanding of the human stuff we are made of and the self-knowledge concerning her own modes of functioning.

Furthermore, exposing "the voice that speaks" (in poetry or in fiction) and giving this voice-persona many guises are trademarks of Atwood's poetic writing that I have stressed throughout. Ever since she began writing poetry she has played with a range of images representing the poetic voice. Atwood's voice-persona has not been portrayed in an attractive way, as I have highlighted in the examples taken from *The Circle Game* to *The Door*. Why should Atwood thus choose to emphasize the unflattering "physical" characteristics when giving us representations of an incarnated voice? I would suggest there are many reasons for this, all to do with the difficult experience of having a special gift for writing (or, as Atwood would say, "a voice"): in her early poetry, Atwood stresses the importance of the "voice" in relation to an entity that the reader could call "the one that does the living" (that is "[t]he thing that calls itself / I", CG 50). Since it is not an easy thing for the latter to compose with the voice, the very existence of the "voice" is often experienced by "the one that does the living" as a tiresome entity. But in "Shadow Voice" for example, it is also perceived, as the one that gives "water... clean crusts / ...words / flowing in your veins / to keep you going", AC, 7) and therefore the voice is the very source of nourishment.

In her later poetry, Atwood recurrently portrays the voice-persona as an aging persona. This provides an opportunity for the author to develop several of her recurring themes, mainly the themes of depression and oppression but also companionship, acceptance and survival strategies. To these, one must add another theme, from her own experience as a celebrated author: Atwood's meta-iconography, to use York's expression, that is a discourse which highlights society's need for and treatment of celebrities. Indeed Atwood mocks the way authors are turned into icons, weaving a great deal of humour into many meta-poetic poems.

Having highlighted, in this volume, the specificities of Atwood's different voices, even the public persona voice – which Atwood does not place under the same aesthetic obligation as the poetic voice – , I would like to emphasize once more the importance of poetry in comparison to prose. Atwood herself repetitively states the importance of poetry, as, for example, in her speech "An End to Audience?": "I believe that poetry is the heart of language, the activity through which language is renewed and kept alive" (SW 346). A chronological reading of Atwood's work suggests that up until 1995, poetry precedes prose. Dividing her work into three periods, one notices how each volume of poetry is the "seed planted for the next novel". In the first period, Atwood devotes more time to poetry and then alternates rigorously between poetry and prose. The balance between the two forms gradually tilts in favor of fiction, in the second period: indeed, the alternation between the two forms is no longer systematic but the poetry remains the source of inspiration for the prose. Finally, in the third period, Atwood writes little "traditional" poetry, but instead develops a new form: that of the prose poems which are often highly meta-fictional in nature. In this third period, Atwood does not abandon poetry altogether. Her later poetry (*Morning in the Burned House, Bottle, The Tent, The Door*) extensively explores the theme of aging and aging icons which are further developed in her fiction from 1995 onwards. Atwood's active participation in the poetry context named after her ("The Atties") also demonstrates her continuing love of poetry.

It is clear that much of the innovation in Atwood's artistic creation finds its origin in the poetry. However, it is important here to point out that the fecundity of poetry is obviously not an exclusively Atwoodian characteristic, but rather, inherent to the very nature of poetry itself. Poetry stretches language into realms of great complexity by exploiting the tension between form and content. Yet, as a result of this tension, poetry cannot settle anything. The fragmented nature of the verse, its deliberate opposition to the continuity of prose writing, is the sign of an impossible reconciliation amply illustrated by Atwood's double-headed image. The reader is forced to play a more active role, because of the difficulty involved in coming to terms with the tension between what one sees and what one hears when reading poetry. The play on both language and visual form stimulates the reader to reflect on possible polyphonies and contradictions in the poem and thus use this extremely tight form of writing to explore the paradoxes of our human condition. Poems are not dreams offering a romantic or idealistic vision of life, and as their scope is limited through being addressed to an individual reader, they cannot reform society. But they *do* have something to offer in that they can help us explore restrictions, contradictions, hopes, and desires. Poetry will lead the way to the understanding of our mode of being, as well as the inevitable paradoxes and new forms of resistance to the social, the cultural, and the political. Poems do not produce a voice that functions merely as an echo chamber of existing discourses, but they work within tensions which we eventually learn to see as "permanently unresolved" – to use Munro's expression, (Munro 197). This better understanding and acceptance of something "permanently unresolved", mirrors the very nature of poetry. It is then hardly surprising that such teachings (which are offered both to the poet and the reader) should result in the production of potential material for novels and that Atwood's signature should be characterized by a two-headedness staged in a multi-faceted manner throughout the corpus. Through working on Atwood's poetry, the reader learns to grow to be attentive to a polyphony of voices. We learn to listen, and to integrate the different components of our extended identity. We learn to resist the unsatisfactory bargains offered by society and to cultivate the willpower to remain in this fragile state of equilibrium which allows us to explore both light and darkness. And thus, we follow the voice of the persona of "Interlunar" that says:

> I wish to show you the darkness
> you are so afraid of
>
> Trust me. This darkness is
> a place you can enter and be
> as safe in as you are anywhere;
> you can put one foot in front of the other
> and believe the sides of your eyes.
> Memorize. You will know it
> again in your own time...
> We have come to the edge:...
> The lake, vast and dimensionless,
> doubles everything, the stars,
> the boulders, itself, even the darkness
> that you can walk so long in
> it becomes light. (I 102–103)

Although I am tempted to end with this beautiful poem which I never tire of quoting, I will add one last word about my own reasons for carrying out this investigation concerning Atwood's voice. The journey undertaken here is part of a vast collective critical enterprise. I started taking part in it over a decade ago when Reena Kandhpur and myself were preparing questions to interview Margaret Atwood so as to capture her voice-print, to deepen our understanding of her voice-persona and to apprehend the origin of her inspiration and her own voice: "What prompted you to write this image...?"; "What prompted you to write that poem...?" These were unanswerable questions, as Atwood soon responded. And once again, she affirms this in 2011 in her introduction *In Other Worlds: SF and the Human Imagination*:

> Everyone wants to know this about writers: What is your inspiration? What put you up to it? They're never satisfied with such explanations as "Because it was there" or "I don't know what came over me." They want specifics.
>
> So let me try this:
>
> As a young child, living briefly in the winter of 1944-5 in an old house in Sault Ste. Marie, I used to get up before anyone else was awake and climb to the cold but spacious attic, where in a state of solipsistic bliss I would build strange habitations and quasi-people with a bunch of sticks and spools called Tinkertoy. What I really wanted to make was the windmill pictured on the box, but my set didn't have the necessary parts, and as it was war-time I was unlikely ever to possess the missing items.
>
> Some say that the art one makes as an adult supplies the absence of things longed for in childhood. I don't know whether or not this is true. If I'd been able to create that windmill, would I have become a writer? [...] We'll never know the answer to that question but it's one theory. (IOW 11)

While Atwood's many questions about and representations of the poetic voice reveal, I would suggest, her own fascination with the origin and nature of "a voice"[3] and while the above image of the author's early creativity may contribute to the self-mythologizing of the author, Atwood clearly states that the anecdote she gives us here is only an attempt at illustrating "one theory" about becoming a writer. The critic, no more than the writer, can explain the trajectory from childhood creativity to the affirmation of artistic talent. Therefore I will not venture to connect the dots between Atwood's opus and her first creation of "strange habitations and quasi-people" made from a Tinkertoy construction set. I cannot trace the source of her inspirations as a writer, no more than I can reveal the secret behind "a voice" since this secret is the mystery of artistic creation

---

[3] *Negotiating with the Dead* provides an illustration of the questions Atwood raised in connection with those themes.

itself. But there is one thing I *can* do and that is simply share the pleasure I experience in reading her work and contemplating her many poetical images, including the one I have quoted to conclude this volume – that of Margaret Atwood as a child, experiencing "solipsistic bliss" as she plays with a handful of sticks, alone in a spacious and cold attic. And I can point out the protean windmill of her poetry and fiction echoing the author as she says, quite simply, in terms she equally could have used back then when she was a child: "Meanwhile […] I hope you have as much fun with [my windmill] as I have had." (IOW 11)

Bibliography

Atwood's Work

Novels

Atwood, Margaret. 1980. *The Edible Woman*. 1969. London: Virago Press.
---. *Surfacing*. 1972, 1979. London: Virago Press.
---. *Lady Oracle*. 1976. London: Virago Press, 1982.
---. *Life Before Man*. 1979. London: Vintage, 1996.
---. *Bodily Harm*. 1981. London: Vintage, 1996.
---. *The Handmaid's Tale*. 1985. London: Vintage, 1996.
---. *Cat's Eye*. 1988. London: Virago Press, 1990.
---. *The Robber Bride*. 1993. London: Virago Press, 1994.
---. *Alias Grace*. 1996. London: Virago Press, 1997.
---. *The Blind Assassin*. London: Bloomsbury, 2000.
---. *Oryx and Crake*. London: Bloomsbury, 2003.
---. *The Year of the Flood: a Novel*. New York: Nan A. Talese / Doubleday, 2009.
---. *Maddaddam*. New York: Random House, 2013.

Short Fiction

---. *Dancing Girls*. 1977. London: Virago Press, 1996.
---. *Bluebeard's Egg*. 1983. London: Vintage, 1996.
---. *Wilderness Tips*. 1991. London: Virago Press, 1992.
---. *The Labrador Fiasco*. London: Bloomsbury, 1996.
---. *The Penelopiad*. Edinburgh: Canongate, 2005.
---. *Moral Disorder*. London: Bloomsbury Pub., 2006.

Prose Poems

---. *Murder in Dark*. 1983. London: Virago Press, 1994.
---. *Good Bones*. 1992. London: Virago Press, 1993.
---. *Bottle*. Hay: Hay Festival Press, 2004.
---. *The Tent*. London: Doubleday, 2006.

Poetry

---. *The Circle Game*. 1964. Toronto: Anansi, 1998.
---. *The Animals in That Country*. Toronto: Oxford UP, 1968.
---. *The Journals of Susanna Moodie*. Toronto: Oxford UP, 1970.
---. *Le Journal de Susanna Moodie*. Trans. Christine Evain. Paris: Bruno Doucey, 2010.
---. *Procedures for Underground*. Toronto: Oxford UP, 1970.
---. *Power Politics*. 1971. Toronto: Anansi, 1996.
---. *You Are Happy*. Toronto: Oxford UP, 1974.
---. *Two-Headed Poems*. Toronto: Oxford UP, 1978.
---. *True Stories*. Toronto: Oxford UP, 1981.
---. *Interlunar*. Toronto: Oxford UP, 1984.
---. *Morning in the Burned House*. Toronto: McClelland & Stewart, 1995.
---. *The Door*. Boston: Houghton Mifflin, 2007

Anthologies

---. *Selected Poems I:* 1965-1975. Toronto: Oxford UP, 1976.
---. *Selected Poems II:* 1976-1986. Toronto: Oxford UP, 1986.
---. *Eating Fire, Selected Poetry 1965-1995*. London: Virago Press, 1998.
Atwood, Margaret and Charles Pachter. *The Journals of Susanna Moodie*. 1970. London: Bloomsbury, 1997.

Critical Work

Atwood, Margaret. *Survival: A Thematic Guide to Canadian Literature*. Toronto: Anansi, 1972.
---. "Canadian Monsters: Some Aspects of the Supernatural in Canadian Fiction." *The Canadian Imagination: Dimensions of a Literary Culture*. Ed. David Staines. Cambridge, Mass. London: Harvard UP, 1977. 97-122.
---. *Days of the Rebels: 1815-1840*. Toronto: Natural Science of Canada, 1977.
---. *Second Words: Selected Critical Prose*. Toronto: Anansi. 1982.
---. *Strange Things: The Malevolent North in Canadian Literature*. Oxford : Clarendon Press, 1995.
---. *Negotiating with the Dead*. Toronto: Cambridge UP, 2002.
---. *Moving Targets*. Toronto: Anansi, 2004

---. *Curious Pursuits: Occasional Writing 1970-2005*. London: Virago. 2005

---. *Writing with Intent: Essays, Reviews, Personal Prose – 1983-2005*. New York: Carroll & Graf Publishers, 2005.

---. *Payback: Debt and the Shadow Side of Wealth*. Toronto : Anansi, 2008.

---. *In Other Worlds: SF and the Human Imagination*. New York: Doubleday, 2011.

Atwood, Margaret and Charles Pachter. *The Journals of Susanna Moodie*. 1970. London : Bloomsbury, 1997.

Atwood, Margaret and Victor-Lévy Beaulieu. *Two Solicitudes: Conversations*. Toronto: McClelland & Stewart, 1998.

Atwood, Margaret and Earl G Ingersoll. *Margaret Atwood: Conversations*. Princeton: Ontario Review Press, 1990.

---. *Waltzing Again: New and Selected Conversations with Margaret Atwood*. Princeton, NJ; New York: Ontario Review Press, 2006.

Critical Work on Margaret Atwood and Literary Analysis

Attridge, Derek. *Poetic Rhythm: An Introduction*. Cambridge; New York: Cambridge University Press, 1995.

Barthes, Roland. *Fragments d'un discours amoureux*. Paris: Éditions du Seuil, 1977.

Baudrillard, Jean. *La Société de consommation: ses mythes, ses structures*. Paris: Denoël, 1986.

Birney, Earle. *The Collected Poems of Earle Birney. Vol. 1. Vol. 1.* Toronto: McClelland and Stewart, 1975.

Blott, Anne. "Journey to light [*Interlunar*]." *Critical Essays on Margaret Atwood*. Ed. Judith McCombs. Boston, Mass.: G.K. Hall, 1988. 275-279.

Bradford, Richard. *The Look of It: a Theory of Visual Form in English Poetry*. Cork: Cork University Press, 1993.

Brown, Brené. *The Gifts of Imperfection: Let Go of Who You Think You're Supposed to Be and Embrace Who You Are*. Center City, Minn.: Hazelden, 2010.

Bugeja, Michael J. *The Art and Craft of Poetry*. Cincinnati, Ohio: Writer's Digest Books, 1994.

Butler, Robert Olen. *From Where You Dream: The Process of Writing Fiction*. Ed. Janet Burroway. New York: Grove Press, 2005.

Carman, Taylor and Mark B. N Hansen. *The Cambridge Companion to Merleau-Ponty*. Cambridge, U.K.; New York: Cambridge University Press, 2005.

Carper, Thomas and Derek Attridge. *Meter and Meaning: An Introduction to Rhythm in Poetry*. New York: Routledge, 2003.

Céline, Louis-Ferdinand, Pascal Fouché and Philippe Sollers. *Lettres à la N.R.F. choix 1931-1961*. Paris: Gallimard, 2011.

Collins, Billy. *Sailing Alone Around the Room: New and Selected Poems*. New York: Random House, 2001.

Cooley, Dennis. "Nearer by Far: The Upset 'I' in Margaret Atwood's Poetry." *Margaret Atwood: Writing and Subjectivity : New Critical Essays*. Ed. Nicholson, Colin. New York: St. Martin's Press, 1994. 68-93.

Davey, Frank. *Margaret Atwood: a Feminist Poetics*. Vancouver: Talonbooks, 1984.

Davidson, Arnold E and Cathy N Davidson. *The Art of Margaret Atwood: Essays in Criticism*. Toronto: Anansi, 1981.

Djwa, Sandra. "Back to the Primal: The Apprenticeship of Margaret Atwood." *Various Atwoods: Essays on the Later Poems, Short Fiction, and Novels*. Ed. Lorraine Mary York. Concord, Ontario: Anansi, 1995.13-46.

Drury, John. *The Poetry Dictionary*. Cincinnati, Ohio: Story Press, 1995.

Eakin, Paul John. *How Our Lives Become Stories: Making Selves*. Ithaca, N.Y.: Cornell University Press, 1999.

Egan, Susanna. *Mirror Talk: Genres of Crisis in Contemporary Autobiography*. Chapel Hill: University of North Carolina Press, 1999.

Estés, Clarissa Pinkola. *Women Who Run with the Wolves: Myths and Stories of the Wild Woman Archetype*. New York: Ballantine Books, 1992.

Evain, Christine. "Repérage et traduction des métaphores créatives atwoodiennes." *La traduction de la poésie, outil de critique littéraire*. Attal, Jean-Pierre et Florence Lautel-Ribstein. Perros-Guirec : La Tribune Internationale des Langues Vivantes, Anagrammes, 46-47 (mai 2009) : 182-193.

---. "La réconciliation intime dans la poésie de Margaret Atwood." *Atwood on her work: "Poems open the doors. Novels are the corridors"*. Eds. Christine Evain and Reena Khandpur. CRINI/CEC Canadensis series, Nantes : Université de Nantes, 2006. 53-74

Evain, Christine, Reena Khandpur, eds. *Atwood on her Work: "Poems open the doors. Novels are the corridors"*. CRINI/CEC Canadensis series, Nantes : Université de Nantes, 2006.

Foucault, Michel. *Power/knowledge: Selected Interviews and Other Writings, 1972-1977*. Trans. Colin Gordon. New York: Pantheon Books, 1980.

Frame, Janet. *An Autobiography ; To the Island*. Auckland, NZ: Random House New Zealand, 1990.

Fredman, Stephen. *The Grounding of American Poetry: Charles Olson and the Emersonian Tradition*. Cambridge; New York: Cambridge University Press, 1993.

Frye, Northrop. *The Bush Garden: Essays on the Canadian Imagination*. Toronto: Anansi, 1971.

Genette, Gérard. *Paratextes*. Paris: Ed. du Seuil, 1987.

---. *Paratexts: Thresholds of Interpretation*. Cambridge; New York, NY, USA: Cambridge University Press, 1997.

Gibson, Douglas. *Stories About Storytellers Publishing Alice Munro, Robertson Davies, Alistair MacLeod, Pierre Trudeau, and Others*. Toronto: ECW Press, 2011.

Gilmore, Leigh. *Autobiographics: a Feminist Theory of Women's Self-representation*. Ithaca: Cornell University Press, 1994.

Grace, Sherrill. "Atwood and the 'Autobiographical Pact' – for Reingard Nischik." *Margaret Atwood: The Open Eye*. Eds. John Moss and Tobi Kozakewich. Ottawa: University of Ottawa Press, 2006. 121-134.

Greco, Albert N. *The Book Publishing Industry in the United States*. Boston: Allyn & Bacon, 1996.

Gross, Gerald. *Editors on Editing*. New York: Harper & Row, 1985.

Guignery, Vanessa. *Novelists in the New Millennium: Conversations with Writers*. Basingstoke, Hampshire; New York: Palgrave Macmillan, 2013.

---, ed. *Voices and Silence in the Contemporary Novel in English*. 1 vol. Newcastle-upon-Tyne, United Kingdom: Cambridge Scholars, 2009.

Hengen, Shannon Eileen, Ashley Thomson. *Margaret Atwood: a Reference Guide, 1988-2005*. Lanham, Md.: Scarecrow Press, 2007.

Hengen, Shannon. "Strange Visions: Atwood's Interlunar and Technopoetics." *Margaret Atwood's Assassinations: Recent Poetry and Fiction*. Ed.

Wilson, Sharon R. Columbus, OH: Ohio State University Press, 2003. 42-53.

---. "Sensory Appeal in *The Atwood Stories* on TV." *Atwood on her work: "Poems open the doors. Novels are the corridors"*. Eds. Christine Evain and Reena Khandpur. CRINI/CEC Canadensis series, Nantes : Université de Nantes, 2006. 35-42

Hood, Bruce M. *The Self Illusion*. London: Constable, 2012.

Howells, Coral Ann. *Margaret Atwood*. New York: Palgrave Macmillan, 2005.

---. *The Cambridge Companion to Margaret Atwood*. Cambridge, UK; New York: Cambridge University Press, 2006.

Howells, Coral Ann. "Writing History, from *The Journals of Susanna Moodie* to *The Blind Assassin*." *Margaret Atwood: The Open Eye*. Eds. John Moss and Tobi Kozakewich. Ottawa: University of Ottawa Press, 2006. 107-120.

Howells, Coral Ann and Lynette Hunter. *Narrative Strategies in Canadian Literature: Feminism and Postcolonialism*. Milton Keynes [Eng.]; Philadelphia: Open University Press, 1991.

Hyde, Lewis. *The Gift: Imagination and the Erotic Life of Property*. New York: Vintage Books, 1983.

Jamieson, Sara. "'*It's Still You*': Aging and Identity in Atwood's Poetry." *Margaret Atwood: The Open Eye*. Eds. John Moss and Tobi Kozakewich. Ottawa: University of Ottawa Press, 2006. 269-278.

Jarraway, Davis. "Com[ing] Through Darkness': Margaret Atwood's 'I'-Opening Lyricism." *Margaret Atwood: The Open Eye*. Eds. John Moss and Tobi Kozakewich. Ottawa: University of Ottawa Press, 2006. 279-290.

Kappeler, Susanne. *The Pornography of Representation*. Minneapolis: University of Minnesota Press, 1986.

King, James. *Jack: a Life with Writers : the Story of Jack McClelland*. Toronto: Knopf Canada, 1999.

Kuhn, Cynthia G. *Self-fashioning in Margaret Atwood's Fiction: Dress, Culture, and Identity*. New York: Peter Lang, 2005.

Lakoff, George and Mark Johnson. *Metaphors We Live By*. Chicago: University of Chicago Press, 1980.

Lejeune, Philippe. *Le pacte autobiographique*. Paris: Seuil, 1975.

---. *On Autobiography*. Ed. Paul John Eakin. Trans. Katherine Leary. Minneapolis: University of Minnesota Press, 1989.

Lessing, Doris May. *Walking in the Shade: Volume Two of My Autobiography, 1949-1962*. New York: HarperCollinsPublishers, 1997.

Lewis, Barry. *Kazuo Ishiguro*. Manchester: Manchester University Press, 2000.

Maulpoix, Jean-Michel. *La poésie comme l'amour: essai sur la relation lyrique*. Paris: Mercure de France, 1998.

---. "La quatrième personne du singulier: esquisse de portrait du sujet lyrique moderne". *Figures du sujet lyrique*. Ed. Dominique Rabaté. Paris: PUF, 1996.

McCombs, Judith, ed. *Critical Essays on Margaret Atwood*. Boston, Mass.: G.K. Hall, 1988.

---. "From *'Places, Migrations'* to *The Circle Game*: Atwood's Canadian and Female Metamorphoses." *Margaret Atwood: Writing and Subjectivity: New Critical Essays*. Ed. Nicholson, Colin. New York: St. Martin's Press, 1994. 51-67.

Merleau-Ponty, Maurice. *Phénoménologie de la perception*. Paris: Gallimard, 1945.

---. *Signes*. Paris: Gallimard, 1960.

---. *The Visible and the Invisible; Followed by Working Notes. Ed.* Claude Lefort. Trans. Alphonso Lingis. Evanston: Northwestern University Press, 1968.

Mogel, Leonard. *Making It in Book Publishing*. New York, NY: Macmillan, 1996.

Moss, John George and Tobi Kozakewich, eds. *Margaret Atwood: The Open Eye*. Ottawa: University of Ottawa Press, 2006.

Moss, Laura. "Margaret Atwood: Branding an Icon Abroad." *Margaret Atwood: The Open Eye*. Eds. John Moss and Tobi Kozakewich. Ottawa: University of Ottawa Press, 2006. 19-34.

Munro, Alice. *The Moons of Jupiter: Stories*. New York: Knopf: Distributed by Random House, 1983.

Nicholson, Colin. *Margaret Atwood: Writing and Subjectivity: New Critical Essays*. New York: St. Martin's Press, 1994.

Nietzsche, Friedrich Wilhelm. *Contribution à la généalogie de la morale: un écrit polémique*. Trans. Angèle Kremer-Marietti. Paris: Union générale d'éditions, 1974. 10/18.

Nischik, Reingard M. *Margaret Atwood: Works and Impact*. Rochester, NY: Camden House, 2000.

Oltarzewska, Jagna. *Témoignage, Identité, Survie : Stratégies feminines de lutte et d'émancipation dans l'œuvre romanesque de Margaret Atwood*. PhD. Paris X University, 1999.

Pache, Walter. "A Certain Frivolity: Margaret Atwood's Literary Criticism" *Margaret Atwood: Works and Impact*. Ed. Nischik, Reingard M. Rochester, NY: Camden House, 2000. 120-135.

Rabaté, Dominique, ed. *Figures du sujet lyrique*. Paris: Presses Universitaires de France, 2001.

Rosenberg, Betty. *Genreflecting: a Guide to Reading Interests in Genre Fiction*. Westport, Connecticut: Libraries Unlimited, 1982.

Siaud-Facchin, Jeanne. *L'enfant surdoué: l'aider à grandir, l'aider à réussir*. Paris: Odile Jacob, 2002.

Seligman in Nischik "Working with Margaret Atwood." *Margaret Atwood: Works and Impact*. Ed. Nischik, Reingard M. Rochester, NY: Camden House, 2000. 287-288.

Smith, Sidonie and Julia Watson. *Reading Autobiography: a Guide for Interpreting Life Narratives*. Minneapolis: University of Minnesota Press, 2001.

Somacarrera, Pilar. "*Power Politics*/ Power Politics: Atwood and Foucault." *Margaret Atwood: The Open Eye*. Eds. John Moss and Tobi Kozakewich. Ottawa: University of Ottawa Press, 2006. 291-303.

Sugars, Cynthia. "'Saying Boo to Colonialism': *Surfacing*, Tom Thomson, and the National Ghost." *Margaret Atwood: The Open Eye*. Eds. John Moss and Tobi Kozakewich. Ottawa: University of Ottawa Press, 2006. 137-158.

Sullivan, Rosemary. *The Red Shoes: Margaret Atwood Starting Out*. Toronto: HarperFlamingo Canada, 1998.

Talese, Nan A. "Charted and Uncharted Courses." *Margaret Atwood: Works and Impact*. Ed. Nischik, Reingard M. Rochester, NY: Camden House, 2000. 289-290.

Twigg, Alan. *For Openers: Conversations with 24 Canadian Writers*. Madiera Park, B.C.: Harbour Pub., 1981.

Van Spanckeren, Kathryn. "Humanizing the Fox: Atwood's Poetic Tricksters and Morning in the Burned House." *Margaret Atwood's Assassinations: Recent Poetry and Fiction*. Ed. Wilson, Sharon R. Columbus, OH: Ohio State University Press, 2003. 102-120.

Wagner-Martin. "'Giving Way to Bedrock': Atwood's Later Poems." *Various Atwoods: Essays on the Later Poems, Short Fiction, and Novels*. Ed. York, Lorraine Mary. Concord, Ont.: Anansi, 1995. 71-88.

Wasson, John M. *Subject and Structure an Anthology for Writers*. 2d Ed. Toronto: Little and Brown, 1966.

Wilson, Sharon R. *Margaret Atwood's Fairy Tale Sexual Politics*. Jackson, Miss.: Univ. Press of Mississippi, 1993.

---. Ed. *Margaret Atwood's Assassinations: Recent Poetry and Fiction*. Columbus, OH: Ohio State University Press, 2003.

York, Lorraine Mary, ed. *Various Atwoods: Essays on the Later Poems, Short Fiction, and Novels*. Concord, Ont.: Anansi, 1995.

---. "'A Slightly Uneasy Eminence': The Celebrity of Margaret Atwood." *Margaret Atwood: The Open Eye*. Eds. John Moss and Tobi Kozakewich. Ottawa: University of Ottawa Press, 2006. 35-48.

Press or Critical Articles on the Internet

Atwood, Margaret. "Atwood in the Twittersphere." NYRblog. March 29, 2010. http://www.nybooks.com/blogs/nyrblog/2010/mar/29/atwood-in-the-twittersphere/, accessed January 8, 2014.

---. "Why Wattpad Works." *The Guardian*, July 6, 2012. http://www.theguardian.com/books/2012/jul/06/margaret-atwood-wattpad-online-writing, accessed January 8, 2014.

Bradshaw, James. "Atwood Promotes New Book via Live Theatre." *The Globe and Mail*, August 17, 2009. http://www.theglobeandmail.com/arts/atwood-promotes-new-book-via-live-theatre/article1201400/, accessed January 8, 2014.

Burkeman, Oliver. "Atwood Sign of the Times Draws Blank." *The Guardian*, March 6, 2006. http://www.theguardian.com/world/2006/mar/06/topstories3.books, accessed February 7, 2014.

Cripps, Charlotte. "Twihaiku? Micropoetry? The Rise of Twitter Poetry." *The Independent*, July 16, 2013. http://www.independent.co.uk/arts-entertainment/books/features/twihaiku-micropoetry-the-rise-of-twitter-poetry-8711637.html, accessed November 10, 2013.

DeMara, Bruce. "Margaret Atwood Offers More Bang for the Book." *The Toronto Star*, August 18, 2009.
http://www.thestar.com/entertainment/books/2009/08/18/margaret_atwood_offers_more_bang_for_the_book.html, accessed January 8, 2014.

Doyle, Sady. "Dystopia, for the 'Lulz'." *These Times*, August 22, 2013.
https://inthesetimes.com/article/15415/margaret_atwoods_dystopia_for_the_lulz/, accessed January 8, 2014.

Flood, Alison. "Margaret Atwood Takes to Stage with Emmerdale and Only Fools Stars." *The Guardian*, August 19, 2009.
http://www.theguardian.com/books/2009/aug/19/margaret-atwood-emmerdale-tour, accessed January 8, 2014.

Gillett, Sue. "Senses of Cinema – Angel from the Mirror City: Jane Campion's Janet Frame." Sense of Cinema (10), November, 2000. http://sensesofcinema.com/2000/10/angel/, accessed March 4, 2014.

Harris, Sam. "The Illusion of the Self: An Interview with Bruce Hood." May 22, 2012. http://www.samharris.org/blog/item/the-illusion-of-the-self2/, accessed January 7, 2014.

Hawkins, Kaitlin. "Tales on Tweet." www.worldliteraturetoday.org, September 6, 2012.
http://www.worldliteraturetoday.org/tales-tweet#.Um916aywUVg, accessed October 29, 2013.

Hunt, Stephen. "Artistic Worlds Collide for Choreographers at Alberta Dance Festival." www.calgaryherald.com, August 31, 2013.
http://www.calgaryherald.com/entertainment/Artistic+worlds+collide+choreographers+Alberta+Dance/8854113/story.html, accessed November 10, 2013.

Johnson, Brian. "In The Wake of the Flood. Margaret Atwood | The Year Of The Flood." March 9, 2013. http://yearoftheflood.com/in-the-wake-of-the-flood/, accessed January 12, 2014.

Kelly, Margo. "Margaret Atwood Says Twitter, Internet Boost Literacy." December 5, 2011. http://www.cbc.ca/1.1057001, accessed January 8, 2014.

Kemp, Peter. "New Fiction: 'MaddAddam': Darkness and Light." *The Economist*, September 21, 2013.
http://www.economist.com/node/21586464, accessed October 29, 2013.

Lennon, Robert. "Margaret Atwood's Latest Novel a Love Letter to Literature." *The Globe and Mail*, August 30, 2013. http://www.theglobeandmail.com/arts/books-and-media/book-reviews/margaret-atwoods-latest-novel-a-love-letter-to-literature/article14041469/, accessed October 29, 2013.

Miller, Max. "How Twitter Is Like African Tribal Drums: Margaret Atwood." Big Think. Jan 2, 2011. http://bigthink.com/videos/how-twitter-is-like-african-tribal-drums, accessed January 8, 2014.

Press release (gjjur4356). "In the Wake of the Flood." Docstoc.com. March 2011. http://www.docstoc.com/docs/74700803/1-In-the-Wake-of-the-Flood, accessed January 8, 2014.

Roberts, Michele. "Book Review: MaddAddam, By Margaret Atwood." *The Independent*, August 16, 2013. http://www.independent.co.uk/arts-entertainment/books/reviews/book-review-maddaddam-by-margaret-atwood-8771138.html, accessed October 29, 2013.

Samson, Nathalie. "LongPen Goes Digital as iDoLVine." *Quill & Quire*, May 17, 2011. http://www.quillandquire.com/blog/index.php/digital-publishing-and-technology/the-longpen-goes-digital-as-idolvine/, accessed January 8, 2014.

Turner, Edwin. "Margaret Atwood Talks About Twitter." Biblioklept. 2012. http://biblioklept.org/2012/01/10/margaret-atwood-talks-about-twitter-video/, accessed January 8, 2014.

Ventura, Héliane. "Introduction. Journal of the Short Story in English." *Les Cahiers de la nouvelle* (55). 2011. http://jsse.revues.org/1057, accessed February 27, 2014.

Viner, Katharine. "Double Bluff." *The Guardian*, September 16, 2000. http://www.theguardian.com/books/2000/sep/16/fiction.bookerprize2000, accessed January 12, 2014.

Zoratti, Ben. "Choreographer's Adaptation of Margaret Atwood's Dystopian Novel Strikes Current Chord." *Winnipeg Free Press*, March 7, 2014. http://www.winnipegfreepress.com/arts-and-life/entertainment/arts/timely-tale-227490411.html, accessed November 10, 2013.

INDEX

ATWOOD'S POEMS

A

A Boat, 53, 73
A Descent Through Carpet, 48, 51
A Foundling, 44, 50
A Man Looks, 72
A Meal, 13, 19, 93
A Place, 66, 69
　Fragments, 66, 69, 173
A Sad Child, 84
A Sibyl, xiii, 14, 17, 18, 77, 88, 102, 140
A Voice, xii, xiii, 135
After the Flood, We, 47, 51, 65, 69, 94
Aging Female Poet on Laundry Day, 32, 36
Animals in That Country (The), x, 4, 46, 48, 49, 51, 99, 172

B

Bad News, 98
Book of Ancestors, 7, 95
Bored, 79
Bottle II, 13, 14, 18
Bread, 71, 72

C

Camera, 20, 21, 93
Circe/Mud Poems, 72, 75
Cyclops, 72

D

Delayed Message, 23

E

Enough of these Discouragements, 3
Eurydice, 6, 8, 28, 74, 75, 76

F

February, 84, 179, 181
Fishing for Eel Totems, 24
Five Poems for Grandmothers, 33, 34, 36

G

Gertrude Talks Back, 72, 73, 98
Girl and Horse, 1928, 20, 29

H

Happy Endings, 97
Heart Test With An Echo Chamber, 73
Helen of Troy Does Counter Dancing, 9
Hotel, 96

I

In the Secular Night, 84
Interlunar, x, 4, 6, 8, 9, 28, 41, 73, 86, 87, 89, 168, 172, 173, 175
Is / Not, 81

L

Last Poem, 96
Late August, 81
Late Night, 96
Let Us Now Praise Stupid Women, 98
Letter from Persephone, 8
Lying Here, 6, 41

M

Marsh, Hawk, 83
Migration, 66
   CPR, 66
Miss July Grows Older, 31, 102
Mourning for Cats, 9
My Mother Dwindles, 9

N

Note Towards a Poem That Can Never Be Written, 83
Notes from Various Pasts, xiii, 51

O

On the Streets, Love, 77
Orpheus (1), 8, 74
Orpheus II, 28
Owl and Pussycat, Some Years Later, 129, 135

P

Portfolio of Ancestors, 81
Pre-Amphibian, 69
Procedures for Underground, x, xiii, 4, 5, 6, 15, 17, 23, 25, 27, 52, 53, 70, 73, 74, 92, 172
Progressive Insanities of a Pioneer, 4, 19
Projected slide of an Unknown Soldier, 72

R

Returning from the dead, 73, 74

S

Sekhmet, The Lion-Headed Goddess of War, Violent Storms, Pestilence, and Recovery From Illness, Contemplates the Desert in The Metropolitan Museum of Art, 9
Shadow Voice, xiii, 70, 73, 74, 75, 76, 78, 84, 102, 166
Shapechangers in Winter, 36, 37, 38, 133, 135
Siren Song, 52, 70, 99
Songs of the Transformed, 49, 72
Speeches for Dr Frankenstein, 72, 99
Spell for the Director of Protocol, 88

T

There is Only One of Everything, 7, 81, 94, 95
There Was Once, 98
This Is a Photograph of Me, 12, 18, 29

U

Unpopular Gals, 98

V

Variation on the Word *Love*, 96

W

What Do You Want From Me, 41

Y

You Heard the Man You Love, 10

TITLES AND AUTHORS

A

Art of Margaret Atwood (The)
  Essays in Criticism, xvii, 163, 174
Alias Grace, xi, 59, 98, 99, 118, 119, 171
Art and Craft of Poetry (The), xiv, 173
Attridge, Derek, 18, 21, 173, 174
Atwood and the 'Autobiographical Pact', 119, 126, 127, 129, 161, 175
Atwood on her Work
Autobiographics
  a Feminist Theory of Women's Self-representation, 127, 128, 130, 161, 175
Autobiography (An)
  To the Island, 49, 180

B

Back to the Primal
  The Apprenticeship of Margaret Atwood, 174
Barnes, Julian, xvii
Barthes, Roland, xiv, 96, 116, 173
Baudrillard, Jean, 122, 173
Birney, Earle, 58, 173
Blind Assassin (The), xi, 43, 59, 99, 118, 119, 150, 161, 171, 176
Blott, Anne, 8, 173
Bodily Harm, x, 43, 95, 96, 100, 122, 123, 171
Book Publishing Industry in the United States (The), 116, 175

Bottle, x, 3, 13, 14, 18, 32, 73, 79, 140, 167, 171
Bradford, Richard, xv, 101, 173
Bradshaw, James, 179
Brown, Brené, 102
Bugeja, Michael J., xiv, 173
Burkeman, Oliver, 179
Bush Garden (The)
  Essays on the Canadian Imagination, 46, 58, 72, 175
Butler, Robert Olen, 151, 173

C

Cambridge Companion to Margaret Atwood (The), 8, 25, 37, 56, 59, 176
Cambridge Companion to Merleau-Ponty (The), 62, 63, 174
Carman, Taylor, 62, 63, 174
Carper, Thomas, 174
Céline, Louis-Ferdinand, 174
Certain Frivolity (A)
  Margaret Atwood's Literary Criticism, 58, 178
Charted and Uncharted Courses, xviii
Circle Game (The), x, xiii, xix, 4, 6, 11, 12, 13, 14, 17, 18, 19, 20, 21, 22, 29, 46, 47, 48, 51, 65, 66, 67, 68, 77, 83, 91, 92, 93, 94, 99, 100, 106, 125, 166, 172, 177
Clarissa Pinkola Estés Releases Her Master Work as a Live Online Series from SoundsTrue.com, 33
Cohen, Leonard, 164
Collected Poems of Earle Birney (The), 58, 173

Collins, Billy, xii, 174
Com[ing] Through Darkness'
 Margaret Atwood's 'I'-Opening Lyricism, 176
Contribution à la généalogie de la morale
 un écrit polémique., 88, 177
Cooley, Dennis, 41, 174
Cripps, Charlotte, 179
Curious Pursuits, xi, 173
Curious Pursuits XE "Curious Pursuits"
 Occasional Writing 1970-2005, xi, 173

D

D. H. Laurence, 111
Dancing Girls, x, 114, 171
Davey, Frank, xvi, 1, 19, 20, 23, 24, 25, 26, 29, 68, 92, 163, 164, 174
Davidson, Arnold E, xvii, 163, 174
Davies, Robertson, 108, 175
DeMara, Bruce, 180
Dennis, Carl, 15
Derrida, Jacques, xviii
Djwa, Sandra,, xvii, 57, 174
Door (The), x, 2, 4, 9, 135, 166, 167, 172
Doyle, Sady, 180

E

Eakin, Paul John, 127, 174, 176
Eco, Umberto, xvi
Edible Woman (The), x, 25, 92, 93, 100, 114, 118, 122, 149, 171
Editors on Editing, 116, 175
Egan, Susanna, 127, 174
Enfant surdoué (L')
 l'aider à grandir, l'aider à réussir, 80, 86, 88, 178
Estés, Clarissa Pinkola, 174

F

Figures du sujet lyrique, 178
Flood, Alison, 180
Visible and the Invisible (The), 62, 63, 174, 177
For Openers
 Conversations with 24 Canadian Writers, 115, 178
Foucault, Michel, 41, 42, 43, 175
Fragments d'un discours amoureux, 173
Frame, Janet, 49, 175
Fredman, Stephen, 90, 91, 102, 175
Freud, 24, 36
From *'Places, Migrations'* to *The Circle Game*
 Atwood's Canadian and Female Metamorphoses., 66, 177
From Where You Dream
 The Process of Writing Fiction, 151, 173
Frye, Northrop, 46, 58, 72, 175

G

Genette, Gérard, 97, 136, 175
Genreflecting
 a Guide to Reading Interests in Genre Fiction, 178
Gibson, Douglas, xvii, 108, 175
Gifts of Imperfection (The)
 Let Go of Who You Think You're Supposed to Be and Embrace Who You Are, 173
Gillett, Sue, 180
Gilmore, Leigh, 127, 128, 130, 161, 175
Good Bones, x, 3, 72, 73, 97, 98, 99, 171
Grace, Sherrill, 119, 126, 127, 129, 161, 175
Greco, Albert, 116, 175
Gross, Gerald, 116, 175
Grounding of American Poetry (The)

Charles Olson and the
Emersonian Tradition, 90, 91,
102, 175
Guignery, Vanessa, xiv, xvi, 102,
109, 175

H

Handmaid's Tale (The), xi, 43, 98,
114, 149, 152, 171
Hansen, Mark B. N, 62, 63, 174
Harris, Sam, 180
Hawkins, Kaitlin, 180
Hébert, Anne, 164
Hengen, Shannon, xvii, 8, 152, 175
Hood, Bruce, 37, 176, 180
*How Our Lives Become Stories
Making Selves*, 127, 174, 176
Howells, Coral Ann, 8, 25, 37, 56,
59, 176
Humanizing the Fox
Atwood's Poetic Tricksters and
Morning in the Burned
House., 178
Hunt, Stephen, 180
Hunter, Lynette, 8, 176
Hutcheon, Linda, 59
Hyde, Lewis, 111, 112, 113, 116,
120, 123, 176

I

Illusion of the Self (The)
An Interview with Bruce Hood,
180
*In Other Worlds
SF and the Human Imagination*,
xi, 164, 169, 170, 173
Ingersoll, Earl, 56, 101, 111, 114,
115, 116, 120, 173
Introduction to a Special issue of
the *Journal of the Short Story* on
Alice Munro, 124, 181
'It's Still You'
Aging and Identity in Atwood's
Poetry, 176

J

*Jack
a Life with Writers
the Story of Jack McClelland*,
114, 176
Jamieson, Sara, 34, 35, 36, 37, 38,
40, 133, 176
Jarraway, Davis, 2, 176
Johnson, Brian, 180
Journals of Susanna Moodie (The),
x, 23, 51, 59
Journey to light [*Interlunar*], 173
Joyce, James, 57, 66

K

Kappeler, Susanne, 122, 176
Kazuo Ishiguro, 61, 111, 112, 120,
176, 177
Kelly, Margo, 180
Khandpur, Reena, 52, 64, 65, 71,
91, 134, 152, 158, 174, 175, 176
King, James, 114, 176
King, Stephen, 116
Kozakewich, Tobi, 2, 5, 23, 40, 43,
58, 59, 126, 127, 129, 133, 162,
175, 176, 177, 178, 179
Kuhn, Cynthia G., 176
Kundera, Milan, xvi

L

*La poésie comme l'amour
essai sur la relation lyrique*, 76,
177
*La quatrième personne du singulier
esquisse de portrait du sujet
lyrique moderne*, 76
*La Société de consommation
ses mythes, ses structures*, 122,
173
Lady Oracle, x, 25, 92, 94, 95, 97,
100, 120, 171

Lakoff, George, 163, 176
Lejeune, Philippe, 125, 126, 127, 176
Lennon, Robert, 181
LePan, Douglas, 164
Lessing, Doris, 108, 109, 177
Lettres à la N.R.F. choix 1931-1961, 155, 174
Life Before Man, x, 95, 96, 100, 119, 131, 171
LongPen goes digital as iDoLVine, 138
Look of It (The)
  a Theory of Visual Form in English Poetry, xv, 101, 173

M

MacLeod, Alistair, 108, 175
Macpherson, Jay, 164
Maddaddam, xi, 10, 136, 140, 171
Making It in Book Publishing, 116, 177
Manguel, Alberto, 155
Margaret Atwood
  a Feminist Poetics, xvi, 1, 19, 20, 23, 24, 25, 26, 29, 68, 92, 163, 164, 174
  a Reference Guide, xvii, 175
  Branding an Icon Abroad, 58, 177
  Conversations, 173
  The Open Eye, 175, 176, 177, 178, 179
  Works and Impact, xvii, 1, 114, 119, 130, 175, 177, 178
  Writing and Subjectivity
    New Critical Essays, 45, 66, 174, 177
Maulpoix, Jean-Michel, 76, 177
McClelland, Jack, 114, 172, 173, 176
McCombs, Judith, 8, 45, 66, 95, 173, 177
Merleau-Ponty, Maurice, 62, 63, 174, 177

Metaphors We Live By, 163, 176
Meter and Meaning
  An Introduction to Rhythm in Poetry, 174
Miller, Max, 181
Mirror Talk
  Genres of Crisis in Contemporary Autobiography., 127, 174
Mogel, Leonard, 116, 177
Moodie, Susanna, x, xiii, xv, xvi, 4, 5, 23, 24, 25, 46, 50, 51, 53, 57, 72, 99, 172, 173, 176
Moons of Jupiter (The), 177
Moral Disorder, xi, 171
Morning in the Burned House, x, 4, 8, 9, 29, 31, 32, 33, 34, 35, 36, 38, 39, 41, 72, 75, 79, 80, 83, 84, 85, 97, 99, 100, 133, 135, 154, 167, 172, 178
Moss, John, 2, 5, 23, 40, 43, 58, 59, 126, 127, 129, 133, 162, 175, 176, 177, 178, 179
Moving Targets, xi, 172
Munro, Alice, 108, 124, 168, 175, 177
Murder in the Dark, x, 3, 71, 97, 98, 99

N

Narrative Strategies in Canadian Literature
  Feminism and Postcolonialism, 8, 176
Nearer by Far
  The Upset 'I' in Margaret Atwood's Poetry, 174
Negotiating with the Dead, xi, xii, xx, 11, 15, 16, 17, 57, 70, 73, 107, 109, 110, 111, 112, 113, 114, 115, 124, 126, 127, 128, 129, 130, 131, 138, 146, 147, 158, 159, 169, 172
Newlove, John, 164
Nicholson, Colin, 45, 66, 174, 177

Nietzsche, Friedrich, 88, 177
Nischik, Reingard, xvii, 1, 114, 119, 130, 175, 177, 178
Novelists in the New Millennium Conversations with Writers., xvi, 175

O

Oltarzewska, Jagna, 66, 178
On Autobiography, 125, 126, 127, 176
Oryx and Crake, xi, 10, 99, 149, 171

P

Pache, Walter, 58, 178
Pacte autobiographique (Le), 125, 126, 127, 176
Paratextes, 97, 136, 175
Paratexts
 Thresholds of Interpretation. Cambridge
  Cambridge University Press, 1997., 97, 136, 175
Payback, xi, 173
Penelopiad (The), xi, 171
Poetic Rhythm
 An Introduction, 173
Poetry Dictionary (The), xiv, xvi, xviii, 15, 21, 54, 174
Pornography of Representation (The), 122, 176
Power Politics, x, 4, 6, 7, 19, 20, 23, 41, 43, 68, 72, 74, 93, 100, 142, 172, 178
Power Politics/ Power Politics Atwood and Foucault, 178

R

Rabaté, Dominique, 178
Reading Autobiography
 a Guide for Interpreting Life Narratives, 127, 178
Red Shoes (The)
 Margaret Atwood Starting Out, 1, 2, 45, 71, 72, 178
Rilke, Rainer Maria, 17, 19, 111
Roberts, Michele, 181
Rosenberg, Betty, 178

S

Sailing Alone Around the Room
 New and Selected Poems, xii, 174
Samson, Nathalie, 181
Saying Boo to Colonialism'
 Surfacing, Tom Thomson, and the National Ghost., 178
Second Words
 Selected Critical Prose, xi, 172
Self Illusion (The), 37, 176, 180
Self-fashioning in Margaret Atwood's Fiction
 Dress, Culture, and Identity, 176
Seligman, xvii, 178
Sensory Appeal in *The Atwood Stories* on TV, 152, 176
Siaud-Facchin, Jeanne, 80, 86, 88, 178
Smith, Sidonie, 127, 178
Sollers, Philippe, 155, 174
Somacarrera, Pilar, 5, 42, 43, 178
Steel, Danielle, 116
Stories About Storytellers
 Publishing Alice Munro, Robertson Davies, Alistair MacLeod, Pierre Trudeau, and Others, xvii, 108, 175
Strange Things
 The Malevolent North in Canadian Literature, xi, 58, 172
Subject and Structure an Anthology for Writers, 90, 179
Sugars, Cynthia, 5, 23, 178

Sullivan, Rosemary, 1, 2, 45, 71, 72, 178
Surfacing, x, 23, 24, 25, 59, 92, 93, 94, 100, 119, 122, 171, 178
Survival
  A Thematic Guide to Canadian Literature, xi, 45, 51, 56, 57, 58, 66, 95, 109, 114, 165, 172

T

Talese, xviii, 171, 178
Témoignage, Identité, Survie
  Stratégies feminines de lutte et d'émancipation dans l'œuvre romanesque de Margaret Atwood, 66, 178
Tent (The), x, 4, 29, 31, 32, 133, 135, 167, 171
The Gift
  Imagination and the Erotic Life of Property, 111, 176
TOC conference, 142, 157
True Stories, x, 1, 4, 7, 8, 43, 44, 60, 61, 62, 71, 72, 77, 83, 95, 96, 100, 142, 161, 172
Turner, Edwin, 181
Twigg, Alan, 115, 178
Twihaiku? Micropoetry? The rise of Twitter poetry, 141
Two-Headed Poems, x, xix, 7, 11, 33, 34, 36, 65, 83, 95

V

Van Spanckeren, Kathryn, 39, 178
Various Atwoods, xvii, xviii, 163, 174, 179
  Essays on the Later Poems, Short Fiction, and Novels, xvii, xviii, 163, 174, 179
Ventura, Héliane, 124, 181
Viner, Katharine, 181
Virgil, 17

W

Wagner-Martin, 2, 179
Walking in the Shade, 177
Waltzing Again
  New and Selected Conversations with Margaret Atwood, 173
Wasson, John, 90, 179
Watson,, 127, 178
Wilderness Tips, xi, 56, 171
Wilson, Sharon, 8, 9, 39, 176, 178, 179
Women Who Run with the Wolves
  Myths and Stories of the Wild Woman Archetype, 174
Working with Margaret Atwood, xvii
Writing with Intent, xi, 173

Y

Year of the Flood (The), xi, 10, 136, 148, 149, 152, 153, 155, 171
York, Lorraine, xvii, xviii, 2, 57, 130, 131, 142, 153, 163, 164, 166, 171, 173, 174, 175, 176, 177, 179
You Are Happy, x, 7, 52, 53, 70, 72, 81, 89, 94, 99

Z

Zoratti, Jen., 181